Really not interested in the Deaf?

by

Doug Alker

Published by
    Doug Alker
    PO Box 11   dougalker@yahoo.com.
    Darwen
    Lancashire BB3 3GH
    e-mail: fdalker@aol.com

A catalouge record for this book is available from the British Library

Printed by Darwen Press

5

Contents

Contents

Preface

This book is about Deaf people and how their lives are blighted by society. Hopefully it will give hearing and also deaf people in the world some real understanding of what it is like to be Deaf in this world. To comprehend that it is beyond not being able to hear. That the issue is how society is constructed to respond to people with whom they cannot easily communicate without using sound.

It will not be a comfortable read for many. But then, nor is the reality of Deaf people's lives very comforting.

Although this book is all about Deaf issues, it is not to decry deaf or hard of hearing people and their legitimate problems. We need to understand the differences and respect each other's views. It does not help to lump us together in one treatment group.

However I pitch the book, to the Deaf or the non-Deaf, I cannot please everyone. Some will be fully aware of the issues I cover, while others will be groping in the dark. I have written it with the lay audience in mind. The Deaf issues need to be explained to give them some understanding of what we Deaf face. I hope I have managed to write about the issues in a way that it is not too boring for those who already know of them.

My chosen style of writing wouldn't win any prizes for the most traditional use of English. It is more staccato than usual, to indicate the that it comes from someone who is Deaf and not a hearing person. I hope that you enjoy the book as much as you are shocked by it!

Some may wince at the frequent use of the seemingly politically incorrect term "the Deaf". The "politically correct" terms like "people who are Deaf", etc were actually coined by non-Deaf people. In BSL we still sign "the Deaf". So, it feels right to me to use it here, as does the use of "Deaf people" in other contexts.

The names of Deaf people (except Paddy Ladd) involved in the RNID story have been changed to protect the individuals and their careers. The names of any culpable hearing people have, of course, been left as they are.

Like many writers, I struggled with the gender issue. Male or female? I have mixed them without any real criteria, with a greater use of the male simply because that is what I am. No sexism intended.

I would like to acknowledge the various people who have commented, criticised or contributed. Most, for the usual Deaf reasons, prefer to remain anonymous.

Prologue

Keeping them in their Place

To disarm the strong and arm the weak would be to change the social order, which it's my job to preserve. Justice is the means by which established injustices are sanctioned.

Anatole France

Imagine if you will this familiar scenario: a news conference attended by politicians, artists, writers and activists. In addition to these guests, there are hundreds of media reporters. Representatives from the print media. From radio. And, of course, television. Carefully made-up and coiffed talking heads occupy the stage overlooking the frantic scene. High above the auditorium, they are speaking with one another in muted voices, considering the significance of this event.

In front of the stage, a simple podium serves as a magnet for a vast and brilliant array of lights and microphones. A banner is draped behind the podium in dramatic fashion. In bold colours it reads: "The National Organisation of Minority Women - the Future is Ours!"

A tall, dignified woman of African descent, dressed in a colourful *dashiki*, moves toward the podium, flanked by several other women, their dark skin characterised by serious and determined expressions.

A hush that is almost physical greets the woman as she adjusts the microphone up to her height. She is well-known to the assembled media reporters. Her near-celebrity status as writer, activist, and academic who has been arrested many times in support of women's causes around the globe gives her an aura of authority and command.

"Good morning," she begins, her dark, piercing eyes seeming to embrace everyone in the auditorium. "It is my pleasure and my honour to introduce you to the person who will lead minority women into the future, the person who will guide us and our agenda into the new millennium... Albert Pringle."

She steps aside as she makes a broad gesture of welcome toward Mr. Pringle - a short, white man in his later years, a man whose thinning gray hair is carefully combed across his pink scalp.

11

Mr. Pringle timidly takes to the podium and adjusts the microphone down to his height...

Now, could you imagine the reception such an announcement would receive? A white man (conservative and old school to boot!) named as the leader of an organisation dedicated to the advancement of minority women? Outrageous! Chauvinism run amok! Colonialism rearing its arrogant head!

Commentators and editorial writers would be in absolute agreement: How could a white man possibly be sufficiently sensitive to the needs of minority women to lead such an organisation?

Now, imagine that, in addition to Mr. Pringle's leadership role, the entire governing board of the National Organisation of Minority Women was comprised of other white men, with the exception of a couple of carefully selected "half-caste" men included for appearance's sake. All, as it turns out, from the same upper socio-economic background as Mr. Pringle. Can you imagine it?

It strains the imagination, doesn't it? In fact, such a scenario is so implausible as to be quickly dismissed as fantasy - an insulting and demeaning fantasy at that. Unless... unless you substituted "The Royal National Institute for Deaf People" for "The National Organisation of Minority Women."

Then the scenario could not be dismissed at all. It could not be dismissed because it would not be considered either insulting nor demeaning. It could not be dismissed because it could not even be considered fantasy. It could not be dismissed because, quite simply, it is reality. Certainly, it was the reality for the first ninety years of the RNID's existence.

Then, on November 25th, 1994 the RNID broke with this astounding run of arrogance, announcing my appointment as its first ever Deaf Chief Executive Officer.

November 25th. That date resonated with meaning for Deaf people. (The significance of the use of the capital D is clarified in the next chapter.) It marked the beginning of a genuine advance. For the first time, we had reason to hope that our fundamental needs, needs that could only be understood by another Deaf person, would be recognised and respected. For the first time, we had reason to believe that the complexities of the world of the deaf and the Deaf would not be lost in the background noise of the hearing world. For the first time, the profound condescension of the hearing, the belief that they "knew best what Deaf people needed", could be answered with dignity and authority.

For the first time, the Deaf had the opportunity to answer the belief, both stated and unstated, that we were "not competent enough to run" our own organisations.

Is it any wonder that my appointment was greeted with such high hopes by the Deaf? We had finally arrived! Of course there was a certain pomposity to the RNID's appointment. Their underlying message was along the lines that Deaf people hadn't been really up to the responsibility of leadership of our own organisation until that point, that they had been "grooming" us for leadership.

As if Deaf people only came into existence with the establishment of the RNID! As if the Deaf were child-like beings needing to be protected and managed by the RNID's paternalistic 'kindness'!

As long as there have been people, there have been Deaf people. For too long, deafness had been synonymous in the minds of hearing people with dumbness and retardation. However, the limitations of Deaf people has a great deal more to do with the failure of educational systems to address the specific communication needs we have than with any inherent lack of ability or intelligence. The system dubbed as "oralism", which I will discuss in detail in Chapter Six, has been a profound failure.

Evaluated objectively, the failure of oralism should be a condemnation of the arrogance of hearing 'specialists'. Instead, it has been used as one more weapon in the arsenal of those who would minimise the potential of Deaf people, used as one more weapon by those more interested in maintaining their own positions and control over the Deaf than with any advancement for Deaf people.

All that appeared to be changed on November 25th. My appointment marked a "new beginning". My appointment was seen as the first huge step toward Deaf people "owning" our own organisations and our own agenda. We had waited so long for this opportunity.

Such high hopes! Such determination!

It all ended just over two years later with the March 4th 1997 press release explaining my departure from the RNID. "Doug Alker wanted the freedom and time to tackle issues close to his heart..."

The wording suggested that I was abandoning leadership of the premier organisation of the Deaf in order to deal with things that I cared about. That is, issues pertaining to the Deaf. The suggestion that I could do that better *apart* from the RNID, rather than leading it, was ludicrous at best. Yet there it was, in the press release.

As the hopes of the Deaf had soared just two years earlier, the despair at the news of my departure was deep. The news was even more shocking to those who knew me personally. If any quality defined me in their eyes it was tenacity. I don't give up easily.

Deaf people recognised that quality in me. Yet suddenly, they were being told that I was leaving the RNID in order to pursue matters of concern to the Deaf. But where better to pursue these matters than at the head of the RNID?

What had happened?

My sudden departure left the Deaf world shocked and suspicious. The additional two years of enforced silence have done little to ease that shock or suspicion.

In contrast to my silence, the hearing Chair of the RNID spoke incessantly, trying to ease those suspicions. But no wall of verbiage could stem the tide of anger and suspicion amongst Deaf people and those who genuinely care about Deaf issues. My very deafening silence on this for the two years since I left the RNID only served to reinforce the feeling that something was seriously amiss.

For ten years, ten years that had culminated in my appointment as Chief Executive of the RNID, the organisation had been changing in positive ways. For the first time in its history, the RNID had gained some semblance of credibility amongst those whose agenda it was supposed to be representing. Deaf people were taking on roles of responsibility throughout the Deaf organisations, locally and nationally.

There was a palpable sense of hope amongst the Deaf. We were moving forward.

Then, overnight, the tide of hope was stemmed. Control of the RNID returned to the hearing. A Palace coup, which none of us had foreseen, had been carried out with ruthless efficiency.

14

Many Deaf people guessed I had either left on principle or had been forced out, or both. In either case, something was very, very wrong.

So, I continued my work for the Deaf cause outside the RNID and without working alongside them. For two long years, I have toiled silently and determinedly. I will continue to toil determinedly but I am no longer compelled to do so in silence. My two years in the wilderness are over! The period of enforced silence has now come to an end. The story of what really happened at the RNID can be told.

The painful and nasty sequence of events that took place during the five-year period beginning in 1994 and ending in 1998, is emblematic of the way the Deaf have been treated for far too long. It is the story of how those who hold certain parochial views of deafness have used their position, their wealth and their power to limit the advance of Deaf people. It is the story of those with personal ambitions and vested interests who have been more than willing to sacrifice the good of Deaf people for their own sense of self.

There are those who will vehemently deny the things written in this book. My only wish is that their denials were true. Unfortunately, they are not. What is written here is the truth. And the truth is always its own defence.

I have a friend who has been involved in politics for a long time. He has a saying that he is particularly fond of, "Turn on the lights and let the cockroaches scurry."

In these pages, I fully intend to "turn on the lights". I will leave it to you to determine who should scurry away from the light.

However, if the only purpose of my book is to exact some petty retribution on the people who played a role in these events of my life then it would be a small book indeed. My story is woven into a much larger tapestry. It is also the story of the long-standing oppression of Deaf people. It is also the story of the fight to achieve dignity in the face of this oppression.

Some might suggest that "oppression" is too strong a term for the experiences of Deaf people. I would challenge that suggestion. You need only consider the reality of a Deaf person's life to realise just how oppressive society is towards us.

15

The oppression of a Deaf person begins at birth. From the earliest moments of life, the structures of society, which control the health and education systems conspire to minimise the ability of a hearing parent to communicate with his or her Deaf child.

"No, you mustn't use sign language," they are told. "You must speak to your child."

"But.. but he can't hear us!"

"No matter. You must speak. Otherwise, your child will never be able to get along in the world."

These professionals prey on vulnerable parents with their paternalistic attitudes and their talk of "normalcy". Parents who come to them, frightened and concerned. Parents who are worried because their child doesn't answer when they call his name, who doesn't jump at loud noises ("I dropped a dish the other night and it shattered. Tommy didn't even blink...") Parents who fear that there is something wrong with *them* if their child is Deaf.

"Hmm, hmm," the kindly doctor says, nodding his head as they voice their fears. "Let's take a look, eh?"

Little Tommy is put on the examination table. He is poked and prodded with various instruments. The doctor peers into his ears. He claps his hands behind the child's head.

The doctor frowns. "You'll have to see a specialist."

"What is it, doctor?"

"Can you help him?"

The mother begins to cry. The father tries to appear brave, compressing his lips. Will he ever be able to take his son to football matches?

The specialist is even more frightening than the family doctor. He puts headphones on little Tommy and turns a number of dials.

"Hmm," he says. "Hmm."

"What shall we do?"

"The boy is deaf," the specialist announces. "He cannot hear." He then goes on to say how dreadfully important it is that they speak to him.

"But he can't hear us..."

"You must do this or your child will never be normal."

Normal. Now, there's a goal for you!

These doctors and professionals (and, as a result of their lead, most of society) perceive Deaf children as deficient and incapable of being 'normal'. Looking at what they cannot do rather than seeing them as functioning human beings.

Now, it is true that the inability to hear poses a real challenge in a world that depends on sounds to communicate. But it is simply that, a challenge. Not an insurmountable obstacle. Yet these professionals insist that parents and teachers should only speak to Deaf children.

It doesn't matter to them that there are very clear indications that the use only of 'speech' and 'hearing' fails to enable communication at vital stages in a Deaf child's development. That it actually diminishes the child's cognitive ability to communicate. All that matters is that this is the "way it's done" so that the child will be 'normal'.

Decades of failure have not convinced these professionals of the folly of their advice. Speaking to children who are deaf (with a lower case d) might provide some benefit. Their hearing deficits are less severe. However, speaking to children who are Deaf (with an upper case D) is pointless. Their hearing deficit is profound.

Forcing Deaf children to 'hear' is as insulting as it is futile. This practice also glosses over the important and complex distinctions between Deafness and deafness. Distinctions which are explained in the next chapter.

If this practice is not oppressive to Deaf children, I don't know what is.

Society compounds this insult by imposing its own perceptions on Deaf children. The inability to hear will most obviously result in difficulty with speech. However, neither the inability to hear or speak should ever be construed to mean that the Deaf child does not have a normal brain or intelligence. Far from it. Deaf children have the same cognitive abilities as any other children.

17

Unfortunately, as countless studies have demonstrated, if a child's cognitive abilities are oppressed for any reason (nutrition, poverty, illness, abusive environments) they do not develop at the same rate as those children who benefit from having their cognitive abilities enriched.

For Deaf children, the failure of society and the educational system to provide enriching input of information and for stunting their ability to express themselves as they would like to can often result in slower development. Adding insult to injury by forcing Deaf children to hear and speak when they do not have the facility to do so is cruel and oppressive.

It would be no different than forcing a child to wear very dark glasses and then, in a darkened room, asking him to read a book. Doing so would be denounced as wickedly cruel. As it should be.

But when a similar practice is imposed on the Deaf. Then it seems to make perfect sense to some people.

Why can't society accept that Deaf children who are allowed and encouraged to use sign language actually do flourish? When will the educational establishment recognise that Deaf children who sign are better adjusted and make more progress?

Isn't *that* what is meant by 'normal'?

However, the insistence on the ability to 'hear' speech is a major stumbling block in a Deaf child's progress. As a result, Deaf children are inevitably classified as slow or stupid or both.

But all this is not really about a Deaf child's intelligence or ability. It is about an educational system being geared toward programming children to fail.

Children, regardless of their ability to hear or not, will not develop positive self-esteem if they are held back or forced to limit their expectations for success and future prospects.

It is difficult to convey the frustration a Deaf child experiences when he realises that vital information is being transmitted in a code that others have the key to understanding but that he is doomed to never quite grasp. How can a Deaf child register a protest about this unfair situation when the words that he would speak are shredded as they work their way through his vocal cords, leaving his listener without a clue to decipher what he is trying to say?

18

With such a 'stellar' education, young Deaf people must then go out into the world and obtain meaningful employment.

It's no wonder a personnel officer, looking over a young Deaf person's application, balks at hiring someone he cannot converse with. Society has not only failed to educate the Deaf. It has made even less progress in aiding the hearing to understand and respond to the legitimate needs of the Deaf.

Thus, the unemployment rate for Deaf people is roughly double the national average. Those who are able to find employment are invariably underemployed or given menial positions.

Once in the workplace, they are further isolated. Prospects for promotion are virtually zero.

Deaf people are no different than anyone else when it comes to the things they want for their lives. They desire success. They know they are capable of more than they are being allowed to achieve.

Creative, intelligent, hopeful people are left to watch less able hearing colleagues move forward professionally, leaving them behind.

Is this not oppression?

Young Deaf people, like all young people, hunger for an active and exciting social life. They go to all the places other young people go - pubs, clubs, discos. There, people cluster around chatting. Young men approach the girls to offer them a drink or to ask them for a dance. Because the young Deaf cannot do this, they are often even more isolated than in the workplace.

How often is a young person expected to feel rejected before he turns away and avoids these painful and oppressive situations?

The Deaf fare no better in community activities. Most of the major functions in our society are based on sound. The spoken word. Music. Telephony. Radio. These are the lynchpins of community interaction. As a result, Deaf people are denied the opportunity to participate in a broad range of information, services and opportunities. In short, Deaf people are prevented from full participation and behaving as full citizens in the communities where they live.

If the sound barrier is not oppressive enough, there remains the negative attitude of many hearing people. All too often they react in one of two very predictable ways toward a Deaf person - condescendingly or negatively.

One might empathise with a lay hearing person's difficulty in reacting appropriately toward a Deaf person. But there is absolutely no excuse for the behaviour and attitude of so many of the people who are involved with Deaf people and the organisations which represent them.

Medical professionals, manufacturers of hearing and other aids, teachers of a particular genre, counsellors - whole industries have blossomed to the benefit of those who say they are helping the Deaf. They strive to 'normalise' Deaf people and usually persist even when they are patently failing.

It is they who benefit. They who profit. We Deaf struggle on, progressing (when we do) *in spite of* these professionals, not because of them. Is there a better definition of oppression than limiting the progress of another for your own benefit?

There are also those who have the need to appear benevolent. And those who wish to satisfy their need for the control and power that eludes them in the under world. They seek it in the Deaf world. Their paternalistic behaviour certainly oppress us.

Does not society applaud the efforts of these oppressors? Gala Balls. Philanthropic events. Church recognition. Honours.

Is it not all an appalling and destructive sham?

Then, there are some parents of Deaf children, especially those in the middle and upper classes, who often struggle with profound shame because they have given birth to children who are not 'normal'. How to compensate? How to overcome their self-imposed guilt? Ah, to become involved in organisations and activities with the aim of 'normalising' their Deaf children.

Clearly, it seems they aim to sublimate their shame, rather than the legitimate needs of their Deaf children.

It is an understatement to say it is unfortunate that these are the very people who control the money and the agendas of Deaf organisations. Because their real agendas are often so contrary to the needs of the Deaf, they make the situation worse for Deaf people. Oh, they are expert at appearing to aid the Deaf. However, appearances are often deceiving.

20

In evaluating the truth of what I'm saying, ask yourself this: What is the benefit to these hearing people who are running organisations for the Deaf? You will almost always find that there is financial gain, power, or relief from the stigma of having given birth to 'imperfect' children.

Because of these oppressive goals, the perceptions and attitudes of the entire hearing public have been tainted. Policies and educational standards have been devised and determined by these selfish hearing oriented goals.

These goals determine the terms of how the world deals with the Deaf.

These people are not the only hearing people who work in organisations for the Deaf. There are those with genuinely positive approaches to Deafness. However, because they, correctly, place Deaf people before themselves, they are not often visible in the Deaf world or in the media. They certainly do not control it or wish to.

Because they refuse to be paternalistic. Because they value the dignity of Deaf people over photo opportunities. Because they shun the Society pages. Because of this and more, they do not put themselves in positions of running these organisations.

So, the damaging, selfish and negative leaders continue to consolidate control.

Where does that leave us, the Deaf? We are blocked at every pass from leading normal lives, as normal Deaf people. We have grown up trying to please parents who have been told by professionals to speak to us and teach us in inappropriate and unsuccessful ways, leaving us with profound frustration and feelings of diminished self-worth.

Damnit, we *tried* to hear! But we couldn't and we can't!

What did this insistence on hearing get us? Not normalcy. Not an education. Not dignity. Only a sense of guilt and lack of worth. Only a belief in our own failure.

How could we understand that our below-par performance was a function of faulty educational methods, not our own ability? How could we know that speaking and lip-reading are unfair expectations for people without the capacity to hear?

21

So, we came to depend on hearing people to help us and we felt obligated to hearing people for their help.

This is hardly the fertile environment for great thinkers and artists, for achievement and leadership.

However, in the 1980s, a change began to occur, accelerating in the 1990s. A new political and social environment brought changes in many areas of society, not least of them areas concerned with the Deaf. Thinkers began to suggest that because Deaf people are different in behaviour, perception and cognition they require different approaches to education and socialisation.

The general trend toward rights and independence brought specific gains to Deaf people's lives. Visibility on television has helped to reduce the stigma of Deafness. Sign language classes have become more and more popular, with nearly 20,000 people taking the British Sign Language (BSL) examinations every year.

Deaf people were being perceived as a distinct cultural minority with a unique language. A new sensibility entered the societal lexicon. It was possible and acceptable to be a normal Deaf person rather than an abnormal hearing person.

By the middle of the 1990s, a number of Deaf people gained greater leadership roles in the major Deaf organisations in the UK. Jeff McWhinney at the British Deaf Association, Susan Daniels at the National Deaf Children's Society and Mabel Davis who became Britain's first Deaf head teacher for nearly a century represent just the tip of the iceberg.

These gains came about almost in spite of those in control of the organisations. These advances took place in a changing societal context but they have also been the result of *individual* determination and courage.

Of additional significance is that like many others, the three people I've mentioned above brought one other skill to their successful achievement - the ability to sign. Even when their education had been based on an oralist method, they used sign language in adult life.

Of perhaps greater significance is that these "successes" are all working in the Deaf field. It is a massive indictment to education and to the field that it has taken over 100 years for such Deaf successes to emerge. It is also a condemnation of the wider society that we do not yet have Deaf successes in mainstream agencies.

Likewise, the appointment of a Deaf person to the head of the RNID, the largest voluntary organisation for d/Deaf people in the world, had great impact. The RNID has an annual budget in excess of £30 million and a paid staff of more than 1,000. With the first non-verbal, BSL using Deaf person to head the RNID, the hopes of Deaf people rose.

This appointment was thought to represent a powerful vote of confidence in Deaf people. We could move forward with the support of hearing people. It was widely believed that the appointment would be the first of many similar appointments. The new world with its broad horizons awaited us...the 'Brave New World' was arriving.

However, as we know, those hopes and dreams were dashed.

So, my story begins in 1985. Before then, the RNID was a traditional, paternalistic organisation, a Victorian philanthropy set up by those 'well-meaning' missionary types who had a deep concern for the welfare of the "deaf and dumb". For most of its history, the RNID tended to be dominated by audiologists, ENT (Ear, Nose and Throat) medical professionals and, of course, 'do-gooders'.

The fifty member Management Committee was made up almost entirely of hearing people. Good people. People who patted themselves on the back and applauded one another for their good and decent work. Oh, there was the occasional Deaf person and a smattering of deaf people. Not enough to cause any concern.

The organisation operated as a typical voluntary organisation. The focus of its work was on things like hearing aids, mental health and social work. In terms of modern management methods and political philosophy, it was still in the dark ages. When Deaf people in the United Kingdom first became politicised, the RNID was ill-suited to appropriately respond.

Indeed, in those early years the RNID was known by Deaf people and their allies as the "Really Not Interested in the Deaf".

This is my story. This is the story of a decade of the RNID. And it is the story of Deaf people.

23

Chapter One

Who Are We?

I never cared about the sound of radios and bands;
What hurts me most is, I never heard
My parents' signing hands.

Stephen J. Bellitz

Before we pick up the story again in the next Chapter, it is necessary to explain an important distinction on which much of this story hangs.

On first glance, it might appear to you that the term "deaf" should be self-evident. It means... what? Someone who is unable to hear? Someone with some degree of significant hearing loss? Someone who was born without the ability to hear? Someone who lost the ability to hear later in life due to a traumatic accident?

All of the above?

Some of the above?

As it turns out, what might appear to be a very simple and straightforward term is, like most 'simple and straightforward' things, much more nuanced and complex when examined more closely.

Deaf.

As I have noted in the previous Chapter, I use the term Deaf (with an upper case D) to refer to people like myself, people who usually have a profound hearing loss. We cannot hear conversations or use the telephone. I use the term deaf (with a lower case d) to refer to most other degrees of hearing loss. A rough distinction would be in the ability to use the telephone. The deaf can and the Deaf can't.

24

It is a fundamental and important distinction, both in terms of how deafness is dealt with institutionally and educationally and how the Deaf (or deaf) perceive themselves.

On the one hand, deafness (lower case) is likely to be something that you have some familiarity with. There is that elderly relative or friend who requires you to raise your voice significantly to be understood.

"This one," they might point, indicating that you must speak into their 'good' ear for them to hear you.

You might find yourself shouting during general conversations when you visit with this relative or friend because the background noise in their home, whether from the radio or the television, is turned up to high volume. Others in the house, like yourself, are likely to scrunch up their faces and make dramatic gestures about plugging their own ears when visiting.

Strictly speaking, your relative or friend is not deaf. He or she is simply hard of hearing. They are able to hear even if what they hear is faint or fading. With the use of a hearing aid, they have little trouble communicating effectively with speech. Their situation is analogous to those of us who have difficulty reading words at a normal distance but whose reading is improved dramatically with the use of spectacles.

In the United Kingdom, there are nearly eight million people who fall somewhere in the category of "hard of hearing" or "hearing impaired". Their hearing loss might be minor - they may have trouble picking up the sound of rustling leaves - or it may be more significant - to the point where they have difficulty in following a normal conversation from a short distance.

Over a third, around three million, of these people with impaired hearing people wear hearing aids to compensate for their hearing deficit. Most of them then manage to have verbal communication and use the telephone. The rest clearly do not have a hearing loss that is significant enough to have effect on their lives.

That hard of hearing (deaf) relative is almost a caricature on television and in the cinema. We can picture him cupping his hand to his ear and uttering the famous request to repeat whatever was said, "Eh?" He might be heroic, having suffered hearing loss during the war, or sad, having lost his hearing due to illness. In either case, he is cranky or adorable, depending on the mood of the filmmaker.

That is not the case with those of us who are so deaf that we cannot hear. We have a profound hearing loss. Yelling at us or turning up the volume will not make any difference. We are Deaf (upper case).

In a world in which sound creates its own geography, we Deaf people are often lost without a map.

We cannot rely on sounds to guide us. We have to use visual cues and on visual forms of communication, like sign language. You are likely to be familiar with sign language from seeing Sign Language Interpreters signing at public events to give access to Deaf people in attendance.

Being Deaf is not just a question of audiograms. The audiological graphs mapping out the amount of hearing over the range of sound frequencies. It is to do with the fact that we cannot follow in group spoken conversations, even with a hearing aid. Some Deaf people may even wear such aids but they just give a mumble of indecipherable sounds. Their purpose is to do with offering a sense of security (e.g. in knowing when a car goes past). Or to reduce the feeling of isolation that complete silence could bring. Because the aural burble of spoken conversation mean nothing, their cognitive processes are not based on spoken words.

For deaf people, some adjustment on the person (i.e. hearing aid) is sufficient to enable participation in society. Not so with the Deaf. *Their access is possible only if the environment is adjusted to include them as equal members of society. That makes Deafness a social and political issue.* It is a struggle for the recognition of and the necessity of that adjustment.

Thus, the difference between a deaf person and a Deaf person is more fundamental than the ability to hear or carry a spoken conversation. Deaf people define themselves in ways that deaf people would likely not feel comfortable with.

These Deaf people form a group (or "community") of around 100,000 sign language users in the United Kingdom. This number is sure to grow as more individuals with profound to severe hearing loss accept their identity as Deaf people rather than suffer in a state of denial that grants them no benefit or comfort. When we count in deaf and hearing people who can use sign language this number increases to around 250,000 users.

This distinction between Deaf and deaf might seem arbitrary at first but it makes perfect sense. To refer again to the analogy of sight, although we might hear someone complain about a cricket umpire who made a bad call as being "blind", we know that a blind person is a person who does not have sight and who requires the assistance of a guide dog or a white stick to move safely along the streets.

People who wear glasses, regardless of the degree of their sight deficit, are not categorised as being "blind". While they may be considered blind in a cultural sense (if the lenses of their glasses appear thick enough) and while some people may say that they are 'blind', they are no more blind than a person who is hard of hearing and uses a hearing aid is 'Deaf'. In some ways it is rather silly to call hearing aid wearers "deaf". It is tantamount to calling spectacle wearers blind. Calling them "deaf" is a misnomer. After all, the word "deaf" means without hearing or cannot hear. "Hearing impaired" would be a more appropriate term for these 'deaf' people.

Although I am sure that societal and cultural considerations and confusions have contributed to the mix of understandings of what it means to be 'deaf', the end result is a mish mash of policies and services that do not adequately address the needs of those who most require assistance to overcome their social exclusion.

Add to the mix a third group of deaf people who deserve a special categorisation, those who lost their hearing later in their lives after having enjoyed normal hearing. While they are unable to hear even with hearing aids, they have normal speech. These people tend not to classify themselves as being 'Deaf'. They want to maintain their careers, relationships and social interactions just as they had always done - in a manner and environment dependent upon sound.

27

For personal, practical and political purposes, it is best to classify them as 'deaf' rather than 'Deaf' despite their absolute hearing impairment.

There, now we have three tidy groups for classification, right? Not exactly. The reality is even more complex than this. There are many areas of overlap, with some people falling in the grey area between categories. Exactly where they fit in depends on the unique circumstances of their lives - the extent of their hearing loss, their situation, how they classify themselves and how others classify them.

I am not certain why this is difficult to fathom for so many people. There is an intuitive understanding that a person with a limp is qualitatively less 'disabled' than a person confined to a wheelchair. Not only is the degree of their disabilities different, but this difference also demands a completely different set of understandings regarding how they function in the world and how they are perceived.

I can point to many of such examples - comparing a person with a white cane to a person wearing glasses, differences in skin colour, language difficulties of immigrants - and while each of these examples will be convincing there remains something that makes it difficult to apply the same concept to people with varying degrees of hearing impairment. Perhaps the difficulty lies in the fact that deafness is a hidden disability.

It is not difficult to spot a person in a wheelchair. It is equally apparent when a blind person crosses a road. Immigrants are generally identifiable by their appearance as well as their language. However, a Deaf person appears no different than anyone else.

A hearing person may casually ask a Deaf person, who is not looking at him, for directions only to discover that the Deaf person does not respond to his enquiry. This might result in anger or annoyance, with the hearing person feeling that he has been somehow 'slighted' and will come away from the encounter with a negative feeling toward Deaf people. But the hearing person has not been slighted.

That same hearing person might ask a deaf person (hearing impaired) for the same directions. He may get a response along the lines of, "Sorry, could you speak a bit louder. Can't hear so well in that ear."

"Sorry, mate," the hearing person will say before repeating the enquiry more loudly.

Clearly, the reality of the Deaf person and the deaf person are as different as the reality of the person who wears reading glasses from the blind person. Yet, the expectations of society do not acknowledge the distinction in the case of deafness.

Education systems respond differently to those with poor eyesight and those who are blind, going so far as to create a completely unique written language (Braille) for the blind. Society correctly spends an incredible amount of money to create access to buildings and public transport for people with physical impairments.

And yet... when it comes to deafness, society and those institutions dedicated to the 'well-being' of the Deaf, seem not to be able to recognise that there is a significant difference between deaf and Deaf, a difference as absolute as that between blindness and the need for reading glasses.

The deaf and the Deaf have very different needs and realities. Even if they are perceived as being the same by the vast majority of those who hear, they perceive themselves very differently. Those who are deaf want to hear again. They want to be 'normal' and to return to a life experience, which they have enjoyed to a greater degree in the past. For them, hearing loss is a source of frustration. They want to be 'cured' or, failing that, they want devices that can minimise their hearing loss.

We who are Deaf do not share this desire. To the extent that each person must accept who they are (should a short person go through life miserable because he is not as tall as a basketball player?) We Deaf people do not expend energy wanting to be 'normal' as defined by a hearing person.

We want to be normal, as we would define it - on our terms. As Deaf people. Our interior terrain will never be marked by sound. We will never have an auditory geography. What we desire is the ability to achieve all that we are capable of as people and as individuals while recognising and respecting this reality.

The absence of sound is just the way it is. Our reactions and our behaviour are wholly appropriate in a soundless environment.

Those of us who have been Deaf from birth or a very young age have cognitive processes that, while fully functioning, develop differently from those of deaf or hearing people. A child who can hear is exposed to a phenomenal amount of input that is sound-based.

"Cootchy, cootchy coo."

"Mah-mah."

Walks in a pram in which everything is being pointed out by name. Music. Street sounds. Birds. Aeroplanes overhead. Footsteps approaching the cot.

The sound of his own crying.

These sounds are coordinated with visual clues to create a particular tapestry of experience. In the hearing baby's brain, the sound of his crying is followed by the sound of mother's footsteps approaching, which is followed by the appearance of his mother.

Sound allows a hearing child to anticipate events differently than a Deaf child can. The Deaf child relies solely on visual input. His cognitive processes develop on the basis of visual sequences alone. As a result, a Deaf child thinks and makes deductions in a qualitatively different way than a hearing child.

Similarly, the development of language will be different for the hearing and the Deaf child. For the hearing child, the acquisition of language will depend on hearing the language being spoken around him. It will also be the result of a sound-based understanding of the world. The hearing child will hear footsteps then the sound of a door opening. This will be translated into, "Daddy is home!" even before Daddy walks through the door.

Thought, in the hearing child, is articulated in a language based on words.

In contrast, the Deaf child relies exclusively on visual cues. A Deaf child in the same situation as the hearing child above would not hear footsteps or the sound of the door opening. He would however *see* the door opening and he would *see* Daddy coming into the room. As a result, his thought process (and the way it would be communicated in sign language) is "Door open Daddy walk." In the order that events appeared in vision.

Naturally, the reality of communication and experience, of the subtle interplay of cognitive processes, is much, much more complex than this. But this very simplistic example should give you a clear idea of the fundamental difference between the hearing and the Deaf in this regard.

Spoken English would be a second language for the Deaf child, learned after his native BSL (British Sign Language). This is too often overlooked or minimised by educators in their attempts to 'normalise' Deaf children. Would an English family living in China expect their child to speak Chinese before English? Or would English be the child's 'mother tongue' and Chinese a comfortable second language?

The consequences for forcing a child to not develop his true native language are often disastrous. Note the distinction between "native" (innate) and "mother" (environmental) languages. For the hearing they are one and the same. But with the Deaf, even if they have hearing parents, they are different. Language and communication skills are so fundamentally intertwined with cognitive development that to retard one significantly hampers the development of the other. Those who would force Deaf children to be taught by the precepts of oralism, where the use of sign language is prohibited, doom them to frustration. The native language is corrupted and submerged before it has emerged sufficiently to form the basis of cognition.

Deaf children should be allowed to develop communication skills naturally, utilising sign language and other visual means. Once they are fluent in their ability to communicate and their cognitive skills are developing, then they are in a strong position to learn a second language, English. The wisdom of this approach is evident in the experience of many Deaf people, myself included.

Of course, a deaf child who is able to hear a considerable amount of sound, even if it is sometimes misheard due to his hearing impairment, has special needs that require some combination of these two approaches so that he will develop language and cognitive skills.

For Deaf people, the accommodations that must be made to allow us to function in a society that is sound-based, while operating with cognitive processes that are visually based, means that we exist with fundamentally different cultural imperatives than those of hearing people - and those of deaf people.

Our life experiences in education, employment, and socialising are profoundly different from hearing or deaf people. The ability to communicate effectively with speech is a Rubicon, which we cannot easily cross. The ability to hear, however compromised, is an essential tool in a sound-based society. It allows the deaf to do reasonably well in educational settings, in employment and in social settings. For the most part, they are perceived and treated as being the same as hearing people.

Which is how they see themselves. The deaf would never identify themselves as Deaf, as people who cannot hear enough to be able to communicate in a speaking environment. They consider themselves full members in the hearing world. They do not want to be Deaf.

It may help to further clarify the distinctions between the two clearly different groups if we refer to the auditory map that I mentioned earlier.

First, picture a huge white area, based on the geography of sound. It is populated by those who have the facility, the internal sound based geography so to speak. They are primarily hearing. This white area also includes our 8 million who have a hearing impairment. With or without hearing aids they function well enough in that world of sound. They have the necessary internal aural geography.

Within this white map we have a black area, which is not based on a geography of sound. Area of silence where aural cues are largely meaningless. This is populated by those who do not have the facility to operate normally in the world of sound. They have an internal geography based primarily on visual stimulus, like sign language. These are the Deaf. Their normal modes of communication, thoughts and experiences are different from those in the white area.

Because it is based on sound, they are socially excluded from that 'white' environment. They do not have the means to interact in that setting. The Deaf then face problems in education, employment and social interaction. They require political or medical actions to enable them involvement in the white areas on an equal basis to others. As medical solutions do not work, they are therefore, dependent on political solutions.

Those deaf people in the outside white area do not need such measures, nor do they want them.

Then there is a grey circle round the rim of the black area. It consists of people who are not sure where they are.

They could be deaf people who want to be hearing but do not quite have sufficient hearing to manage in a world of sound. They don't want to be Deaf and use sign language.

Or they could be people with profound hearing loss who have been influenced by oralism. Our "speaking" Deaf. They clearly cannot function normally in the outer 'white' world. Nor can they function in the Deafworld.

These people chose to remain in this state of limbo. Confused people in "no mans land". Neither hearing nor Deaf. The Greys.

Also within that grey area are those that I have dubbed as the "career d/Deaf". People with hearing deficits who do not want to be deaf or Deaf. Then when it suits them for their own political reasons they become deaf or even Deaf. They go round proclaiming, "I am deaf," as if it needs to be broadcast.

All organisations involved with d/Deaf (a term used to cover all who cannot use the telephone normally) people should be working *only* within the black and grey circles or else they are working under false pretences. They are not wanted or needed in the white area. Visions on Deaf (and deaf) rights refer to the political black and grey areas only. In terms of numbers, we are looking at around 500,000 d/Deaf people. If we want to play the "numbers game", we can stretch it to 1 (one) million people. No more.

On those grounds, it is inappropriate for bodies like the RNID to "represent" these 8.7 million hearing impaired (deaf?) people. As it would be for the RNIB to represent all those who wear spectacles.

The Royal National Institute for Spectacle Wearers? Oh yeah! The Royal National Institute for Hearing Impaired would be more appropriate, that is if those people do want to be represented by a charity. Which they clearly don't.

Witness the number of people who register onto the telephone relay service for those who cannot use the phone normally. It has consistently been around 18,000 people. Where are the 8 million? Clearly they are able to access the telephone normally and so are not Deaf (or even deaf!).

This leads to the question of who is to represent those in the black area in the political arena? Who ought to dictate policies that affect these people? And who should be on the governing bodies of these organisations? It is quite clear from the arguments that I have presented that it can only be those from the black area - the Deaf. Those for whom participation in the wider world require political solutions.

Not the hearing impaired or deaf – in the same way as we could not have spectacle users controlling policies for blind members of the RNIB! It would be as inappropriate as having hearing people to represent the Deaf. Clearly nonsense.

We do have organisations and new Paternalists that use the deaf (hearing impaired) to suit their own political purposes. Whether to play the 8 million numbers game or to make the composition of governing bodies look better, they are misleading everyone. This is not helping the cause of the Deaf. In fact it is holding us back, as it prevents the development of appropriate policies and practices.

Deaf people should control bodies like the RNID – as Black people do with Black organisations and women with Women's organisations.

The deaf (hearing impaired) view themselves as normal members and participants in society. On the other hand, for the Deaf, the very term "society" has a negative connotation. While we live *in* society, we are not *a part of* society. We are people who live on isolated islands floating in the sea of society. Our black circles on a white sea. We can see the society. The society can see us. But there is a distance and an "apartness" that cannot be easily bridged.

Society is tolerant of deaf people. That inquiry for directions I discussed earlier, while met with initial annoyance, is repeated more loudly. The deaf get a second chance. The Deaf rarely do.

We are looked down upon. We are treated in a condescending manner, a dismissive manner or as 'village idiots'. People can utter negative things to our faces, secure in their belief that we cannot 'hear' them. These behaviours and the attitudes that fuel them create near-insurmountable obstacles to our attempts to become integrated into the society where we live.

But how can we live comfortably in a society that imposes such cruel expectations upon us? A blind child is not expected to look up into the sky and count the number of birds flying overhead. A crippled child in a wheelchair is not expected to run a race and win.

"That's cruel and distasteful!" any reasonable person would say to the very suggestion of those things. Yet, that same 'reasonable' person seems not to have any problem with the expectation that a Deaf child hear. Lorraine Fletcher, the mother of a Deaf child hit it on the head when she exclaimed, "With a blind child, the approach is to maximise the use of the existing senses to compensate for the loss of one. Whereas with a Deaf child, the focus is on maximising the use of the deficient sense! Ridiculous!"

Her frustration and anger were right on target. Society has worked to find ways of helping a blind person compensate for the loss of sight either through increased use of hearing or touch (beeps in elevators and at crosswalks, Braille to assist in reading). However, society expects the Deaf to hear!

Ridiculous indeed!

Hearing society responds to the deaf child and adult by acknowledging and understanding the limitations of their hearing ability. However, that same hearing society views Deaf people as a bit "dim".

Society justifies this in part because people seem to genuinely believe that they know what it is like to be Deaf.

"Here you go," they say, plugging their ears with their fingers. "Like this then."

Their experiential simulation misses the point completely. Being Deaf is not simply the inability to hear. Remember, the hearing person standing there like an idiot with his fingers in his ears has an entire sound-based internal geography.

"What? What did you say? I can't hear you?" he replies to a question. "Hmm," he thinks to himself. "So this must be what it's like to be deaf..."

Because society depends on a sound-based geography, Deaf people are strangers. Without a guide or an effective map, we cannot manage for ourselves in society. In other words, being Deaf is as much a social handicap as a physical one.

We are like strangers in a strange land, a land where the natives view us with a spectrum of emotions that range from fear to pity. Our Deafness is not only defined by ourselves but by the reactions and attitudes of society.

Being Deaf means confronting social prejudices. Being Deaf means being an outsider in a society that is based on sound. Being Deaf means having to communicate - or not communicate - in an environment dominated by sound.

These realities define our existence from our very earliest years. As children, at a communications disadvantage, we struggle to understand the lessons our teachers try to teach us using speech and, as a result, we are invariably classified as being either "stupid" or "slow". As young adults, we are unable to converse at parties or pubs. Hearing people often avoid us as if we are lepers. As adults, we miss trains because we are unable to hear verbal announcements. We watch our friends go on to meaningful employment while we are left behind. We stay in hotels with the knowledge that we cannot hear the fire alarm.

We cannot understand our Doctors. We do not become involved in local politics or community affairs.

Do you still think that understanding what it is like to be Deaf is as simple as sticking your fingers in your ears? Is it this simplistic presumption that is at the heart of society's reaction to Deaf people? As Lorraine Fletcher noted, it's only with the Deaf that society insists on maximising the deficient sense - as if the deficiency could, or should, be easily remedied.

Sound is so essential to hearing people that they seem to have a primal fear of Deaf people in a way that they don't fear people with most other handicaps. Could this fear be at the root of society's insistence that Deaf people be made 'normal'.

Perhaps.

However, the source of the fear is of less importance than its consequences, which have allowed certain people to act as gatekeepers to determine who has rights and who does not. Society's reliance on so-called 'experts' - Doctors, Audiologists, and others with a vested interest in their paternalistic medical model - has shaped too many negative perspectives of the Deaf.

This is where we Deaf are too often defined by our physical limitation. As a result, our humanity is determined by our deafness rather than our humanity. The 'problem' is located in the individual Deaf person. We are rendered apart from the rest of humanity.

This medical model, which focuses on cure, support, the denial of deafness and on rehabilitation might have a very real role in the lives of the deaf. It has absolutely no relevance in the lives of the Deaf.

During the decade, a new model has emerged, a social model. This model emphasises the humanity of the Deaf. As such, it presumes the 'normalcy' of Deafness as part of the full spectrum of human beings in a society. It emphasises our rights as people. Rather than focus on the physical limitation of Deafness, this model examines the social factors that limit our ability to function fully to our capabilities.

This social model examines attitudes, education, the inaccessibility of information - the very social structures that bar Deaf people from full participation - and concludes that the problem of a Deaf person functioning in society is a societal problem, *not* a physical and individual disability in itself.

This is a profound and powerful shift in focus and attention. It is revolutionary. Whereas the medical model fosters negative perceptions regarding deafness, and fails to make a clear and useful distinction between deafness and Deafness, the social model addresses these failures directly and effectively.

The failures of the educational system to adequately teach Deaf people can be seen as results from flawed philosophies and policies – based primarily on the presumptions of the medical model. By lumping the deaf and the Deaf together and insisting on oralism, which could be effective for some deaf children, ensures that the vast majority of Deaf children have had little or no chance of succeeding.

Why has this faulty and destructive model been allowed to operate for so long? I wish I could suggest that ignorance and prejudice were the only reasons. However, I fear that the real and fundamental reason is much more sinister. Power and profit.

The medical model has been held in place by those who directly profit from it. The doctors and audiologists, the manufacturers of devices designed to 'normalise' Deaf people. And of course, the 'benevolent' Paternalists. These people are the prime drivers behind the medical model.

The social model has politicised Deaf issues, much to the distress of those who would maintain control over the Deaf. The social model threatens the money machine.

It is in this context, the sea of change brought about by the emergence of the social model, that our story begins. The story of the RNID in 1985. Prior to this, unchallenged by social thinkers, the RNID had reflected the condescending attitude, which had defined it from its inception. Rather than lead in advocacy for the legitimate needs and goals of Deaf people, it occupied a primary role in holding the Deaf back by perpetuating the medical model of deafness.

However, in 1985, with the winds of change blowing, the RNID decided that it, too, needed to think about modernising, primarily on an institutional level. The consequences of that decision could not have been anticipated by anyone.

Chapter Two

Metamorphosis

The fundamental premise of a revolution is that the existing social structure has become incapable of solving the urgent problems of the development of the nation.

Leon Trotsky

Up to the 1980's the Deaf were generally seen as defective and in need of paternalistic support. Deafness was a 'charitable cause'. The major organisations like the RNID had a prime focus on cure and normalisation. Even the largest 'consumer' organisation, the British Deaf Association (BDA) was run by hearing people.

As a result of the corrosive effects of their poor education, social situation and paternalistic entrapment Deaf people had acquired a sense of inferiority and worthlessness. This began to be challenged by a small number of Deaf people and their hearing allies. They began to take to task how they were being treated and the negative attitudes around them. They made Deafness a political issue. In 1976 Paddy Ladd, Raymond Lee and others set up the National Union of the Deaf (NUD) to raise consciousness of Deaf people's rights and also to fight against the failure of the education system to educate Deaf children.

Their battle was informed by examples from abroad like the USA and Sweden, with their liberal policies on rights for disabled and Deaf people. Speakers were invited from these two countries to key British Deaf conferences. Several central issues then came about at around the same time, which had significant effects on the subsequently rapid advance of Deaf politics in the UK.

Information came over to the UK in the early 1970s from US researchers that American Sign Language was a language in its own right with its own distinctive grammar and structure, which was different from that of spoken English. This had implications for the sign language used in the UK. Instead of being dismissed as a parody of animal gestures, it had to be contended with as a legitimate language. Research projects were then set up at Bristol and Durham Universities to explore this. The results confirmed that British Sign Language (BSL) was indeed a different – but equally legitimate – language from spoken English.

Then a book came over to the UK from the US, "When the Mind Hears" by Harlan Lane, a hearing American language psychologist, which tracked the history of Deaf people. It had an explosive effect in the UK as Deaf people began to realise their own identities as Deaf people rather than as pseudo-hearing people.

In 1981, Arthur Verney, a hearing child of Deaf parents, became the General Secretary of the British Deaf Association (BDA). Up to that point, the BDA had been an organisation "of" Deaf people run mainly by Social worker types, with its main focus on the social and sports activities of Deaf people. Verney changed the BDA into a political campaigning organisation. No doubt he was provoked into this by the rise of the NUD, which threatened to draw attention away from the BDA and consign it to a floating fun house without any real meaning. Under Verney's leadership the BDA developed into a real fighting force for the rights of Deaf people. He made a point of involving Deaf people into the campaigns.

At the same time, there was a strong nationwide movement by disabled people for their rights. Successive Governments, for various reasons (whether socialism or the need to cut the welfare budget) espoused policies for the independence of disabled people. As Deaf people were legally classified under the disability banner, they got dragged into these issues whether they liked it or not.

This was the background where the new era of the RNID and for many Deaf people, the "golden era" of the RNID began in 1985. That was not its original aim. The Management Committee (as the Board of Trustees was known then) had intended simply for the organisation to become more efficient. 1985 was the heart of Thatcherism. Prime Minister Thatcher was brow-beating the nation into becoming a more powerful market economy.

Thatcher saw public services as being bloated bureaucracies, wasteful and inefficient. She wanted the public services to buy into private sector management methods. And, as you might recall, when the "Iron Lady" wanted something, she generally got it.

In this environment, charities, particularly those dependent on public funding, were told in no uncertain terms to get their accounts in order. In other words, the "winds of change" that were blowing were fiduciary, not

41

philosophical. The RNID had no intention of relinquishing its fundamental colonialism. Their creed, then and forever, was to "help the d/Deaf people". Which, to many Deaf people, always translated into keeping "Deaf people effectively neutered in society."

The Management Committee's first move toward modernisation was to recruit Mike Whitlam from another charity, Save the Children Fund, as their first Chief Executive Officer. Previously, they had a General Secretary as its head.

The move was a smart one in that Whitlam quickly and effectively restructured the RNID to become more efficient. He split the work of the RNID and its staff into six Departments; Finance and Administration, Residential Services, Advocacy and Information, Fundraising, Regional Services and Technical Services. Each Department was headed by a Director with full responsibility for the budget and activities within that Department. The group formed by the CEO and Directors was the Senior Management Team (SMT).

However, as any leader knows, in order for an organisation to be truly effective, it must have a vision with a clearly articulated mission statement. In order to draft this mission statement, Whitlam assessed the situation both inside and outside the d/Deaf world.

Nothing ever happens in a vacuum. Just as Thatcherism had prompted the RNID to make the management changes that Whitlam put in place, the social and political environment played a significant role in determining the way he would articulate the RNID's vision and mission.

After years of social democratic politics and labour unions, Margaret Thatcher represented a determined insistence on individual initiative. She wanted everyone "off the dole". This political environment promoted the independence of individuals and minimised the concepts of dependence. In this context, the disabled were seen to have very real rights. It had to be this way. If disabled people had no rights, then the government could not very well pull the social service rug out from under them.

While the truly sick and infirm continued to receive care, the feeling was that those who were capable should be out running their own lives. It was in this climate that the BDA, under the leadership of Verney, began to aggressively promote the rights of Deaf people.

The BDA's leadership was not surprising. Unlike the RNID, which emphasised the needs of the deaf, the BDA always had its primary focus on the Deaf.

This trend toward empowerment was reinforced by international events. Deaf people, particularly in the Scandinavian countries, had made tremendous strides toward equality and participation. Verney and the BDA took the lead in raising the consciousness of Deaf people and in making politicians aware of the issues of Deaf rights.

Progress on all these fronts was changing the political environment of Deafness. "Quality of life" issues as defined by such paternalistic organisations as the RNID were no longer the only items on the table. Core issues such as equality and full rights as citizens were demanding attention.

Whitlam was smart enough to take the measure of all these trends and he was able to see that the key to any progress in the field of deafness that was not determined by and limited by the medical model was BSL. He was also quick enough to realise that the RNID could not have any meaningful role in that progress without targeting Deaf people.

In short, he came to the conclusion that it wasn't just the winds of change that were blowing but the winds of revolution. Only the Deaf represented a real political body. The deaf had no serious desire to change the world. They had no need to. They encountered some relatively minor frustrations but they considered themselves, correctly, to be part of the normal, hearing world. The Deaf were a different matter. We had suffered with real oppression, prejudice and adversity.

Whitlam formulated the vision of the RNID simply and directly, "Deaf people have the right to full citizenship."

Not only had he changed the direction and emphasis of the RNID but Whitlam had also managed to hijack BDA's political agenda. In doing this, he was strongly supported by two of his Directors - Stuart Etherington and me. As I will explain in the next chapter, I had joined the staff of the RNID in 1987.

Whitlam made it clear that the RNID was not abandoning the needs of the deaf. However, he made it equally clear that when it came to the leading edge of its political agenda, it was the Deaf and their issues that would define the RNID.

Along with this vision came a transformation of operating principles for the RNID. The shift was at once subtle and profound. Rather than reaching out to help these "poor d/Deaf people" the mission of the RNID was becoming to create a social environment where the inability to hear was less of a disadvantage, so that individual d/Deaf people could take control of their own lives.

Rather than, for example, using RNID staff and resources to advise individual d/Deaf callers on legal issues, they were referred to their local agencies such as the Citizen's Advice Bureau. The RNID staff would then contact the local agencies to make sure that they were following it through.

The RNID wasn't going to "do it for them" any longer. Instead, the RNID was going to work to make all the local service agencies be more responsive to Deaf people.

Whitlam and his six Directors (the SMT) were out in front of this trend. The political agenda was being changed without directly consulting Deaf people. This sea of change was startling to many people. Including Deaf people. Whitlam's vision meant promoting a positive face on Deafness rather than portraying Deaf people as victims in need of assistance.

"Revolutionary" is almost an understatement for the significance of this change. For a charity to become so overtly political rather than rely on the "tried and true" methods of portraying the Deaf as pathetic called into question the RNID's ability to make money. After all, anyone who has done charity work knows that sympathy for the pathetic is a great motivator for those willing to donate.

No one should minimise the courage that Whitlam displayed by changing the message from "they need help" to "they can do it!" In addition to courage, Whitlam showed passion and creativity in bringing this message home. The first advertisement to hit the streets as a result of this showed a long poster with an ear at either end. The copy read: "Because they're not working, it doesn't mean there's nothing between them."

The Management Committee of the RNID was probably a mite uneasy about some of these trends. Whitlam was a voice and a presence they had not anticipated. But they dared not move against him. In spite of their discomfort with the direction of Whitlam's leadership, they had to be cautious about moving against success. And Whitlam was clearly successful.

Besides, it took the Committee a while to fully appreciate just how effectively Whitlam was turning the RNID around. After all, these 'good people' only pop in for meetings every three months or so. They wouldn't realise what had happened until it was too late to do anything about it.

Whitlam was a man for his time, perfectly suited for the ethos of the Thatcher era. Along with his six Directors, he decentralised the work of the organisation. As a result, the RNID was well-positioned to benefit from any opportunities arising from government action.

Etherington, the Director of Advocacy and Information, and I, Director of Community Services, worked tirelessly to support Whitlam's directives. Etherington provided the strategic wisdom to realise the RNID's new goals. I provided the "Deaf view", along with the philosophical justification for those goals.

Just as Whitlam had our support, we were supported by a number of strong Divisional Managers. John Healey headed Campaigns. (He later moved to a similar post at the TUC before becoming one of the new breed of Labour MPs.) Sheila Grew, Jean Greaves, Lynne Hawcroft, Helen Fraquet and Jim Edwards formed a powerful and forward-thinking group of Principal Regional Officers.

By working in the real world rather than the 'ivory tower' of the headquarters, they had direct knowledge and commitment to rights issues. They could see where we needed to go and they supported Whitlam's changes whole-heartedly.

Thatcher's government pushed for competitive tendering of the statutory social services. As a result, many Local Authorities began to contract out their social services for Deaf people among other things. While responsibilities under the Mental Health Act and the Children Act generally remained within the authority's own staff, sign language interpreting and the provision of equipment to Deaf people were offered to outside contractors.

Against the general opinion of other charities, Whitlam brought the RNID into the culture of competitive bidding for contracts. He recognised more than just the opportunity to make the RNID more efficient. He saw an opportunity to change the entire ethos of services for Deaf people away from the traditional paternalistic model.

"Don't you see the significance of splitting the interpreting role from social work?" he would ask, astonished if anyone failed to immediately spot the sense of it.

Most people working in Deaf services failed to spot the logic, or preferred not to. They argued and fought against the move. They were horrified at the thought of the Social Workers losing their near-absolute grip on all Deaf services.

They might have been late in seeing the Whitlam's changes coming, but once they realised what was happening, they began to fight tooth and nail.

But, as I've noted above, they were too late.

Soon afterwards the RNID began to obtain contracts to provide Interpreting Services in some areas, taking these services away from the Social Workers. Most of the Local Authorities followed suit. Social Service Departments were then left to focus on those situations and individuals that required specific social work skills.

There was an added, unforeseen bonus to the outside contracts. Many Local Authorities specified that the contracted work be for work within the Authority's domain only. Any other interpreting requirement, such as those for health, further education, police, courts, or the private sector had to be paid for by those bodies.

Making this interpreting service successful meant more work for the Deaf organisations. They had to campaign to get the various community agencies to accept their responsibilities. But once done, it forced community agencies to acknowledge their role and responsibility in providing and paying for access for Deaf people.

Whitlam refused to limit the role of the RNID. In the past, the RNID had been a service provider only. The BDA had been the campaigning organisation. Whitlam insisted that the RNID do both. He was the one to establish the Department of Advocacy and Information under the directorship of Stuart Etherington. Suddenly, the RNID was playing a key role in campaigning, public relations, advertising and Parliamentary lobbying.

The Advocacy Department's first campaigning victory was rescuing the telephone relay service from being shut down due to a cut in project funding. The project was to overcome the barrier that Deaf people had in accessing the telephone network, by operating it through a relay system. With this system, the Deaf person who had textphone equipment would contact the relay service, which also had a textphone. The operator would then contact the hearing person that the Deaf person wished to speak to and pass on the message. The spoken responses from the called person were then typed by the operator to the Deaf person.

Because of this victory, Deaf people with text-phones were able to continue to benefit from this service. That embryo project went on to become the fully-fledged "Typetalk" service run by the RNID under a multi million pound contract from British Telecom (BT).

This new "campaigning arm" of the RNID in no way interfered with the services it had traditionally offered. It continued to provide residential care, Interpreting, Deaf awareness training and testing hearing-assistive devices.

Whitlam's greatest success was to place Deaf issues firmly in the public arena. He revived the "RNID Conference" which addressed all aspects of deafness. The Harrogate Conference was a resounding success. Such well-known public figures as Lord Blum-Cooper spoke and chaired workshops. Many of its recommendations continue to have a positive impact today.

In 1982 the BDA originated the idea of having Deaf people attend Party Political Conferences, funding a handful of Deaf delegates and demanding that they be given access via Interpreters. Whitlam went one step further; he went to each Political Party and offered the RNID as the agency to provide the Interpreters for their Conferences.

The RNID also muscled into the BDA initiative of setting up sponsored meetings at the Party Political Conferences to bring Deaf issues directly into the political arena. One example of how effectively this was accomplished was a breakfast meeting during a Labour Party conference at Brighton. The then Leader of the Opposition, Neil Kinnock, and his wife were joined at breakfast by a number of Deaf children from the local Deaf school, Hamilton Lodge. It was a great public relations coup as the media flocked in to take pictures of the Kinnocks conversing with the signing Deaf children.

Soon the RNID began to dominate political action on Deaf issues.

Just as Whitlam had led the RNID in the charitable and political spheres, he moved in the commercial sphere as well. He used a manager seconded from BT to establish "Sound Advantage", a company designed to sell deaf-related equipment. Visual alarms and text-phones among many other innovative and important devices were made available not only to the Local Authorities but also to individual Deaf buyers. Because the company was linked to the RNID's Technical Department, which undertook all testing of equipment, buyers knew they were getting the best quality and value available.

Marilyn Rykstrom was brought in to head the new Fundraising Department. She was successful in bringing in the funds to support the RNID's expanding agenda by going beyond the usual fund-raising methods to establish some very original and creative events, events which did more than simply bring in funds. They created an image and established a network

Perhaps Whitlam's most important vision was recognising that, at some point, leadership of a d/Deaf organisation must be provided by Deaf people. Toward this aim, he recruited me in 1987 to be the first Deaf Director/Senior Manager at the RNID. He also gave his full support for my recruitment of a team of Deaf Regional Officers and Interpreters.

Having come to the RNID from outside the Deaf world, Whitlam was not weighed down by preconceptions regarding Deaf people. Unlike so many in the field, including the traditionalists at the RNID and the Board of Trustees, he took Deaf people as they were. He encouraged us to believe we could do whatever was wanted if we set our minds to it.

His example and approach to creating a rights culture both inside and outside the RNID inspired many Deaf people who had never had any objective reason to be hopeful about the future. He represented the hope that there might be a light at the end of the tunnel.

"It's so blasted obvious, isn't it?" Whitlam said when he determined that wouldn't it *just make sense* if the people who worked at RNID could communicate with *all* d/Deaf people, including those who used sign language.

"But learning to sign is so difficult," many hearing members of staff protested. Whitlam would have none of that. Setting an example, he went out and learned to sign. And he expected everyone else to follow suit. Not just those on the front lines that had direct contact with Deaf people but the entire staff, including the normally cloistered finance department.

"Every last one," he said. "At least up to Stage One level" (the standard set by the Council for the Advancement of Communication with Deaf People - CACDP).

He set up in-house classes and employed full-time BSL tutors within the RNID. You can imagine what happened. The RNID went from an "anti-sign" organisational culture to one where sign language became almost... well, sexy.

It is remarkable to look back and measure what Mike Whitlam accomplished in four years. The profile of Deafness had never been raised to such a high level. For the first time, Deafness, and not the organisations established to deal with the d/Deaf, was at centre-stage.

Whatever the Management Committee of the RNID felt about this trend, Whitlam had the support of the staff. And Deaf people took to him right away. He was more than a breath of fresh air; he was a voice of genuine reason and vision. He had energy, determination, intelligence and creativity.

He needed all his gifts. In addition to overcoming the reluctance of some of the Board, Whitlam encountered the greatest resistance from many professionals in the field. They were not interested in change. They were interested in "business as usual". Deaf issues were, to them, their issues.

Whitlam's great success at the RNID made him a highly visible and much sought after candidate to head other prominent service organisations. Consequently, he left the RNID in 1989 to become the Director General of the British Red Cross.

Of course, in spite of the many things he'd achieved, there were objectives he had not yet completed.

Etherington succeeded Whitlam as Chief Executive. From the very start, he sensed that the "tide was turning." Although Whitlam had increased the RNID's income nearly three-fold, from £4 million to £11 million, the many projects he'd initiated stretched the budget to its limits. With a recession starting to take hold of the country, cutbacks were almost inevitable.

Perhaps Whitlam, with his incredible combination of character and determination, could have cajoled and pleaded and badgered for enough money to maintain the level of performance. However, Etherington recognised that he was not Whitlam. His wisdom and self-awareness allowed him to exercise control over those ideas he wanted to put on hold.

In addition to the economic environment, Etherington came into leadership saddled with another disadvantage. Deaf people had expected a Deaf person to follow Whitlam. However, the Board was either out of step with the political developments in the Deaf world or it chose to ignore them.

Even with these two realities hampering him, he accomplished quite a bit. While Whitlam was an exceptional tactician, making the most of any situation in front of him to achieve a vision, Etherington was a master strategist. He had the ability to plot out the methods and manner of getting from where we are now to that exalted vision.

While the onset of the recession might have been a horrible crisis, the reality was that it couldn't have come at a better time for Etherington. Although the RNID was not in any serious financial trouble as he took the helm, he knew that it would be if things continued the way they were going. Even under Whitlam, he had believed that the organisation could be more efficiently managed. Now, the situation gave him the opportunity to impose exactly the kind of efficiency he'd envisioned.

Taking a leaf from Thatcher's play book, Etherington created the impression of a crisis in the organisation and then went about providing the necessary hard decisions required to avert disaster. The consequent restructuring resulted in a number of redundancies. One of the hardest hit departments was mine, the Department of Community Services. There was quite an outcry about his decisions but he stuck by them. Whatever else could be said about him, Etherington did not shirk from difficult and unpopular decisions.

He closed the Employment and Education Divisions in spite of the fact that it is these very two issues that Deaf people would put at the head of their agenda. He closed down the Hearing Advisory Service. This decision was roundly protested by some of the Trustees. However, he stuck to it. Even when the issue was raised at the Annual General Meeting, a meeting chaired by the RNID President, Jack Ashley.

A majority vote at the AGM determined that the Senior Management Team should re-examine the decision. However, by the time the Senior Management Team finished looking at the issue, it was too late to do anything about it. Everyone had got used to making do without the Hearing Advisory Service. So it remained closed.

Cost and control were tightened during Etherington's first year. It is to his credit that even with this severe pruning, the quantity and quality of the RNID's services were not diminished. Things had to be done differently, yes. Staff were called upon to do more with less. But they did.

Of course, in any bureaucracy, a hard line at the top will result in some degree of insurrection somewhere down the line. Some staff, who had always appeared to be the very models of integrity, let their fear and instinct for self-preservation get the better of them. Principles be damned, the degree of sycophancy during Etherington's reign was truly staggering.

However, he gained respect if not affection from many people, including Deaf people. He brought his London Business School MBA to play in every aspect of his administration. He relished the intellectual aspects of management. He introduced many new methods into the RNID. Methods borrowed from the private sector such as the concepts of the learning organisation, total quality management, customer care, and staff attitude surveys. It was not long before the RNID was viewed by non-d/Deaf charities as the leader in the charity field when it came to organisational and staff development practices.

Etherington stabilised the RNID by developing an extremely efficient organisation. He also developed a much more potent SMT. So effective was his SMT that he used to boast that, should the RNID go into making washing machines, this Senior Management Team would make a good job of it.

He also devoted time and energy to improving the structure of the Management Committee, converting it to a Board of Trustees. Its size was cut from fifty to fifteen people. A largely academic RNID Assembly was established for those who did not make the final fifteen, to be joined by representatives from all organisations in the Deaf world. Of those fifteen, three were elected from the Assembly. It was a very smart ploy to make it seem as if all the other organisations came under an RNID 'umbrella'.

This Assembly was effectively a neutered body, having the task of presenting the RNID Chair and CEO with bi-annual opportunities to bombard them with some PR about how wonderful the RNID continued to be. Some organisational members have since pulled out of this farce. The majority remain, kept in place by obeisance to the power represented by association with the RNID.

51

After eighteen months of contraction and consolidation, Etherington eased off the reins to allow a period of controlled expansion. The focus of this expansion was for the RNID to become more commercial, to survive and pay its own way through earned income rather than depend on the vagaries of charity.

The development of the Deaf awareness training given by the Regional Training Officers to local agencies was one example. The training was to do with how to deal with d/Deaf customers and work with d/Deaf employees. It was then packaged and marketed as a "Louder than Words" campaign. Commercial Companies and statutory agencies "signed up" to a "Louder than Words Charter" where they committed themselves to ten points which would ensure full access to d/Deaf customers. These points included training for staff, provision of equipment (e.g. textphones) and Interpreters. The RNID would, of course, supply all these – at a price. In addition, the links with these "signed up" Companies offered potential for fundraising, sponsorship or other avenues of financial support.

In this effort, Etherington nearly doubled the annual income to just over £20 million. This amount included a greatly-increased contract with BT to operate "Typetalk".

Etherington had the good sense to value signing Deaf people and he expanded the commercial aspect of the RNID around them. In other words, he was the comfortable inheritor of Whitlam's vision but he developed it with his own methods.

Success has its own inherent failings. With the commercial and organisational success of the RNID, there were many who worried that it had begun to lose its soul. Something is always lost with hard-edged determination. As the millions of pounds began to pile up, little things, human touches were often lost.

There came to be such a professional feel to the RNID that it really could have produced washing machines. There was a palpable sense of "Oh, yes there's those d/Deaf people we have to do something with." As if the raison d'entre of the RNID had got lost in its efficient performance of its mission.

Curiously, in addition to success, this sense could have been the result of what both Whitlam and Etherington chose *not* to touch. Neither bothered with Education despite the fact that it is so crucial to every Deaf person's experience. Perhaps they felt that there was just no money in it. Or, perhaps they saw it as being more appropriately handled under the auspices of the National Deaf Children's Society agenda. Or, perhaps the intense politics of Deaf education was too much for them!

Even with this overlooked item, the significance of what occurred during these seven years cannot be diminished. Deaf issues had progressed from virtual non-existence to the forefront of the political agenda; there had been real progress in changing the perception of the Deaf from 'failed hearing people' to a distinct group of people with a social disability; there had been significant progress in the area of Deaf rights; modern management methods were introduced into the RNID.

Perhaps most significant, there had been a shift in organisational ethos from "how can we help these poor things" or "what is the best treatment for them?" to "what do deaf/Deaf people want?"

It was a profoundly heady time. As these seven years came to an end, the stage was set for the first ever Deaf CEO of the RNID in 1994.

Chapter Three

The Gritty Crusader

You see things as they are and ask, "Why?" I dream things as they never were and ask, "Why not?"

George Bernard Shaw

You must be the change you wish to see in the world.

Mahatma Ghandi

"Doug Alker? Who's Doug Alker?"

Back in 1987 in the early days of Whitlam's tenure at the RNID, these were the words that leapt to people's minds when I was first appointed to the position of Manager in the RNID. They wanted to know the kind of Deaf person who would be occupying the "hallowed halls" of that venerable organisation. Deaf people asked this question with particular urgency. After all, what could any Deaf person be doing "siding with" an organisation hated by so many Deaf people and held in suspicion by so many others? Treason! Switching sides! Going over to the enemy!

Where did I belong in this assembly of blue-rinsed Lady Bountifuls and ambitious wannabe knights? What business did I have rubbing elbows with those parents who had backed destructive education practices, parents who continued to push the same flawed and damaging practices on other Deaf children? How could I side with Educators with their appalling track record, who continued to advocate for failed policies? Or with medicos with their obsession with the ear rather than with the whole person? Or Audiologists. Or 'Missioners' in search of a new people to 'save'. Or the odd Social Worker looking for God knows what?

In spite of the handful of genuinely good eggs, the Committees that made up the RNID were a gathering of people and practices anathema to Deaf people. They were comprised of people who had minimal contact with the Deaf and who generally frowned upon the use of sign language.

"It's like a dance."

"A pantomime."

"Yes, that's it!"

To people with this sensibility, Deaf people really do 'pantomime' and as such are perceived to be lower down on the social and intellectual scale. To them, the 'better' and 'ideal' Deaf people speak and read lips. To get a step up in the estimation of these people, Deaf people are expected to participate in this vaudeville of exaggerated mouthings.

So, what was I doing at the RNID? Let me start at the beginning...

A staunch Lancastrian, born and bred in Wigan, where I spent my first twenty-three years (that is, when I wasn't away at boarding schools), I then moved to Blackburn to work as a Chemist at ICI for nearly a quarter of a century. I was true to my upbringing in most regards, especially in my suspicion and mistrust of politicians. A true northern working class man, I have no patience for people who promise things they can't - or won't - deliver. And I have even less patience for those who subscribe to backroom politics or the "old boys'" network. Both by experience and temperament, I strongly support measures to counter social injustice.

I was born with normal hearing but became completely deaf when I contracted meningitis at two years of age. My parents, concerned with my education and my development, consulted the "experts" at Manchester University Department of Audiology who instructed them not to sign to me.

Good northerners, they followed that advice religiously. What else could they do? After all, could you imagine how concerned they were? They had shepherded me through a dangerous disease with white-knuckled prayers. They were simply grateful that the consequences of the disease had not been worse.

Yet, they were left with a baby boy who was very much different from the baby boy they'd had only a few short weeks before. I no longer turned at the sound of their voices. I no longer smiled at the sound of my name.

They were at once so grateful and so fearful.

They placed themselves in the hands of the Doctors who had cared for me in my illness. These Doctors sent them to the Department of Audiology at Manchester University. Like most parents of Deaf children, they had to learn how to react as they went along. They had no preparation.

In addition to this advice not to sign, my parents were also advised to send me away to a boarding school for Deaf children when I was three. Again, they followed that heart wrenching advice to the letter, sending me away to a residential school at Preston some 20 miles from home, where I stayed even at weekends. In fact, I went home only three times a year - at Easter, Summer and Christmas.

The school at Preston was an interesting experience in that they allowed the use of sign between Deaf children even though the teachers tried to avoid signing with us. However, in spite of their determination to get through by speaking they often, in a nod to practicality, used signing as an aid in getting their lessons across.

After all, what was the point in speaking to us when we didn't understand much of what was being said?

The most glorious time for me at Preston was when I was with the other children on the playground or in the dayroom in the evening. At those times, we were allowed to sign to our hearts content and we 'chatted' away incessantly. We were, in short, just like any other kids. We laughed. We joked. We 'talked' about our teachers, conspiratorially 'whispering' about their strengths and weaknesses.

When I was able to sign, I felt normal and fulfilled. I was aware that I was communicating differently from people with the ability to hear, but I was communicating! There was no stigma attached. I could share my ideas and understand the ideas and feelings of others.

Unfortunately, my use of sign language was brought to an abrupt halt when I was twelve. At that time, I passed the entrance examination allowing me to attend Mary Hare Grammar School in Newbury. The only Grammar school for d/Deaf children in the United Kingdom, it was - and still is - the high temple of oralist education. It would be an understatement to say that I was a bit of a 'heathen' at the gates. Many of the students at Mary Hare were upper crust types and tended to look down at me, and other Northerners with accents, rough edges and hands that tended to weave through the air during conversations. Coming from the school at Preston where we literally wore hobnailed boots and had to fight to stand our ground all this was water off my back.

At Mary Hare sign was forbidden - not only in classrooms but everywhere. We were all - Deaf and deaf alike - expected to speak and to 'listen'. The absurdity of this situation should be apparent to everyone with any sense. Yet it failed to affect the teachers at Mary Hare.

If a student was caught signing, the teaching staff noted his name in a book that they carried around with them. More than three such "speech marks" in a week resulted in detention on Saturday evening while the rest of the school enjoyed the social activities. Detention usually consisted of sitting in a classroom for an hour or two, writing the same line hundreds of times, copying text from Shakespeare or learning a passage by heart for later recitation.

In addition to being held against the individual pupil, speech marks were held against the total of the pupil's House in the annual Speech Trophy Competition. So, using sign incurred not just the wrath of teachers but of peers in one's own House as well.

It was quite a system they had at Mary Hare. I think they took some of the more effective methods directly from the Nazi Youth Movement. The idea that a Deaf child can learn through reading lips is a grotesque farce. At best, a Deaf adult can lip read only a small percentage of words. The rest are largely guessed at. But a child? What kind of person could expect a three-year old Deaf child to read lips? So-called 'experts', that's who!

There were some children who did quite well at school. But they tended to be deaf children who managed well with hearing aids. They were so much like 'normal' children that some of them could even use a telephone. These children should have been mainstreamed at hearing schools. It is the irony of oralism that they aim to 'normalise' Deaf children and yet insist on segregated special schools! Surely, the best place to develop speech and auditory skills would be in a mainstream hearing school. Just as living in France would be the best and most effective way for anyone to acquire fluent French. Logically, there should be no oralist special schools. Such speaking deaf children should be mainstreamed in normal schools. Instead, their presence allowed the staff of

Mary Hare to skew its methods so that we Deaf students were at a profound disadvantage.

Ah, Temple of Enlightened Education! Ah hypocrites! There is no surer sign of the school's failings than to note that it has never invited one of its former pupils as the Speaker on its Annual Speech Day. The Speakers tend to be hearing people or, if they are deaf, they are people who came to deafness late in life. And not former pupils.

The reason for this situation is really quite simple - and damning for the school. Those former Deaf students who have gone on to become successes have invariably gone back to the use of sign language as their primary method of communication. To invite any of them to 'speak' where they would use sign language would only serve to condemn the philosophy and educational methods of the school. The speaking deaf can't have been all that successful if there weren't any that could be invited as Speaker to "prove" their case.

So, the farce is perpetuated. The hearing or deafened people who give the speeches address the students, the majority of whom have absolutely no idea what's being said! Even if lip reading was 100% effective - which it's not - it is impossible to accomplish well from distances greater than ten feet or so. It is a ridiculous exercise in a huge hall.

It was exactly the same at the weekly compulsory service at the local church. You just stared at the priest, not knowing what the sermon was all about. For variety, you could count the number of bits of coloured glass in the stained glass window behind the preacher. The more timid ones who were afraid if the Headmaster spotting that their eyes were not religiously focused on the lips of the priest just counted the number of times they thought he said a certain word like God".

I was considered a success by the school. My academic achievements were heralded as a great personal success and as an argument for the strength of oralism. Like many other Deaf children who had to endure the oral system, I had forced my way through the subjects despite not being able to lip-read or understand most of the oralist teachers. You dared not say, "Please sir, I don't understand what you're saying" or "Please will you repeat what you said". That would be asking for real trouble. You just wore the mandatory headphones, which did not really do much to make sense of what was said. I, like many others, survived by pretending to understand during the classes. I then relied on the textbooks and whatever I had copied down from the blackboard to work out the examples. Being a stubborn and determined character saw me through where so many struggled to keep up with the lessons. What the school failed to acknowledge was that I had achieved academic success *in spite* of the oralist methods they employed, not because of them.

I was angry at this charade of 'school' that we had to play in order to keep out of trouble and to keep the teachers happy. How many more generations of Deaf children must be made into pantomiming clowns for the pleasure of the so-called 'experts'? How many children must suffer through classes in which they have virtually no chance of learning so that teachers can claim that they have taught?

Too many.

And for what?

There are still many Deaf children in such schools, pretending, bluffing their way through and somehow surviving. Or more often, failing and getting blamed for not trying hard or labelled as not being clever enough. Teachers and parents never get to know what suffering they are setting their kids.

This whole farce can be transformed into a meaningful educational experience *overnight*. If only the experts would relinquish their self-serving insistence on forcing a failed philosophy and method on Deaf children. If only they would allow signing.

If only they would allow Deaf children to communicate, to engage in the effective exchange of thoughts and ideas. Then they would learn.

Just like every other child.

When I left Mary Hare in 1959, I was of the profound impression that I was somehow not really Deaf. I was a "cut above" Deaf people who signed. In fact, I felt so ashamed to be associated with Deaf people who signed that I would cross the street rather than have any contact with one of these signing Deaf people.

For a full year, my pride and illusions propelled me forward as I struggled to make my way in the world. I had trouble with shopkeepers, with bus conductors, with police officers. It was embarrassing. More often than not, I could not read their lips and my speech was indecipherable to them.

I had to get over my false pride before I came to recognise just how effective gestures were in helping me in shops. Pointing to an item rather than trying to speak in an incomprehensible voice was more efficient and it saved the grateful shopkeeper a good deal of discomfort.

When I made it visually obvious that I was Deaf, they responded positively. From that point onwards I jettisoned all pretence that I was a pseudo hearing person. I reverted to my true Deaf character.

I've never looked back since then.

At this same time, I became interested in the philosophy of thinkers like Thomas Paine and Jean-Jacques Rousseau and their promotion of human rights. I was learning too about the history and experiences of other oppressed groups, like Black people. I was able to draw some parallels between our experiences. These readings found a haven in my oppressed and angry psyche. They reinforced my beliefs in rights and equality.

It had long been my belief that Deaf people need to become an integral part of society. Barriers to achieving this full integration could - and should - be brought down. I set about to do something about this. During the quarter century between my leaving school and my entering the RNID, I became known as an activist and campaigner on rights issues.

My first battle came not long after I left school. In the 1960s, the Deaf Centres, or Missions as they were called then, were owned by hearing people - usually, the Church and run by Management Committees consisting of bands of hearing 'well-meaning' do-gooders and professionals.

Few of these people ever interacted with Deaf people. That was left to the paid Missioner or Welfare Officers. They did everything. They did social work and also acted as Interpreters. They found jobs and got involved with the homes and families. They preached in the weekly Church service and also organised the social events. You name it, they did it. Their control was so complete that no Deaf person dared cross them for fear of losing their patronage and support.

We Deaf were oppressed colonials, nothing more.

Yah suh. Nah suh.

I was appalled at some of the practices at the Deaf Centres I visited. For example, intelligent and competent Deaf people who managed their weekly household budgets were forced to hand over the takings from the Deaf Club canteen after each of the weekly social evenings so that a Missioner or Welfare Officer could record it in the accounts book and have it banked.

How demeaning! And let me quickly add that the money we're talking about was hardly a king's ransom - the total would amount to approximately 50 pence at current rates. 50 pence!

Children are afforded larger sums. But not the Deaf! The Deaf were deemed incapable of conducting their own affairs. And, true to this self-fulfilling image the Missioners had of us, we danced to the tune they played. We faithfully did what we were told, no matter how demeaning, no matter how ridiculous.

If the system had been consciously constructed in order to render us into comical non-entities it could not have been more effective. As a result of the paternalistic attitude of those agencies created to 'assist' us and the failure of the educational system, we were little more than puppets!

However, the puppet is not a puppet without the manipulation of the puppeteer. We Deaf were embroiled in a relationship with these organisations. They needed us as much as we needed them. We fed off one another.

We were in near-perfect balance. Like the slave and the slave holder. One could not exist without the other. And, in frightening ways, the slave was as reluctant to shrug off slavery, as the slave holder was to relinquish control.

So, you can imagine my popularity with these Missioners when I did everything in my power to upset this tidy little apple cart. My popularity with the Deaf was not much better - at first. It is difficult to discover that your gods have feet of clay. That, after a lifetime of absorbing the message that the Missioners knew what was best, to have a young upstart say that this message was a lie.

The Deaf didn't want to talk about rights. They didn't want them.

But I knew the message was real and it was urgent. If they wouldn't talk about rights under the glare of the Missioner's eyes, surely they would read about them in the privacy of their own homes? I was so determined to get the message out to these Deaf people that I embarked on a publishing venture.

61

In 1962, using my own meagre resources, I published the first edition of "The Argonaut", a journal dedicated to Deaf issues and Deaf rights. The title was taken from Homer's "Odyssey". The tale from ancient Greek mythology where a group of heroes (Argonauts) sailed in search of the Golden Fleece. I saw parallels here in that Deaf people's Golden Fleece was the achievement of our rights.

Without a mailing list, I relied on my cockiness and determination to distribute the journal. I sent six copies to each of the local Deaf Centres around the United Kingdom, using addresses obtained from the RNID's old magazine, with the ironically apt name of "Hearing".

Included with each packet was a covering letter to the Secretary of each Deaf Centre, asking him to distribute the journals to Deaf people whom they thought "might be interested in what the journal had to say."

I said I was cocky and determined. I failed to mention I was also naive. Because the Missioners generally opened the mail addressed to the Club Secretary, almost every copy probably found its way into the rubbish bin rather than the hands of Deaf people. A couple of Missioners - including one nearly revered for his work - wrote back to me and informed me of their refusal to distribute the "Argonaut" to Deaf people.

In the next edition, I challenged these people. I demanded to know what right they had to censor the information Deaf people should have access to. People were horrified at this "attack" on such saintly men. Needless to say, I was not on anyone's Christmas card list that year.

After the third issue of the "Argonaut" my resources ran out and it ceased publication. There must have been a good few sighs of relief. Some people somewhere may still have copies of these magazines, which must now rank as collectors items! Alas, I had not made much progress for Deaf rights other than to anger those people in control.

My defeats with the "Argonaut" and other things left me disgusted. I turned my attention from Deaf issues to my own life, becoming consumed with domestic and work issues. For the next fifteen years, I was effectively "off the radar" of Deaf issues.

Not that I sat around and sulked. I married a hearing woman and raised three hearing daughters. I shared many things with the hearing world, including ambition for advancement in my career.

62

I was determined to work my way up the hierarchy at ICI in Darwen, near Blackburn, where I was employed as a Chemist. ICI had a good reputation for grooming their own managers and sponsored many in-house training courses for prospective managers. I was willing to do whatever I had to do in order to go forward. With a nod to the frustrations of my oralist education, I depended on some of the skills I'd been forced to learn at school. After all, at that time, Interpreters or text phones were not provided.

I made do much as I did in school and with my degree course. While these tutors were hardly trained in teaching the Deaf, their lipreadability was on a par with many of the teachers I'd had in school. I managed by copying the notes the tutors wrote on the board and the notes taken by colleagues at the lectures. Often the tutors would let me have a copy of their own notes. In addition, I prepared for each session in advance by reading the topic to be covered from library books.

The only time I was completely stymied was during group discussions and activities. Rather than ruin these activities for my colleagues, I "followed" them from outside the discussion circles. This was a better option than leaving the room, which would have isolated me from the other people in the course.

Even as my family and career occupied most of my time, my strong sense of independence and the need for social justice were unabated. As my Union experience and the 1960's struggles for Civil Rights had taught me, these things were stronger *outside* the Deaf world than within it. And, as I came to realise in a very real way, the need for justice is shared by everyone.

One day the management at the ICI site where I worked instituted a reorganisation of the non-unionised white-collar staff without bothering to consult with those of us to be affected. We were furious! We knew that they would never dare such a move on the shop floor where the trade unions were strong.

My colleagues shared my anger. However, I went one step further and set up and organised a trade union for the white-collar workers at ICI. Those who did join the Union elected me as their Accredited Representative (the white-collar version of Shop Steward). I was also appointed by the Union (the Association of Scientific, Technical, and Managerial Staff - ASTMS) as the workplace Health and Safety Officer.

63

In the 1970s, the ASTMS sponsored a course on race relations at the Union's Training School in Bishop's Stortford. I was anxious to attend not only because Blackburn had a large ethnic population but also because I had always been very sensitive to ethnic issues, believing then as I do now, that there are many parallels between the subjugation of the Deaf by society and the subjugation of minorities.

Even as I state this, I want to be quick to note I am also very aware of and sensitive to the differences between our experiences. The depth of the prejudice that Black people suffer in our society is much deeper and crueller than that which we Deaf suffer. After all, Deaf people may be isolated and looked down upon but there is little call for us to be killed or deported.

Generally, we are not hated. Sadly, the same cannot be said for many ethnic groups.

For the first time in my experience, a sign language Interpreter was provided so that I could follow the proceedings. This was a revelation!

After that, an Interpreter was present at every ASTMS branch meeting that I attended. Even so, ICI was adamant in continuing to refuse to provide an Interpreter at ICI meetings. This barrier was only breached in the late 1970s when ICI agreed to allow the local Social Worker to interpret at a key dispute resolution meeting.

Mind you, this decision wasn't for *my* benefit but for the company's. I held the cards in this particular case and they wanted to be certain they understood what I was communicating! The reason for their opting for the local social worker rather than a professional Interpreter was that they believed the local Social Worker to be more "trustworthy" than some outside person. They had previous dealings with the social worker when she 'helped' to find a job for a Deaf person.

Even as all these things were going on in my life, I continued to play a full role in the local community. As a lifelong supporter of Wigan Rugby League Club, it was not surprising that I got to play both codes of rugby, League and Union.

All the teams I played for or against consisted entirely of hearing people.

This did not generally present a problem except in Rugby League when I was grappling with an opponent in a tackle and the referee would shout, "Tackled." Because I couldn't hear, I would continue to grapple. My opponent would get mad and lash out at me. I would retaliate and before anyone could blink, there would be a big punch up all around!

Inevitably, I was sent off six times in two years.

I also became involved in local amateur football, first as a fitness trainer for the Deaf soccer team in Blackburn. The team was playing exclusively against hearing teams and getting thrashed every time it took the field. Their improved fitness helped them to keep the score down but they were still lacking in essential skills.

With no one around willing to coach, I enrolled in some Football Association Coaches courses and became a fully qualified FA coach in 1978. I was then, and still am, the first and only Deaf person with such a qualification. This certainly helped as the local Deaf team ended the season as Cup finalists and runners up in their (hearing) League.

I got a lot of support and encouragement here from Tony Waiters the ex Blackpool and England goalkeeper. He was the Football Association Regional Coach for the North West area. When he became Coach at Liverpool F.C., his successor, Ray Minshull the ex Everton goalkeeper also gave me good support. Naturally, there were no Interpreters provided, as general awareness at that time did not extend to the need for such provision.

I managed on these FA Coaching Courses by the same methods that I used on the ICI Management Training Courses. At such courses I was working alongside people like Bobby Robson, Graham Taylor, Don Howe, Dave Sexton, Laurie McMenemy, Howard Wilkinson and Ian St John to name but a few.

Following my success with this Deaf team, I was approached by a hearing amateur team in a much higher league. After a successful spell with this hearing team, I became Coach for the semi-professional Darwen Football Club, playing in the Lancashire Football Combination.

I was then head hunted from there to be the Coach at Bacup Borough, a rival Club in the same league. I eventually became the Manager of that Club. This broadened my responsibilities because I now had to interact with the Press and the fans as well as the players and Club administration. Having an assistant manager aided in making the difficulties of being Deaf in this role more manageable. In the two years that I was Manager, the Club were runners-up in the League Championship and Lancashire Cup Finalists.

After seven years, I had to make the difficult decision to leave semi-professional football. By this time, my increasing involvement in the Deaf world was making it impossible to meet all the commitments football required.

I was reaching a point in my life when my various experiences and strengths were coming together to serve me in a new capacity. I was fortunate that I was able to bring these and other talents to play in my work for Deaf rights.

For example, I had always had an interest in entertainment. When I was at school, I regularly organised Saturday evening social events (that is, when I was not in detention!) and also played a significant role in the School's Drama Club. I still remember one show in particular that I produced.

The show was comprised exclusively of visual comedy sketches. No lip reading required! The other students *loved* the show. The Headmaster, however, was far from pleased. He had expected the usual 'spoken' fare of tortured Shakespeare.

For me, theatre meant that unless you could communicate to the audience and get your message across you have failed. At all costs, you had to find a way to do this. Clearly, in our case speech and lipreading wasn't going to create our bridge with the audience. That didn't matter to a Headmaster whose speakers at the annual Speech or Open Days were incomprehensible to most of the pupils. The annual Carol Concert to which local dignitaries were invited must have sounded truly awful with the whole school trying to 'sing'. How these dignitaries kept straight faces as they politely applauded and uttered the expected complimentary remarks, I don't know!

I also had become interested in performing as a magician and had developed my act to the point of being good enough to obtain paid bookings. Many of my evenings were taken up with engagements at a range of venues as a semi-professional entertainer. My favourite area of activity was in the northern Working Men's Club circuit with their reputably tough audiences. It was an honour when in 1979 I was invited to perform in a Command Performance by the Concert Secretary's Association where I had been selected as the Speciality Act of the Year. I also had a booking as one of the supporting acts for one of Ken Dodd's shows when he was on tour. It was not long before I met the criteria of having so many paid contracts to become a member of the actor's Union, Equity.

My agent raised a number of possibilities for work as a full time entertainer, offering me a booking to do a Summer season at the Robin Hood Holiday Camp in Skegness followed by a possible six month contract to entertain on a winter cruise ship in the Caribbean. After serious consideration, I decided not take the booking, as I could not risk losing my steady job at ICI when I had a young family to support. I acquired a good reputation among other magicians and in 1977 won three of the four trophies on offer at the International Brotherhood of Magicians Convention at Hastings.

My return to the Deaf world after nearly fifteen years was more by accident than design. A local Councillor who was on the Management Committee of the East Lancashire Deaf Society had read a feature article in the local paper about my performance as a magician. She approached me to do a show at the Society's annual Dinner and Dance.

That evening, I met friends I hadn't seen since we were together at Preston Deaf School. From them, I learned that, while my personal world had been propelled forward, the Deaf world was *still* stuck in the antiquated, paternalistic world of the previous century.

"Why don't you do something about it?" I asked.

Oh, they wanted to. They really wanted to. But they were fearful of "rocking the boat".

They were still in that same puppet dance. As frustrated as they were, they still believed they needed the old taskmasters as much as the taskmasters needed them.

They didn't know how to "break the mould".

My experiences of the previous fifteen years in the outside world had of course been nothing *but* a series of ways to break moulds.

Thus, I was convinced that it was a perfect time for my return to the Deaf world. My first move was to rejoin the Deaf Social Club in the Blackburn area. Not long after rejoining, I was elected Chair of the Blackburn Deaf Sports and Social Club.

The Club operated in premises owned and run by the hearing-controlled East Lancashire Deaf Society (ELDS). Because the Management Committee met only every couple of months and had little, if anything, to do with the Deaf users of the premises, they had no idea of what our needs and desires were.

They tended to be very restrictive regarding the activities they would permit on the premises. For example, in line with the missionary tradition, they would not allow a bar to be built. As a result, members would come to the Club at seven and leave again by nine, completing their social evening at a local pub.

I led a small group of Deaf members in an attempt to do something about this situation. With money that we had raised by ourselves, we converted some rooms at the Centre into a bar and lounge area. We did almost all the work ourselves. What we were unable to do, we contracted out to people we employed.

We did *everything*. We applied for the appropriate planning permits. We went to the magistrates' court for the bar license. We took care of the bureaucracy and the physical work without the help of any hearing people, save for the contractors we hired to complete some of the work.

The actual conversion to the facility was completed in a week. As a result, the Management Committee didn't have a clue of what was going on until it was all finished. Because the work was completely professional - using Deaf professional bricklayers, joiners, plasterers, and decorators - and because it improved the facility, they would not dare order it to be torn down.

They actually accepted the conversion with good grace. And why not? It hadn't cost them a penny!

Because of the way it was accomplished, the Deaf Club - and therefore we - had full control over the bar. As Chairman of the Social Club my name was listed on the licence granted by the magistrate!

Around this same time, I was co-opted onto the Society's Management Committee as the "Deaf representative". As you can imagine, the position had little or no power. It was a token position so that the Committee could demonstrate their "commitment" to Deaf people.

I suppose it was presumed that I would accept this tokenism as the terms of my service.

Bad assumption.

When the incumbent Chair of the Committee stepped down, I stood for election. As none of the hearing members of the Committee could agree amongst themselves who would take over, I was elected unopposed as the first-ever Deaf Chair of ELDS.

In 1984!

Seems awfully late in the game for the election of the first-ever Deaf person to a leadership role in a Deaf Society but there you have it in a nutshell, the sad truth of these "caring" organisations.

However, 1984 was an interesting turning point, don't you think? George Orwell would have been amused.

Not only was I the Deaf Chair of the Society's Management Committee, I was the *only Deaf member.* I was determined to put an end to that immediately. My first move upon taking over the leadership of the Committee was to amend the Constitution of the Society to specify that a *minimum* of 51% of the Management Committee had to be Deaf.

I wasn't interested in leadership *per se.* I was interested in revolution.

The hearing members of the Committee found themselves check-mated. They could not and did not, oppose my move.

Fifteen years on, the Constitution of the ELDS is *still* unique in this country in that it determines that control of a Deaf organisation must be in the hands of the people the organisation serves. In 2000 A.D. That is a depressing commentary on the Deaf Associations in the rest of the United Kingdom.

With control of the Management Committee, I set the agenda to be one of developing Deaf rights locally. Curiously, at this point, my biggest battles were being fought with older Deaf members who were uncomfortable or apprehensive of the responsibilities that independence demanded. They preferred the comfort and ease of having Social Workers to cart them around and fill forms for them! It took a long time to change this deep-rooted sense of dependency and inertia.

Once again, I was reminded that as much as the slaves hated their taskmasters, they needed them. Similarly, battered women sometimes find it difficult to leave the man who is abusing them or the home. I believe there is a psychological term for this curious dynamic - the Stockholm Syndrome. It was coined to describe the puzzling reactions of four Swedish Bank employees to their captors. They were held for six days by two convicts who threatened their lives but also showed them kindness. The hostages actually resisted rescue and were eager to defend their captors.

It is an interesting syndrome and one that I observed first-hand as I fought for Deaf rights - there were times that my most passionate opponents were Deaf people, particularly the puppets and the over dependents.

In 1981, the British Deaf Association, under the new leadership of Arthur Verney, was beginning to become more political. However, its Executive Committee continued to be dominated by paternalistic, hearing members. Its Chair, JF Hudson, personified the kind of person who came to be reviled by Deaf people determined to gain independence.

Heady with the success of my efforts at ELDS, I set out to fight the BDA and to force changes at the national level by arguing that local representatives to the BDA should be Deaf, just as the local representatives to the national Women's Forum would undoubtedly be women.

Hudson was not about to have these changes put in place on his watch. Not without a fight. When these reasonable arguments were met with powerful resistance, I established the Deaf Tribune Group in the North West Region to force through these changes.

The Deaf Tribune Group was made up of a number of like-thinking Deaf officials of local Deaf Clubs in the North West area. We met together to share information and views. As a result of our meetings, we came to a consensus on our approach to a number of specific issues on the agenda for up coming BDA regional or national meetings.

"Look," I explained, "if we can present a solid block of votes and manage a 50/50 split of the remaining votes, we should have the majority..."

Our first "target" was to get Deaf control of the BDA's Regional Council responsible for our area, an area that was under the tight control of what we dubbed as the "Yorkshire Mafia". This consisted of Hudson as the Chairman plus a number of leading Social Workers and some of their Deaf drones.

Our strategy was straight out of Al Capone. "You take the west, we'll take the east." The North Regional Council covered both Lancashire and Yorkshire. We hoped to split the Council's coverage so that we could be responsible for Lancashire and the Yorkshire Mafia could be responsible for Yorkshire.

At the meeting at St. Helens in the North West area, we presented the motion to split the region into two. With our Tribune voting as a bloc and many from the Yorkshire region not having bothered to make the trip over the Pennines for such a "boring" event as the Regional AGM, we won the vote by the required two-thirds majority.

The Constitution would be changed.

The newly-formed NW Regional Council insisted that all Committee members be Deaf. Terry Riley was the first Chair. I was the Secretary. Together, we worked to establish the successful model of independence that would hopefully allow other Deaf people to take ownership of their Centres. To this end, we set up a range of innovative activities and training programs to educate and prepare local Deaf activists.

Everything we did was designed to counter the prevailing sense that "Deaf people can't do it" or that "Deaf people aren't ready."

We could and we were.

Taking control of the North Regional Council was never an end in itself. Only a beginning. The goal was to nationalise Deaf control of the Deaf organisations. Our next step was to take control of the hearing-dominated BDA Executive Committee.

71

The moves to bring this change about took place during the BDA Congress at Torquay in 1983. The events of this Congress proved to be a turning point for Deaf rights in the United Kingdom. It was the first time that Deaf people fought for control of the Executive Committee of their own organisation.

We had done our homework well. We reckoned that we had enough votes to oppose the re-nomination of Hudson. Events, as it turned out, aided us. Whether because of the strong opposition or for other reasons, Hudson chose not to run.

Our votes then turned to a more positive reality, electing Jock Young, a Deaf person, as the next Chair. In addition, we gained assurances that future members of the BDA Executive Committee would be Deaf.

As Secretary, I played a key role in the joint campaign by the NW Regional Council and the National Union of the Deaf opposing oralism at the Congress on Education of Deaf Children, held in Manchester in 1985. This Congress shunned the American Psychologist Professor Harlan Lane in spite of the fact that his recently published book, "When the Mind Hears" had struck a powerful chord among Deaf people.

In addition to our activities at the Congress proper, we organised and conducted an "alternative Congress" at the Manchester Deaf Centre every evening. Each evening after the official Congress closed, we opened up the Centre with events to "redress the oralist bias of the Congress".

One evening, Harlan Lane was our speaker. His message went off like a bomb. The atmosphere was electric. The hall was absolutely silent throughout his hour speech. Not a soul there failed to be moved by his passionate talk about oppression and the measures people go to in order to enforce their will.

He managed to galvanise our increasingly strong faith in ourselves and our determination to overcome the oppression of the hearing paternalists.

On another evening, a cabaret show was presented which saw the birth of the Deaf Comedians. It was a group of Deaf people I had set up a year previously to entertain the local Deaf Clubs with Deaf humour. For the first time ever in our Deaf world, we had a complete show consisting of humorous sketches which made fun of the oralist methods and portrayed the real Deaf

72

experience in no uncertain political terms. Satire was relatively unknown in the Deaf world at that time. (Fifteen years later, the Deaf Comedians are now renowned across the globe for their biting and side splitting satire on the negative experiences of Deaf people in society).

Even as these organisational successes were taking place, the changes in my personal and professional life proved to be equally profound. During these years, as I entered my 40s, I found myself divorced and the children were now adults themselves. In certain ways, I was free to do a great deal more for the Deaf cause than I had been at any point in my adult life.

I was frustrated at ICI because I had risen as high as I was going to go in the managerial hierarchy. It seemed that being Deaf was the factor that hindered my promotion in the company.

In spite of this frustration, I was well established there. I was very involved in the community. I saw myself continuing as I was doing for the rest of my life.

Then, in 1984, I received a textphone call from a Deaf colleague working in the BBC. The call came completely unexpectedly. I was asked if I would be interested in working as Researcher for the See Hear television programme.

I was stunned. I didn't know what to say. However, as I considered the offer, it occurred to me that my life seemed to have conspired to bring me to this interesting crossroads. I knew that if things did not work out at See Hear that I would be unable to return to my position at ICI. However, being on my own for the first time in many, many years meant that I could make this gamble without jeopardising anyone else.

I drew a deep breath and made the leap!

I decided to commit to two years at See Hear. I felt that this was sufficient time to decide if I was having any impact. If I fell short at that point, I would return to the NW region.

In many ways, See Hear was a joyful time for me. It was wonderful to be working in a "Deaf friendly" environment. Almost the entire hearing staff was able to converse in sign language. Interpreters were provided in all situations as a matter of course.

73

I travelled the country, meeting a vast number of people and becoming familiar with many different organisations. I gained an insight into the day-to-day workings of the media. I also enjoyed the small victory of nudging the nature of the programming from its paternalistic tone, where Deaf people were "wowed" for being hairdressers, to one where Deaf issues were clearly examined and debated in-depth, and put in a broader political and social context.

I also worked with the renowned Deaf historian, Arthur Dimmock, who outlined things of interest and significance in Deaf history, like illustrations of Queen Victoria using sign language to converse with a Deaf girl she had come to know.

After I left See Hear, I had the opportunity to work with Paddy Ladd on the production of the film, "Pictures in the Mind" which was made for peak time television. Directed by the well known, Nigel Evans, and based on the story from Harlan Lane's book, it was very well received.

Paddy and I participated both as script advisers and performers.

The Research team had located one of the many young Deaf people who had been taught by the oral method and, upon leaving school, was unable to speak, lip read, or sign. As a result, he was unable to communicate with either the hearing or the Deaf.

The movie examined all the influences that brought about this sad and frustrating state of affairs.

This anti-oralist film remains one of the best films on Deaf issues ever produced. In contrast to those syrupy-sweet, disgusting "Mandy" type of films which Deaf people resent with all our hearts. In "Mandy" the climax and indeed the whole focus of the film was when after years of oralist training, the little Deaf girl slowly mumbled out her own name. Incidentally, we are seeing the same syndrome with the current craze for cochlear implants. These stories tend to end with the flow of tears of triumph when the little Deaf kid with the "bionic ear" recognises one single sound made in isolation!

The sad commentary is that other films since "Pictures in the Mind" have not followed suit. Society seems not to be interested in Deaf people, in our opinions, our perspectives, our lives. Certainly, a case of being really not interested in the Deaf!

Over the course of these years, I had inevitably become known as a fighter and campaigner for Deaf rights at all levels. Being willing to withstand the negative feelings of the establishment and the Deaf "grandees", who wanted nothing more than for me to simply go away, I had become a threat to their comfortable, cushy positions.

There were many Deaf people who supported what I was doing but were afraid to speak out. However, as we were beginning to see, change was possible. It was within our grasp. We just needed to have more Deaf people emerge as leaders, pressing for rights. In respect of this, I gave a talk at the BDA Centenary Congress in 1990 where the theme was "Out of the Shell". The choice of this theme was meant to reflect a positive trend for the Deaf, their "coming out". I reckoned that we were deluding ourselves and queried if we were really out of our shell. I asked where were our leaders and what they were doing, contending that our lives were still under the control of paternalists, Social Workers and the Deaf Club Grandees. I argued that it was time to let the younger Deaf people come through and take the lead with their ideas.

Similarly, I gave a talk at the global Deaf Way Conference at Gallaudet University in the USA where I stressed that control of Deaf organisations has to be in hands of Deaf people. The audience there, which included several from this country, agreed and gave me a good hand. Yet back at home these same people were fearful of rocking the boat and upsetting their patronage.

Like many Deaf people, I had an intense dislike of the RNID and all it stood for. To us, "RNID" stood for "Really Not Interested in the Deaf". As a rule, we tried to have as little as possible to do with it. Mistakenly, we thought it had little to do with our lives. Certainly, I thought it had little to do with *my* life.

But that was soon to change.

Derek Burton, one of the RNID Directors, knew me from his days as Superintendent of the Liverpool Deaf Society during the 1960s. He approached me while I was at See Hear and considering a move back north to continue with the political development of Deaf people up there. He wanted me to work for the RNID.

"No way!" I responded immediately. Derek, though, was not easily dissuaded. "Think about it," he suggested. "You never know what the future holds."

Soon afterwards, as a representative of the East Lancashire Deaf Society, I attended the North Regional Association for the Deaf Conference at Kendal where the RNID CEO. Mike Whitlam was the guest Speaker. He impressed me as he laid out his aims for the future of the RNID. He was defining a role that had Deaf rights at its centre. He expressed the need to de-centralise the RNID services so that it could better serve Deaf people.

I shook my head in astonishment. He was saying the very things I had been working towards most of my adult life!

It began to occur to me that working with this Whitlam fellow wasn't as outlandish as it appeared at first blush. Deaf rights would be more easily achieved if we could utilise the RNID's resources

I discussed my thinking with a number of friends, both hearing and Deaf. Arthur Verney was concerned that having a prominent Deaf person join the RNID would give the organisation credibility with Deaf people and with politicians, credibility that they didn't yet have.

"You could be quite the meal ticket for them," he pointed out.

Paddy Ladd and I argued whether it would be best to fight the RNID and all it stood for from the inside or outside.

"Do I go with my Trade Union experience of working from the inside or your approach, to destroy the beast by developing opposing consumer organisations?"

"You know how I feel about it," Paddy said.

As much as the political reality, Paddy worried that if I joined with the RNID, I would be isolated. Deaf people would shun me. It would define me as a Judas and they would turn away from me. In addition, I would be cut off from most of the RNID staff, as they were anti-signing.

There was also apprehension about what I dubbed as the "Lord Pander syndrome", where Trade Union bruisers and activists got absorbed into the establishment once a title was endowed onto them. Being in the establishment can lead to corruption of one's principles and forgetting where one had come from in the first place.

There was also my fear that I could become corrupt or my principles compromised by being drawn into the "establishment". We drew parallels from the Black world, where some Black people had got drawn into the system after joining it and distanced themselves from their roots. They had been bought off so to speak. Politics is full of such people. We had evidence of this in our own Deaf world. Paddy wondered if I would end up the same way.

"Who the hell will you be able to talk with?" he wondered.

My only protection against that would be to maintain constant contact with aware Deaf people like Paddy and to retain my links with the local East Lancashire Deaf Society.

Back and forth. We debated these issues. I lived and breathed this decision over the course of the weeks. It finally came down to whether or not anything of worth could be done through the BDA, because that was the consumer organisation, the one nearest and dearest to Deaf people.

However, as I explained in an earlier chapter, the BDA was in the midst of crisis at the time, Verney and his allies were pitted against the last of the old guard, Deaf and hearing alike. These wars of attrition were causing the organisation to lose its earlier focus, making it ineffective in continuing the work it had begun. I also knew that the old guard there would do all it could to prevent me, or any other radical leader, from becoming its Chief Executive Officer.

So, I drew a deep breath and once more took a leap of faith, this time into the bosom of "the enemy". I decided to move into the RNID

My rationale was that getting RNID resources behind Deaf issues could be the difference between success and failure. I was not blind. I knew that key ministers and politicians would still rather listen to the voice of the RNID rather than Deaf people or consumer organisations.

The RNID's traditional weakness had been its reluctance to have any real contact with Deaf people. Under Whitlam, this weakness was being addressed. I was convinced that, with the right strategy, dedication to work, and political developments, there was a chance I could eventually become the CEO of the RNID.

From the perspective of Deaf people, that would be a major coup. If I could breach the RNID, then others could follow in other organisations.

My goal of the CEO post at the RNID was known to some people in the RNID and in the Deaf world

The fact that Winifred Tumim, (the wife of Judge, later Lord Tumim), was the Chair of the RNID presented something of an obstacle. Paternalistic and largely oralist, she was not liked by many Deaf activists. My first meeting with her came when she condescendingly took over a conversation I had been having with another Deaf person and two Liberal Party politicians. We two were representing the BDA at the 1983 Liberal Democrat Conference at Harrogate. We were lobbying the politicians about Deaf rights.

Tumim blithely butted into the conversation, "Ah, my Deaf people," she said sweetly as she plopped herself down and proceeded to commandeer the discussion.

The two of us edged ourselves out, feeling castrated and demoralised.

When she was interviewed for an article in a national newspaper, she was quoted as saying that her Deaf daughter was like a car without a steering wheel! With attitudes like these, it was highly unlikely that she would allow a Deaf person to be Chief Executive Officer of the RNID, not as long as she was Chair. On that point, I was pretty certain.

My plan then was to address her chairmanship when the time came.

Back to our original question - "Who is Doug Alker?"

This is the person you have now come to know. On April 1st 1987, he became the first-ever Deaf Manager at the RNID. He had a record as a determined fighter for Deaf people's rights.

What would happen next? Would the establishment change Doug Alker, or would Doug Alker change the establishment?

Only time would tell.

Chapter Four

Out of the Frying Pan and Into the Fire

I have learned that success is to be measured not so much by the position in that one has reached as by the obstacles one had to overcome to get there.

Booker T. Washington

In retrospect, my rise at the RNID was both an anomaly and inevitable. A contradiction, yes. But the fact is, in spite of the organisation's mandate to aid the Deaf I was a stranger in a strange land. I was a Deaf person in a place where hearing people had always held sway, hearing people who, remember, had traditionally treated the Deaf as something less than capable, independent human beings.

Still, my rise to prominence and leadership there had the feel of inevitability in that "the time was ripe" for the ascension of a Deaf person to lead the RNID.

On the first of April 1987 I was appointed the Principal Officer in the South East Region. Just two rungs below the Chief Executive on the RNID ladder and a single rung beneath the level of Department Director. My strategy was straightforward. I intended to remain as Principal Officer for two years at which time I anticipated the incumbent Director leaving his post. I would move up to become a Department Director. Two years later, after gaining the experience of a Directorship, I would aim to move up to Chief Executive when Whitlam left the RNID, which I was certain that he would do.

Save for a handful of unanticipated hitches, my ascent went remarkably according to plan.

As Principal Regional Officer for the South East, I was responsible for establishing and setting up a RNID regional office in my area. At that time, the RNID was very centralised, with everything based at the headquarters and only a small number of residential homes for Deaf people with additional difficulties outside of the capital.

When I started, the "Regional Office" was nothing more than me, a Secretary and a couple of rented rooms. Five such offices covered all the regions of the UK. As you can imagine, each of the Regional Officers had a fair amount of ground to cover.

I was responsible for the area that extended from the English Channel at one end to Oxford at the other, and from Brighton in the south to Hertfordshire in the North, an area that included Greater London.

One benefit to having such an anaemic regional operation was that each Regional Office had a great deal of freedom to function as it saw fit. Each Office was responsible for such core activities as running an information service, scheduling talks and lectures to raise awareness of d/Deaf issues and working with the local Social Services agencies. There tended to be little to no contact with the local Deaf Centres. As ridiculous as this was, it was actually a preference of Deaf people, who had little regard for the RNID.

This period was one in which I became familiar with the RNID's system. I had to learn how it and its associated professionals, particularly in Social Services, functioned. I treated this process as an educational one. I was amassing as much understanding of the organisation as I could.

Burton, the Director of Regional Services, along with the four other Principal Regional Officers were invaluable in aiding me during this period. They not only helped me with gaining a firm grasp on how the statutory agencies functioned but also on the office and management systems of the organisations.

Along the way, I found myself in a role I'd never played before – being an advocate for deafened and deaf people. I was devoting time I had previously devoted to Deaf cultural and rights issues to issues of the elderly deaf and the deafened. This was a culture shock of sorts for me. In all honesty, this was not the issue closest to my heart, but it was an essential area of expertise if I expected to make any headway in the RNID.

In addition to learning about the RNID, I moved forward with a mind toward how I could transform it into an organisation more responsive to Deaf needs, how I could establish a new model to enable the RNID to work with local organisations and individual Deaf people on issues that are important to us.

I began my attempt to transform the RNID by establishing connections between the organisation and Deaf individuals to address a broad range of issues that confront the statutory and volunteer agencies that serve us. During these meetings, I came to appreciate just who was who and what was what in these agencies. I also came to understand the key issues as each agency defined them.

I built bridges between the RNID and these local agencies by establishing a number of joint projects, conferences, and seminars. Once I was able to establish some degree of RNID credibility with Local Authorities, I began to take steps to making some impact on influencing their services.

As I mentioned, my intention was to be a Regional Officer for two years. However, I had been in the position for only six months when Burton chose to leave the RNID. Based in Manchester, Burton was loath to move down to London where Whitlam wanted all the Directors to be stationed. Burton's decision to take early retirement was very bad timing from my perspective. I was just getting established. I needed more time to gain credibility in my role.

However, as we all know, there are times when circumstances dictate what we must do. How I would have loved for Burton to have been able to hang on another year or so! But I did not have the luxury of another year of on-the-job training and improving my knowledge of deaf issues.

"You're daft if you apply for that position now!" some of my friends warned me.

Daft or no, I argued that opportunities have a way of presenting themselves at inopportune times. One of my stock of favourite quotes was "Carpe diem", which translated from Latin means "Seize the day". I would take the leap.

Despite my relative lack of RNID experience, I submitted my application for the post that Burton vacated. I knew I would be competing against a strong field of candidates for the post, but, as I'd argued with my friends, I felt that it was important to go for it. The next opportunity might not appear for a few years.

I believe I benefited by having Rev. Brian Murray on the interview panel. Rev. Murray had had a lot of experience with Deaf people in the north of England and was a strong supporter of our causes. However, I have to believe that he was not alone as I was chosen as Director of Regional Services, soon to be renamed Community Services in recognition of the emerging community-oriented ethos emerging at the RNID.

Once again, I had broken new ground at the organisation. I was the first Deaf Director of the RNID.

I was directly responsible for all the Regional Offices and the RNID developments outside of the Head Office, except for the Residential Homes.

In contrast to those recently recruited from the 'outside world', many staff members who had worked in the field for years, had difficulty with a Deaf line Manager. Curious that it should have been so difficult for staff at the RNID but there you have it. Fortunately, and to their credit, I continued to receive the unqualified support of the quintet of Principal Regional Officers. They proved themselves to be far and away more creative in their thinking than most of the Social Workers who were working with the Deaf at the time. They were concerned with Deaf people's rights and the need for Deaf people to be independent, to have control over their own lives.

The entire ethos of the Regional Offices began to become more oriented toward Deaf rights, particularly as more Deaf people were being recruited as regional staff.

These changes all went back to the message Whitlam was sending to everyone involved with the RNID. He wanted more Deaf Managers. He knew this sent an implicit message about how Deaf people should be employed. How could the RNID expect Deaf people to gain greater levels of responsibility if it was unwilling to assign greater responsibility to them?

For the first time in my experience, career issues were being handled promptly and appropriately. Interpreters were provided whenever required as were any necessary equipment, such as text phones (where two people with the equipment can carry a typed conversation with each other over a telephone line). However, no one should be deceived. Text phones and Interpreters, as essential as they are, do not resolve all the difficulties Deaf Managers faced. We are at a considerable disadvantage with hearing employees. In addition to the usual management skills, practices and politics, Deaf Managers confront a full range of issues specific to being Deaf.

Communication is the essential skill in any management situation. Anything that compromises effective communication compromises the relationship. A text phone does not "level the playing field" for telephone use. Deaf Managers are often by-passed as the hearing caller either phones a subordinate or doesn't bother to phone at all, because of the added inconvenience of typing out messages on a textphone.

Without the use of a telephone, a Manager is at a significant disadvantage.

The same degree of disadvantage occurs during meetings. Even when an Interpreter is available, a hearing Manager is able to listen to a whole range of voices. The Interpreter can only interpret one at a time. This does not even call into account the Interpreters varying levels of skill.

Misinterpretation is also a significant problem.

There is also the issue of confidentiality. Often, senior people are not too keen to open out with highly sensitive issues in the presence of a third party (e.g. an Interpreter). They therefore hold back.

Not all members of staff are able to sign well enough and are often reluctant to see the Deaf Manager over any issues of personal concern. At times they would go directly to the person above the Deaf Manager to discuss them and get them resolved. This undermines the Deaf Manager's authority and effectiveness. It is poor practice and gives the Senior Manager a bad impression of the Deaf Manager's ability and effectiveness.

Add to all this the reality and importance of informal communication. A Manager without access to the casual, off-hand comment might be at a disadvantage for anticipating a problem and dealing with it before it becomes a crisis.

All these factors conspire to make promotion prospects particularly dim for Deaf Managers.

Ironically, the situation is a good deal worse for a Deaf Manager in a Deaf-related organisation. In addition to the difficulties I've outlined, a Deaf Manager must overcome the entrenched attitudes of some of the key people in the organisation. From the Boards to the professionals involved, the attitudes are based on the presumption of weakness on the part of the Deaf. Or, perhaps they recognise that their positions or their livelihoods depend on that weakness! However, those RNID staff that were lately recruited from outside of the Deaf field were generally fine, as they did not have such psychological baggage.

Deaf Managers are trebly isolated in Deaf organisations. First, they are isolated from general, hearing society. Second, they are essentially isolated from their peers - hearing Managers. Finally, they are isolated from other Deaf people. This final isolation is often the cruellest. Whether by jealousy or some other reason, Deaf people, like other minorities, sometimes act like crabs in a basket, pulling down those who seek to crawl out.

Of course, the expectations placed on the Deaf Manager often contribute to his or her failure. These expectations are that the responsibilities will be performed flawlessly. There is none of the margin of error extended to hearing Managers. The Deaf Manager is a role model first and foremost. No longer "just a man", he must never falter for fear of damaging the prospects of other Deaf people coming up behind him.

Deaf Managers in Deaf organisations are forced to confront paternalism day and night. They work alongside some people who have no respect for Deaf people. They have to work twice as hard as other Managers just to keep their heads above water – and harder still in order to excel.

Should a Deaf Manager feel down or tired the "red flags" begin to wave.

"He can't do it!"

"I knew it!"

"Can't cope with the pressure!"

"I told you so!"

Whitlam was generally sensitive to these and other difficulties. He knew how easy it was for hearing Managers to undermine the success of a Deaf Manager. Not being Deaf himself, he could not be aware of all the needs of a Deaf person. Still he did his best to anticipate and respond to Deaf needs.

The Regional team of Managers I had were also more than a little sensitive to these issues. They worked hard to adopt practices that would make it easier for me to succeed rather than rely on time-worn practices, which could guarantee my failure. Etherington also acquired a good deal of sensitivity to these matters.

Others, unfortunately, were not nearly so sensitive and often did what they could to undermine the results I was achieving. I do not want to be subtle on this point. It is disturbing on many different levels but it is a reality that people need to appreciate. There were some people who sought to do what they could to undermine me.

As a Director and then later as Chief Executive, I had to be constantly on the alert for this. To be successful on this count, I had to rely on others to be equally alert. It was so simple for a Director or Board member to undermine me, intentionally or unintentionally. Most times, the slight was the result of ignorance and adjustments were made in the future.

Other times, the slight was the result of anything but ignorance!

As Director of Community Services, I was responsible for developing the network of RNID Regional Offices and services to d/Deaf people in the community. The regionalisation of the RNID suited me fine. I found that it enabled the real world of Deaf politics to insinuate itself into the world of the RNID. It enabled the mobilisation of some RNID resources into developing work on Deaf people's rights.

I could envision these developments mushrooming as part of the general call for political rights by the full range of disabled people. Remember, the Government of the time was calling for the greater independence of disabled people. Deaf people needed to be in there to ensure their specific issues were incorporated.

The time was ripe for moving forward.

There was a palpable shift in emphasis in the RNID Regional Offices from helping d/Deaf people to changing the approaches and attitudes of the community agencies so that d/Deaf people could have access to the same services and opportunities as everyone else.

For example, rather than RNID staff finding a job for one Deaf person, attention was paid to training the staff of the local Job Centre to be ready to help any Deaf person who came into the Centre.

One step in achieving this was through Deaf Awareness Training. This training was such a success that there was a demand for more Deaf people to work for Community Services in order to deliver the training. Of course, for every two steps forward, there was a step backward. While there was an increasing demand for more work by Deaf people, there was a shortage of Sign Language (BSL) Interpreters to work with them.

This shortage resulted in the establishment of a Regional Interpreting Service, primarily to cover Deaf staff in the regions. These Interpreters were also hired out to work outside the Regional Office in places such as Job Centres when their services were not required in-house.

The development of the Interpreting service coincided with the advent of the compulsory tendering and the Community Care Act, which encouraged local authorities to contract out their services. The BDA (British Deaf

85

Association) – the obvious candidate to build-up such an out-sourcing of services – was uninterested, leaving the field wide open to the RNID to provide Interpreters to various agencies all over the UK. This move created much-needed bridges between the RNID and many Deaf people. Bridges that had not existed previously. The RNID continued to move in a positive direction when it set up local Deaf User Groups to gain feedback about these new services. Once again, the BDA missed out on an opportunity to provide leadership and establish these services that their own members wanted. And once again, the RNID benefited.

The BDA also ceded control of interpreting training and standards to the RNID. Time and again, the BDA demonstrated a frightening failure of leadership and vision in continuing to miss other opportunities - right up to the present day.

The Regional Managers were set the task of gaining contracts to provide interpreting services from as many Local Authorities as possible. Etherington and I had a "gentleman's bet" of a bottle of champagne to see if the first contract could be signed by April 1989. I lost the bet by just a few weeks as the first contract was signed in May 1989 by East Sussex County Council to provide interpreting services in their area. Contracts from other agencies, including bodies like the Open University, rolled in after that point.

The Regional staff of the RNID began to attend the Association of Directors of Social Services Conferences along with Whitlam, Etherington, and myself. The contacts we made during these meetings enabled us to establish a national network of contacts with Directors of Social Services and the Chairs of the Social Services Committees. Of course, as we had gained in political savvy, our purpose was not just to obtain contracts but also to try influence policies and practices on services for Deaf people.

We lobbied the Government and also the Local Authorities for an increase in funding for Deaf services in general while at the same time pressing for a more effective distribution and deployment of these services. Our successes in all these areas was putting a wooden stake into the heart of the traditional all-encompassing role of the Social Worker with Deaf People.

Many although not all, Social Workers with Deaf people had inherited many of the practices of the thankfully extinct missioners. In their zeal to 'help', they rendered Deaf people nearly helpless, taking over all manner of tasks that Deaf people were more than capable of performing. Heck, they often filled forms for Deaf clients! Who needs help like that?

The 'saintly' Social Worker model clearly did not fit in with the philosophy of independence for Deaf people that we were trying to promote. We believed that many things that Social Workers were devoting their time and energy to, such as distributing equipment to Deaf people or filling in forms for Deaf clients were best done by other people or agencies, which would in turn free the Social Workers to concentrate on the difficult task of supporting those Deaf people who truly needed it.

As rights issues gained in importance, it became clear that such vital services as interpreting should not only be liberated from Social Services but they should become a shared community responsibility. In other words, rather than Social Services providing interpreting for all events, like visits to hospitals, job interviews, etc it was incumbent on the various local bodies to provide interpreting services. The Health Service ought to provide for interpreting within their own domain. Likewise the police, the courts, education services and so on.

Some Social Workers, seeing in this movement a threat to their power and authority, resisted the growing trend of devolving some elements of their traditional role. Often, they were joined in their resistance by local organisations that had no desire to take on greater responsibility. However, with the winds of change finally blowing, they were fighting a battle they could no longer win. For Deaf people, this has to be one of the few and long lasting benefits of Thatcherism!

As the demand exploded for Interpreters, more Interpreters were recruited by the Community Services Department. The demand grew at such an astonishing rate that by 1991 the RNID had nearly 35 full-time Interpreters on staff. Because of the urgent need for them, many of these Interpreters were not yet fully qualified when they were hired. However, the RNID was committed to training them to the CACDP's (Council for the Advancement of Communication with Deaf People) Register of Interpreters level, which was and still is the national standards for sign language interpreting.

As noble as that commitment was, it might have been a bit unrealistic. Training requires appropriate courses and teachers. Unfortunately, there were not enough suitable training courses. A couple of Universities, Durham and Bristol, offered courses but these required a lot of time off work and were very costly. We simply could not afford the fees or the loss of time on the part of interpreters in training. As important was the fact that the training at these locations was not specifically geared to our needs as an employer and service provider.

With these obstacles before us, we opted for the most creative and appropriate solution available - we decided to develop an in-house interpreter training programme to enable our Interpreters to pass the CACDP assessments. We opened our programme to Interpreters from outside of the RNID as well, hoping to ensure that there were plenty of Interpreters available for Deaf people throughout the UK.

The in-house RNID course was so successful that for a period of five or six years nearly 90% of those who passed the annual CACDP Interpreter assessments were coming from our courses!

This training course was just one indication of the RNID's shift in emphasis. The new philosophy, of independence, was particularly strong in two Departments - Community Services and Advocacy and Information. The staff of these Departments initiated a range of regional and national campaigns to promote Deaf rights. There was no better illustration of the shift in the RNID's direction than it's financing of Harlan Lane's 1987 national lecture tour. Lane, the well-known American anti-oralist author on Deaf people's rights, would have been anathema to the "old" RNID.

It seemed that he was almost the poster boy for the "new" RNID.

It was almost impossible to recognise the "old" RNID in the "new". The work of the organisation was almost unrecognisable to those who only knew the "old" staid and traditional RNID. And the change was real – at least on the outside. On the inside, it was a different matter. There were areas in the RNID power structure where the old ways were still firmly entrenched. The old attitudes prevailed most of all at the Board level. They had not shifted very far from their paternalistic ethos and behaviour.

Two years after my appointment as a Director, Whitlam was head-hunted for the post of Director General of the British Red Cross. His dynamic work at the RNID had made him the number one candidate for other social agencies anxious to develop similar growth. Whitlam departed the RNID in the middle of 1989.

Just as with Derek Burton's leaving his post, I wished that Whitlam could have remained for another year or so. That additional year would have allowed some of the developments that we had only just put into play to become established before being affected by leadership changes. In addition, Deaf rights would have moved forward, creating a more positive political climate for the appointment of Deaf leaders.

As I had learned long, long ago, the brass ring doesn't come around often.

The Board as a whole was still not yet comfortable with a Deaf Senior Manager. As troubling as that might be to consider, it was the reality. They were not yet ready for a Deaf person at the top - or indeed as a Director. And this feeling was shared by the two Deaf members of the Board.

However, I don't believe anyone has ever accused me of timidity or of playing it safe.

So, I applied for the post of CEO.

Remember, my ultimate goal in coming to the RNID was to attain this leadership role. That my timetable had been disrupted was unimportant. The reality was, I was being confronted by an incredible opportunity. But I represented the very thing that certain members of the Board found intimidating – control by the signing Deaf. If I was to come to the post of CEO of the RNID, it would not be without a fight. This was not going to be a coronation.

The questions began from the outset. Was I capable? Was I the best candidate? Did I have the right "stuff"?

None of the questions dared tread on the most sensitive topic – or the underlying reality that coloured every aspect of my candidacy. No one publicly mentioned the fact that I was Deaf.

To have done so might have called into question the saintliness of the missionary sensibility. It might also have laid bare the hypocrisy.

If I had envisioned the "worst case scenario" for my interview it could not have been any more of a debacle than it was. My first round interview was with Winifred Tumim, Chair of RNID, and Mary Nunn, Head of Personnel. These fine ladies, sensitive to the needs and the realities of the Deaf had failed to ensure the presence of an interpreter at the interview.

"They're playing you for the fool!" my friends warned me.

"How dare they!"

"Don't do it!"

Don't do it? What? And concede victory to the very people who would take the greatest pleasure in my surrender? No, I could not allow that.

I agreed to go forward without the benefit of an Interpreter rather than to show "weakness" as a Deaf candidate. I was forced to try to lipread the words of the questions and then sort out what they meant. Only when that was done could I form a response in my far-from-perfect speech.

These two ladies never gave any indication if they understood me or not. It was like being in oral school all over again. I might not deliver the correct answer, but I was getting some credit for my good acting. So too did they. Playing their parts well – pleasant, smiling and condescending.

Following this interview, I was engaged in a series of psychometric tests run by an external consultancy company. These too were biased against a Deaf person. Oh, I did just fine with the intelligence tests, where my strengths were readily apparent. However, I was more than a little annoyed by personality profile questions, which were quite obviously based on a hearing person's norms. For example – "When you are in a pub or other similar social situations – how do you react.?"

Now, I doubt that anyone who knows me would ever accuse me of being a wallflower. But the reality is that any Deaf person entering that kind of social situation would do what I would do - hold back in a pub because of the difficulty in communicating through speech. But such an answer was sure to have me labelled as an introvert or a social misfit. The marks and rating were based on the standards of hearing senior managers. If the questions had been adjusted to say (as they ought have been for a post involving work with Deaf people) "If you went into a Deaf Club where everyone was using BSL, how would you react?" I would have been fine and hearing people would end up looking like introverted, social misfits – like chumps.

Despite the obvious difficulties that this initial interview process posed, I managed to make the short list for the final formal interview before a panel of five RNID Trustees. Aside of the Chair, the Treasurer Mark Nicholls would obviously be a key person on that panel.

As I entered the interview room, Tumim opened with (via an Interpreter this time!), "Good morning Doug. Mark has a very important telephone call to make. So, he will ask his questions first and then leave the room to make his call."

No choice was offered. No, "Are you agreeable to this?" Just that this is what is going to happen – full stop!

I was a bit stunned. I felt like responding, "Well, I have a very important interview that could affect my career. I would like him to remain here throughout this interview." But if I had done so, it would probably have been "Bye bye Doug," as a candidate.

So, stiff upper lip was called for yet again!

Nicholls asked his three questions and then left the room after only ten minutes of my 45 minute long interview.

I didn't protest about this strange situation. How could I? I was confronted with a situation that I had little control over. Holding my ground would have destroyed my chances. I very much doubt if they would have done this with a hearing candidate.

As it happened, I did not get the appointment. The appointment went to a fellow Director, Etherington, with whom I had worked well over the previous two years.

I have never had any serious problem with Etherington's appointment. Indeed, it was a wise appointment. But my anger at the process is a separate issue to the final choice. There was no excuse for the attitude I confronted simply because I was Deaf.

In an organisation that is supposedly sensitive to such realities!

I had fought tenaciously throughout my life against exactly the kind of demeaning treatment I had received at the hands of the leadership of the RNID. How could I not be furious? Yes, I was hurt that I did not get the position I had been working towards for years. However, to have lost out on the appointment in the way that I had was beyond galling!

I was determined that no Deaf person should ever be treated as I had been treated again. Therefore, I invoked a grievance against the conduct of my interviews. In taking this action, I had the support of my Trade Union, MSF.

91

Because the RNID did not recognise Trade Unions there was a bit of argy bargy over whether or not to allow my Union Official at my grievance hearing. In the end, the RNID "rules" would not allow for his presence in the hearing. I could only meet my Union advisor before and after the interview, outside of the interview room.

I can't imagine that it would have made any difference anyway. The three-man panel of Board members rejected my grounds for grievance without giving so much as an explanation! The MSF was as livid as I was. They wanted to fight the decision.

"Why?" I asked the Chair of that panel of Trustees (an Audiologist no less!). "Why did you reject my grievance?"

I'm still waiting for the answer.

There were a few difficult days and sleepless nights as I weighed the decision to pursue my grievance. Ultimately, it was only after putting it in a larger context that I decided not to go forward.

There was political change in the country. The Labour Party was in ascendant. The Deaf rights movement was continuing to make important headway on every level.

I reasoned that I would have another opportunity to take over the reins of the RNID. I based my reasoning on my understanding of Etherington. Having worked with him, I had a good read of him and his goals. I knew he regarded the RNID as a stepping stone in his own career progression. He wouldn't be staying terribly long.

Did I enjoy the taste of humble pie?

Did I, heck! But I had to try and keep in mind the larger picture.

I would not allow them to limit me and use my Deafness as their excuse. I would demonstrate that I could accomplish all of my goals. And by doing so, I would be demonstrating that every Deaf person could accomplish his or her goals.

So, I withdrew my grievance and affirmed my support for Etherington.

92

None of that kept me from planning my strategy for the future. This time, I would leave nothing to chance. Due to the age factor, I knew that the next time would be my last chance for the top spot at the RNID. I didn't want to consider not succeeding on my next shot at it. However, I had to account for that possibility as well. If I failed to get it at the second shot, I decided I would quit the RNID and continue with the work on Deaf issues from outside. I would take up from where I had left off some years ago.

However, that was only if I didn't succeed. I didn't plan on that outcome. To that end, I identified my weak areas and set out to remedy them over the next two years so that I would be ready for the time when Etherington moved on.

I determined that, given the direction of the charity world, that I would benefit from the possession of a top management qualification like a MBA. Although such a qualification had never been a requirement in the past, I believed that it was likely to be a requirement for candidates in the future – which it did become. I enrolled on a part-time MBA course at Birmingham University and duly obtained the degree in 1992.

I also set about shoring up my weaknesses in the areas of deaf and deafened issues. I plotted out a two year program for gaining knowledge and experience with the deaf population. However, my own strategy was more than taken care of when Etherington restructured the Senior Management Team in 1990, making me the Director of Research and Development.

In this role, I had quite a broad remit, which more than covered the gaps in my CV. In fact, it went beyond it in that I was to lead the drive for the development of quality in the RNID and its work. This had become a key development in the UK private sector as companies sought to regain the ground they had lost to the Japanese. As Director, I had the opportunity to look at private sector methods and adapt them to suit a charity like the RNID. We were well ahead of other Charities in this respect.

My remit also covered Education and Employment, the Information Services and Policy Research and Development. If Etherington was working with me to strengthen my CV, he could not have assisted me more.

More than the benefit to my CV, my new role gave me the opportunity to continue to pursue Deaf people's rights. I was responsible for quality issues at every level of the organisation, giving me many opportunities to "turn things around".

93

I ensured that for all the RNID services, "quality" had to mean meeting or exceeding customer requirements. It meant that service standards and specifications were to be set primarily by Deaf people as the end customers. With the quality chain starting and ending there, it meant that the standards for all parts of the support infrastructure in the organisation were pitched towards these goals. This effectively gave Deaf people some control over how services were designed and delivered.

"Total Quality Management" became our watchword. The RNID became the first charity to be accepted as a member of the British Quality Association. Typetalk, the telephone relay service run by the RNID obtained BS 5750 certification. In the external climate of quality, consumerism and customer care, the RNID developments fitted in well with the successful approaches that were being used in the private sector. All these developments worked in concert with Etherington's commercialist philosophy.

In addition to quality control, I was also responsible for the RNID's information services. One of my first moves was to act on the decision to shut down the RNID's hearing advisory service. Operated by the RNID for years, it had provided nothing more than a ready excuse for local health clinics to not do what they should have been doing.

While it provided an important service – free hearing testing and advice – it required deaf individuals to come to the RNID Head Office. This ran against the principle that everyone was equally entitled to a good local health service. Yes, some areas did have substandard services. However, rather than letting those areas "off the hook" by providing services, the RNID needed to use its resources and influence to improve those local services.

Perhaps more to the point, only those people able to afford the trip to London could take advantage of the hearing tests at the RNID. As a result, people of more limited means were once again left out in the cold.

The closure of the RNID hearing advisory service was not well liked by those who had taken advantage of it. However, thanks to Etherington's full support, the closure held.

We also stopped advising individuals as to the best hearing aid for them. Instead, we sought to make this decision one which empowered the individual. We made all relevant information available and let the individual decide on the device that would best meet their needs.

Consistent with the philosophy of empowering individuals, a new Social Policy and Research Division was set up within the Department to develop a range of RNID policies on various issues and to undertake social research. This Division also co-ordinated responses to Government policies and initiatives. Previously, these activities had been dealt with on an ad hoc basis, without oversight or coordination of message. Whoever happened to respond to the particular issue just said what they thought was the right thing to say. Naturally, the RNID's message often was conflicting and ambiguous. Establishing this Division was aimed at ensuring a common approach and common message throughout the organisation on key issues. We also believed that it would aid in our attempts to influence Government policies.

When Mike Martin, the Director of the Technical Department retired, that unit too fell under my auspices. Now, in addition to everything else, I had oversight and responsibility for the Division, which evaluated equipment for Deaf people, developed new technical ideas and gave technical support and advice to all locations.

Again, though it might not have been the way I would have plotted it out, my preparation for becoming CEO was very thorough. When Etherington did leave just over three years after his appointment, I was very well prepared to take over the reins of leadership. My responsibilities had covered much of what the RNID did. I had gained valuable knowledge and experience with a broader range of RNID clients. And I had an MBA to boot.

Etherington moved on to the post of Chief Executive of the National Council for Voluntary Organisations in 1994. When he announced that he would be leaving, the RNID Board contracted a top recruitment agency, Saxon Bampfylde, to aid it in its search for a suitable replacement from amongst the more than 300 applicants. Applicants, which included three other RNID Directors besides myself.

When Etherington announced his decision to move on, a small group of Deaf people – unbeknownst to me – organised a "Deaf Chief Now!" campaign. They staged a media campaign including a well-managed demonstration outside of the RNID AGM in October 1994.

Their argument was simple and direct – unless Deaf people are shown to be capable of running their own organisations, how could anyone argue for Deaf people being able to be top managers anyplace else? Of course, this

95

argument was fuelled by lifetimes of frustration at being held down by the paternalistic, hearing power mongers who controlled the organisations "dedicated to their well-being".

The campaign was inspired by the one carried out in 1988 at Gallaudet University in the USA, where Deaf people and their allies successfully overturned a decision to appoint a hearing person as the President of the University. Their actions had hung heavily on the consciences of many Deaf people in the UK ever since.

How could we sit back and do nothing about a similar situation over here?

The protesters were only too aware of the symbolic significance of breaching the RNID "fortress". They knew, as did every Deaf person, that the RNID was the strongest bastion of the "old" thinking. If they - if we - could gain control of the RNID then we could overcome any other obstacles in our path!

I don't know if these protesters helped or hurt my candidacy. Certainly they called attention to the need for a Deaf CEO at the RNID but their actions also served to feed into the Board's "siege mentality", causing them to redouble their efforts to find someone who was so good that it could "sell" him or her to anyone and everyone.

Some members of the RNID Board and staff looked down at the protesters. "They should show some maturity," one of these members sniffed. "They should just swallow any decision to appoint a hearing person and count their blessings until the next time around."

It was painfully obvious that in spite of the work of people like Whitlam and Etherington, the RNID had not changed internally as much as we hoped. The feeling in the RNID seemed to be taking hold that at best a deaf person should be appointed Chief Executive. Such a person would allow the Board to "have its cake and eat it too". The Board could praise such a person as being the epitome of everything that the RNID stood for. After all, such a person could hear and speak. Wouldn't that be the perfect leader for an institution with close links to oralism?

A signing, Deaf person? How could such a person represent the RNID?

I might be deaf but I was not blind to the sentiment on the Board. I had ample experience with these people to not leave anything to chance. Who could know just how far they had shifted in their previous negative stance regarding having a Deaf Chief Executive? The likelihood was that they were even more firmly set against it – not more flexible in considering it.

I could not afford to leave anything to chance. I pored over all my potential weaknesses. I made lists upon lists, searching for that one "stone" left unturned. I asked friends to try to view me and my candidacy with brutal candour.

"You're Deaf," they said.

"Thanks for the insight," I replied.

I went so far as to employ a Public Relations Consultant, Veronica Crichton, out of my own pocket to work on aspects of my personal image. I relied on her judgment to steer me through my preparation for the interviews. My reasoning was simple. If all the top politicians and business people utilised such expertise, why not me?

I even tried to prepare myself for instances of unfairness and humiliation. I was as ready as I could be.

Just before the first of the interviews, a friend knowing of my liking for rugby said, "Good luck in sidestepping past these people."

"I am more likely to crash over the line for the try with all of them clinging onto me!" I replied.

Three other RNID Directors, Elaine Sola, Brian Hindson and Karl Holweger, had also applied for the post. Whatever else this portended, it also meant that, should I be given the position, I was likely to be faced with three unhappy key Directors.

There were three rounds in the selection process following the initial short-listing. First, an interview with the recruitment agency. Then, a round with the RNID Chair, Brigadier Jim Grear and finally an interview with a panel of five RNID Trustees.

The first one was the most difficult of the three. This was with a professional recruiter who knew what he was doing and how to search out any weakness that a candidate might possess. Such people weren't concerned with their standing in the charity world. They pulled no punches in their questioning. They were perfectly nice but there was no question that they would succeed in getting to the bottom of each candidate.

I came out of that first round completely exhausted. I didn't know what to think about how it had gone. When I was asked, I shrugged my shoulders. I hadn't a clue how I had got on or how they would evaluate all my answers.

Fortunately, I did well on this first round and made my way onto the final short list of eight candidates. The other RNID Director that had made it to the first round had been eliminated, leaving me as the sole internal candidate. One of the eight finalists pulled out before the final interview, leaving a field of seven people.

A couple of days before my final interview, 25th November 1994, the BSL Interpreter I had lined up dropped out due to illness.

I couldn't believe my bad luck! At this point in the process, I had begun to look for signs and significance in all sorts of outlandish places. A curious glance from a Board member could have me trying to sort out its significance for hours. Thank God I was never the superstitious sort or I'm sure I would have been reading tea leaves or consulting the oracles throughout the process.

Fortunately, I was able to locate a suitable replacement Interpreter at short notice. We had to meet in a Central London hotel on the night before to prepare him for my likely answers to the range of questions that I could be asked. To his credit, he did a great job on the day. I was confident that I had answered all the questions well enough and that if I did not get appointed it would not be due to any failing on my part but due to factors over which I had absolutely no control.

The Chair, Grear, an ex-Army Brigadier General who had seen action in Northern Ireland, was a honourable chap with no deaf background and, therefore, no big hang ups on Deaf politics. Like most senior Army Officers, he was trained to assess a situation and to do the right thing – regardless of the circumstances. This situation was no exception. His thinking was straightforward and pragmatic. If appointing a Deaf person was the right thing to do - even if it could cause him a good bit of personal hassle in overcoming communication barriers - then he would do it.

There has been precious little acknowledgement of Grear's integrity and courage in this matter and in those that followed. He deserves praise in supporting my appointment as the first ever Deaf Chief Executive of the RNID.

Finally, my personal goal and my dream had come true! It was actually second to my original wish to become a Senior Manager at ICI. That would have been a real achievement, but it was not to be.

I wasted little time revelling in my victory at the RNID. It was more of a great relief for me than elation as I had continued to suspect that some obstacle would be erected in front of me. My attaining this position was just the beginning! Now it was time to move the RNID forward toward greater things than it had ever considered before - things that Deaf people needed and wanted to see done. Even to a Deaf Manager of a mainstream organisation!

I wanted the RNID to use its power and influence, its position and its resources to make things, as they should be. I wanted the RNID to truly lead when it came to Deaf rights and have the Deaf "on board" with us.

Over the previous eight years, the RNID had gone through developmental transformations. First, under Whitlam it became a charity as a managed enterprise. Then with Etherington at the helm, with his conception of charity as business. As outsiders to the Deaf world, they brought into the RNID the wider world philosophies. They had the courage to do what they felt was right even in the face of severe opposition from the establishment. Their ability to play it both ways and at the same time direct the ship in the right direction helped in carrying everyone in our field into the world of modern philosophies and management methods.

Now it was time for the RNID to be a Charity closer to Deaf people while at the same time, continuing with the practices and the foundations laid down by both Whitlam and Etherington.

The question was, could I provide the leadership that could make that happen?

Chapter Five

Riding for Glory on Our Backs!

It is not from the benevolence of the butcher, the brewer, or the baker, that we expect our dinner, but from their regard to their own interest. We address ourselves not to their humanity but their self love.

Wealth of Nations – **Adam Smith**

No one would have remembered the Good Samaritan if he'd only had good intentions. He had money as well.

Margaret Thatcher

The distressed and downtrodden in society have always depended on the kindness of strangers – the kindness of those good Samaritans who reach out to others in need, helping them through life's difficult and trying moments. From the motorist who stops to help another motorist with the flat tyre, to the dedicated individuals who work in soup kitchens to make certain that the poor and hungry are fed, these Samaritans perform a vital human and societal function.

In addition to these simple acts of kindness, there are also those individuals whose status and means demand a qualitatively – and quantitatively – different approach. These "Carnegie" type Samaritans, philanthropists, who donate millions upon millions to museums, libraries, and charities, are the backbone of institutionalised "samaritanism". They are the ones who establish the trusts, who sit upon the Boards of charities, who have their photographs taken and published on the society pages. They are the ones that are held up by normative society as the secular saints.

These people need the distressed and downtrodden as much as the distressed and downtrodden need them.

I would be unfair to them and to Deaf people if I denied the many Deaf people who have benefited from these Samaritans over the years. When Deaf people were generally uneducated, unemployed and destitute the

100

kindness of such people brought immeasurable comfort and support. However, those years are long gone. Charity has evolved from the doing of kind acts to becoming an institution. It has become an industry, one that has long ago shed the skin of its original concept, that of helping people in distress. It has become a sort of a culture or, worse, a habit that these philanthropists need even more than the 'distressed and downtrodden' victims of their benevolence.

The 'kindness of these strangers' has become something of a prison to the people they seek to help. Deaf people have become just one example of such an imprisoned group.

When a Samaritan or philanthropist goes beyond the alleviation of pain or destitution, when he extends beyond the alleviation of hunger or illness to the point where he seeks to take control of people's lives, then the Samaritan ceases to be charitable. It becomes *paternalism*. Once the Samaritan imposes conditions upon his charity and tries to manage the lives of those he professes to help, his 'charity' is only the kindly mask of an insidious paternalism. It is condescending, cold and calculating.

It is anything but charitable.

The reasons why paternalism runs amok are complex but they centre on the power and prestige that such 'charity' bestows upon the 'Samaritan'.

Paternalism might rise from 'good intentions' but it translates into interference in the lives of those who need help. The needy become objectified. They lose their humanity, their individual dignity, and their integrity.

In the eyes of these 'Samaritans', the consumers never know what is best for themselves. Only they, the 'Samaritans', know what is best.

Now, there are clearly people in society who need this kind of care because the nature of their needs are so desperate. However, in too many cases, the Samaritan either oversteps boundaries or overstays their welcome.

As the saying goes: "Give a man a fish and you feed him for a single meal. Give a man a fishing rod, and you give him the means to feed himself for life." These paternalistic 'Samaritans' seem determined to pile the needy

101

man's plate with fish, feeding him an infinite number of meals but never providing for the greatest gift a charity can give a person in need – dignity and the means to take care of himself.

Paternalism is a curse word in the Deaf world because we have suffered under its yoke for so long. This 'kindness' has probably done more, apart from oralism to hold us back than any other single attitude in society.

This paternalism generally takes two forms. First, there is the traditional concept of paternalism (overt acts of help and benevolence whether or not the recipients need it) that still exists in certain bodies like the RNID and local organisations like that of the Blackpool and Fylde Deaf Society - where they insisted on a literacy test before Deaf people were eligible to stand for election as Trustees of the Deaf Charity.

As befits pure paternalism, this literacy ruling does not apply to hearing people who wish to become Trustees of the Deaf Charity! These people actually believe that they can and are helping Deaf people.

Organisations such as these hold their self interest above all else. They want nothing more than to perpetuate themselves and extend their influence and power. Their Boards are predominately non-Deaf. Some stretch the point by saying they have "deaf people" on their Boards. By doing so they emphasise the lengths they will go to in order to delude. A few of their members may be deaf, yes, but they not Deaf. This is a tactic, which those in power use to deflect attention from this issue. A couple of elderly people who wear hearing aids could be recruited onto the Board. They are presented as an indication that they have "filled their quota" as it were!

Those Boards that do have a Deaf person or two on their Committees, or functioning as advisers, invariably reduce these individuals to mere token roles. They hold no real power or influence. Indeed, the fact that they appoint a Deaf person only as an "advisor" on their Boards is an indictment in itself.

The control of policy decisions in such "d/Deaf" organisations is retained by these Paternalists and 'deaf' people. Crucially, because they represent their Boards on external statutory advisory bodies they retain a wider control on policies that affect Deaf people.

102

What chutzpah! To say that they "represent Deaf people" is ridiculous. You would not find a single organisation representing Black people whose Board consists entirely of white people. Or a women's organisation run entirely by men.

There aren't any!

But a d/Deaf organisation? You'd be hard-pressed to find a d/Deaf organisation in which a single Deaf person had a significant or power-sharing role on the Board. Apart from that consumer organisation, the BDA. How is such an organisation to lead Deaf people when, by their very leadership structure, they send the message that Deaf people are neither worthy, nor capable of taking control of their own lives?

Why do these paternalistic 'Samaritans' sit upon these Boards? Oh, they will usually respond that they are "helping these poor d/Deaf people". In doing so, they mimic the worst traits of Politicians! They will say or do anything that suits their purposes. How can they talk about helping Deaf people when they hardly ever see them?

These paternalistic 'Samaritans' don't even grace the various gatherings of Deaf people with their presence. How could they possibly get a feel of what it is like to be Deaf? How can they possibly appreciate the views of Deaf people on various issues? Yet they just go on making decisions at their Board meetings on policies that affect the lives of Deaf people. They don't have a clue what it is like to be Deaf!

To be fair, there may once have been a place for this type of paternalism way back in the mists of history but there is no excuse for it in today's enlightened climate. Over the past ten or fifteen years, the generic policies and practices have been towards avoiding any hint of paternalism. The principle of encouraging independence of the individual via empowerment has become paramount.

By and large, the Deaf world has been moving away from the traditional concept of paternalism. "Missions to the Deaf and Dumb" are now called Deaf Societies or Associations. Their premises are now "Deaf Centres".

Missioners are no longer with us. But, the traditional attitudes and behaviours still exist in many of these establishments. They are still controlled by hearing "ex-Samaritans".

However, the demise of the old paternalism has led to its replacement by a second and more subtle form, the *new paternalism*.

While most of the hearing people (the ex-Samaritans) involved in the Deaf world as Trustees, Committee members or as professionals would be quick to disown the concept of paternalism - indeed, they would be astonished to have the charge of paternalism levelled at them - they still do all they can to retain control and power over Deaf people's lives. Even as the winds of change blow in their faces! Even as the prevailing philosophies and principles cry out for a "new way"!

It is positively sickening how so many of these people - at all levels - speak their fancy words about the rights of Deaf people while, at the same time, obsessively clinging to their control. Why is it so important to these hearing people that they control these organisations?

They speak words of empowerment but do next to nothing about making it a reality.

Ask them to relinquish the reins if their power and they will respond with almost exactly the same words that the traditional paternalists used.

"Deaf people can't…"

"They are not ready for it."

"They still need me."

The key issues here are voyeurism and exploitation. These people want to be seen to be "doing good". As with the old Paternalists, they get to appear on public platforms for Deaf people. They appear on the society pages. They receive awards "on behalf" of this or that do-good organisation. But, as is still the case with most of these self-serving awards, they go to the paternalistic 'Samaritan', not to the achieving Deaf person.

The Paternalist rides to personal glory on the backs of Deaf people. They hang round our necks, holding back our progress like the albatross in the Ancient Mariner poem.

All this is understandable. There's a great deal to be gained by speaking on behalf of another - skills; status; recognition and good feelings. It is difficult to give these up. Not to mention the power!

Oh, the new Paternalists have learned the politically correct manner of speaking. They have learned to invite a Deaf person or two to sit in on their Committees. But they never concede power or control. They speak the speak but never walk the walk! They know how to create the appearance of empowerment, without ever granting power. Deaf people are also invited onto public platforms, but essentially only to speak about themselves and their personal experiences or troubles. They aren't given the chance to participate in the process of converting them into public policy.

As a Deaf friend succulently puts it, "They use us for 'oration' and not policy making."

This new paternalism, along with vestiges of the old paternalism, defines not only these individuals but also the organisations they control. We have seen so many examples of hearing people on television and radio pressing for access for Deaf people or talking about Deaf issues as if they had suffered such experiences in their own lives. There are plenty of books by hearing people on Deafness. But you can count the books by Deaf people on one hand and still have fingers to spare. It is appropriate for white people write on Black people's experience or the able bodied on what it is like to be disabled?

Unfortunately, both types of paternalism lead to very real and negative consequences for Deaf people:

1. They encourage and reinforce negative perceptions of Deaf people. The posturing of Paternalists encourages the general public to see Deaf people as being "in need". Once perceived to be "in need" we might well as well be!

Responding to this public perception, charities are then set up to "help these poor Deaf people". Like it or not, charities for Deaf people invite paternalism, both deliberate and unwitting. We can't have it both ways. If we truly want to be free of the shackles of paternalism, we have to eschew the charity image.

2. Policies that affect Deaf people are not decided by us. The new paternalism has led to a shift in approach from "helping Deaf people" to "speaking for, or on behalf of them". The "enablement of Deaf people" is carried out in a way that ensures that power does not change hands. Control of policies and services remains in the firm grasp of these people who often, conveniently, happen to be the service providers. They also happen to be in the health, social services and education professions.

3. Organisational paternalism is the control of power by organisations that purport to "speak for Deaf people", enabling them to get what they want in order maintain or enhance their organisations. They will do whatever they need to do in order to get money and influence, regardless of whether or not it is actually what Deaf people want.

A plethora of Deaf charities has grown out of this new paternalism. They are generally run by people with attitude problems or people who are only just barely hanging onto their jobs. Almost all seek to perpetuate their own interests.

Perhaps the crucial distinction to be made in determining whether an organisation and the people running it are self-serving is *whether or not Deaf people participate in a meaningful and power-sharing way in the organisation's decision-making process*. Do these Deaf people have any real power to affect the direction the organisation might take?

Power is the key word. It is what it is all really about.

4. One of the saddest outcomes of the new paternalism is the rise of greater tokenism than has ever before existed in the history of Deaf people. Appearances have become more important than substance. With the old paternalism, it was possible to identify the enemy clearly. But this new paternalism is sneaky. There are Deaf people being wheeled onto Boards of certain organisations as "advisers" so that it looks better for these in control.

106

These 'advisers' are thanked for their input. Then they are promptly ignored and their insights forgotten. These are the "house Deaf", an expression deriving from the slave owners' distinction between the field and house 'niggers', in which the latter were chosen for their compliancy with the slavery system.

This problem of tokenism is often exacerbated by Deaf people themselves, who take advantage of the situation to gain status and power for themselves, even if means being an 'Uncle Jack' or 'Auntie Jane', the Deaf equivalents of the Black people's 'Uncle Toms'. It is also made worse by Deaf people's general apathy to such situations and their reluctance to do anything about them.

5. A more subtle, but no less worrying, aspect of the new paternalism is one in which the progressive themes and issues are taken over by the Paternalists. To give but one example, rather than resisting the concept of user involvement, they claim it for their own agenda. This is known as the *professionalisation of consumerism.* This is where we see Researchers, Managers, Consultants and Commentators who have attached themselves to Deaf issues. They put themselves into the forefront and "speak for Deaf people" from the middle of a group of Deaf people!

6. Paternalism in all its forms is doing enormous damage not only to the Deaf cause but also to our confidence and self esteem. It ensures that we have no control over our own destiny. It ensures that we are not allowed to develop and if we do manage to crawl out from under its weight, then we are either bought out or pushed aside. Many Deaf radicals have been pushed to the sidelines for daring to speak out.

We need to remove the shackles and to throw off the yoke of paternalism. It won't be easy. These people will use any excuse they can to maintain power. They will say that Deaf people are not yet ready or that we need training or whatever.

And they will be right. As long as these Paternalists hold power, we never will be ready. We will never have the training we need. We will never believe in ourselves!

So, what is the best route forward? What do we need to do in order to overthrow the yoke of paternalism? We need: Paternalists to be aware of the negative effect they are having, to step down from their high positions and to work on true empowerment of Deaf people. Deaf people (and their allies) to put pressure on these people to do so. The Chair of every d/Deaf organisation should be deaf. Deaf people to point out examples when they occur, as it is often that people patronise without realising it.

No one should confuse my argument against paternalism with an anti-hearing people sentiment. I am most certainly not against hearing people. Deaf people need our allies and supporters. Those who see that there are situations where Deaf people should be in the lead and are happy to support them from behind. Much as many men got behind the women in their battle for emancipation. It is those hearing people who want themselves at the front for their own personal reasons that we are very much against.

I am talking about driving forward a movement away from professional advocacy to self-advocacy; from speaking on Deaf people's behalf to making it possible for them to speak for themselves. Giving them the fishing rod, so to speak.

As much as I would love these Paternalists to cede that power to Deaf people, I am not so naïve to believe it will happen. These people are not going to give up power so easily.

We have to seize it from them.

And, in time, we will.

Chapter Six

They shall hear - and speak!

Your Englishman, confronted by something abnormal will always pretend that it isn't   there. If, however, you force him to look into it, he'll at once pretend that he sees the object not for what it is but for something that he would like it to be.

James Agate

Readers unfamiliar with the Deaf scene may be puzzled by the emphasis on "oralism" in previous chapters. But no study of Deaf people would be complete unless this struggle and its significance are understood.

Of all the frustrations and obstacles that Deaf people face, none comes close to bogging down their lives as much as education. It should come as no surprise then that it is also the nexus for the most enduring controversies regarding the best ways to serve Deaf children.

The 'lines' are clearly drawn. The educational philosophies and their proponents are easily recognisable. Those who support the oral method, or oralism, the philosophy based on the prohibition of sign language, are almost invariably hearing people. Those who oppose this method are invariably Deaf.

This point alone should, in and of itself, lend a simple but incredible insight to the debate. The Deaf have suffered through the system – and have had their lives, their self-esteem and their prospects suffer as a result.

The 'successes' of the oralist method have been successes for the proponents of it, not for those who were subjected to it. Significantly, almost all Deaf 'successes' use sign language, even if they have been orally educated.

Mind you, Deaf people are not the only opponents of this draconian method of education. Others who oppose it include professionals like Social Workers and Mental Health Workers who have to address the so called 'successes' of that method, the Deaf adult outcomes of this 'wonderful' method of education. The scrapheap.

The history of Deaf education is rooted in profound prejudice. We had been perceived as being ineducable by such authorities as Aristotle (who posited that it is impossible to reason without the ability to hear) and St. Augustine (who suggested that faith comes only through hearing). Pretty heady intellectual and theological company, isn't it? Imagine what it must have been like to have been considered little more than a base animal by such noble gentlemen. After all, what is a human being without faith? Not much more than a beast of the field if you're a 'believer' like St. Augustine. And even if you are considered a viable 'child of God', Aristotle consigned you to being an idiot.

Some row to hoe, yes?

But we "hoed it". We managed to suffer through the centuries of abuse to a point where we were actually considered educatable. And then, lo and behold! to the point where we were actually being educated! (Aristotle, eat your words) It's no wonder that some people believe we should be grateful for the few crumbs that have fallen our way from the feast of life.

It goes without saying that these historical luminaries were not Deaf. They, like most gods with feet of clay, passed judgement based on their own, erroneous assumptions.

That we continue to this day to be subjected to these same erroneous assumptions by so many people is the source of astonishment and frustration. But we are. That is the reality of our situation. That must be our starting point. It is sad but it is true. Even in our own day, too many 'authorities' on Deaf issues continue to be self-righteous hearing people.

Among those who were instrumental in demonstrating that Deaf children could be educated were the French priests the Abbés De L'Epée and Sicard. Like many conscientious priests, the Abbé De L'Epée was very concerned that Deaf people were not receiving the sacraments. According to the belief of the Church, failure to receive the sacraments consigned them to Hell. Yet he did not know how to help them.

Then, one day, he noticed two Deaf girls communicating to each other in their own sign language. He observed them carefully and soon was able to communicate simple ideas with them. After a short time, he had learned their language and found that he could communicate even lofty, religious ideas to them.

He could teach them the sacraments (St. Augustine, where are you now?) Stories of the French Abbés successes in educating the Deaf 'imbeciles' became quite popular. To be fair, there were no real measures in those days like the National Curriculum or GCSE, but from the 1780's onwards Deaf people were gaining an education and even writing books (e.g. Pierre Desloges, Francois Berthier and others). It should be noted that most of the important Deaf writers during the next century were French, where education via sign language was the norm.

Wouldn't it have been insightful if an educator had made note of that fact before imposing the cruelty of oralism on generations of Deaf children? But no, our English arrogance would never have acknowledged any French wisdom. We never bothered to note that we in the UK, with all our bragging about the British Empire, could not boast a single Deaf writer before the 1950's.

Prior to the 1780's, there were individual recorded instances of attempts to educate Deaf people. Especially in the Mediterranean countries where Roman law forbade the inheritance of family fortunes by those who could not speak. Noblemen hired monks to spend countless hours teaching their Deaf sons (daughters were cut off from inheritance as a matter of course) to utter a few words. One such Spanish monk, Pedro Ponce, did this for an 18 year old Deaf son of a Mayor to utter a few words. Clearly, this could hardly be considered education. It was more along the lines of mimicking, like teaching a parrot to talk. Polly doesn't have any clue what the noises it utters mean, but it got extra nuts from the master.

However, the die had been cast. There was a powerful dynamic in place for the Deaf sons of rich people to be able to 'perform speech' as a mean to gain inheritance and also to overcome the stigma that existed within their social circles of producing 'inferior' offsprings. These wealthy parents were willing to pay anyone who could make their Deaf children 'normal'.

'Experts' in the art of getting Deaf children to speak and then to be educated through speech began to show up on their doorsteps. Most of these tuitions were paid for privately on a one-to-one basis. However, when there were enough parents around who could afford to pay the fees, special private schools for Deaf children were set up. Their methods remained focused on speech although there is evidence that some used signs to supplement the speech training.

In the UK, such schools were set up from the 1780's. These schools' philosophy was to teach Deaf children to speak and lipread. They would then be able to 'learn' just like normal, hearing children solely through reading the lips of the teachers.

Such methods, which strictly forbid the use of sign language "because it could corrupt Deaf children", is what we call oralism. The foundation of this educational philosophy is a belief that it is best to normalise Deaf children within the wider society. Not surprisingly, this found greatest favour with the upper classes in society who had a historic sense of shame and stigma in having an 'imperfect' child. It was these noble people who would go the furthest in their efforts to normalise their children or, failing that, to exclude them from their social circles.

Being from wealthy families, the parents of the Deaf children in such schools wielded enormous power through their establishment contacts. They had access to the MPs who inevitably moved in their social circles. As a result, government policy mirrored the prejudice of these parents. Despite the successes of sign language based methods in France, the oralist approach dominated in this country.

Even as these Deaf children of privilege were 'benefiting' (?) from the oralist method of education, there was another educational dynamic at work. Deaf children born to poor parents, parents without influence or connections, were being educated according to the tradition that had begun in France.

In 1880, for reasons that I have yet to be able to fathom, a resolution was passed at the International Congress on Deaf Education in Milan that banned the use of sign language in the education of Deaf children. Although I would like nothing more than to find some good intention behind this crass move, my cynicism (and life experience) always seems to get the best of me and I cannot help but assign less noble reasons for this decision.

People of means and connections have a terrible track record when it comes to levelling the playing field for themselves and their children. They exist in a cloud of entitlement, which cannot accept merit that does not begin, and end with them. I wonder if the Milan decision wasn't the result of a realisation that the signing Deaf schools were getting too good for the liking of the Oralists.

If these Oralists realised success was being achieved by some other method, for poor children no less! They would be confronted with two options. One, of course, would be to change their methods to more closely resemble the successful methods being used elsewhere. The second would be to outlaw the successful method so that only their method was in play.

We know what the decision was in Milan.

Perhaps we will quibble over the reasoning.

Perhaps you disagree with my cynical interpretation. Perhaps you are right. However, I ask you to come up with some other explanation for such a destructive decision. My experience has taught me that these Oralists would never have even bothered with the poor Deaf children if not for one simple reality – they were learning! They were succeeding where Deaf children subjected to the oralist method were not doing too well. As a result, the educational method of these poor children – signing – was held to blame. This was a threat to the oralist establishment, which was seeing failure and frustration as the norm. If the signing Deaf students and schools were not succeeding the oralists would not have bothered to try to squash them – they would have simply allowed them to die out as their oralism produced superior results. They would have taken the Darwinian high road.

But, my experience has taught me that the Oralists rarely, if ever, take the high road.

That's my opinion. Knock it down if you can!

It should come as no surprise that the Milan resolution was adopted by most governments. After all, it was rigged by the wealthy with their rich social and political contacts. Educational systems for the Deaf were erected on the oralists' premise.

Predictably, that resolution and its consequences was the start of a constant stream of failures in the education of Deaf children. And, as we know from any number of social studies, a failure in education inevitably leads to negative social implications, implications even more damaging for Deaf people who could not hear or speak. Just as predictably, the full blame for these failures was placed by the oralist teachers squarely on the shoulders of Deaf children.

"They are not clever enough," these educators claimed.

"They don't try!"

"They don't work hard enough!"

"They can't be taught!"

"There is something else there - a learning difficulty!"

The system never once pointed its finger inward! Never once blamed itself for the cruelty - and failure - it inflicted (and continues to inflict!) upon Deaf children.

Over the succeeding 120 years, the oralist professionals have been adamant on their stance and have refused to examine their approach and philosophy, much less change it. In fact, they have actually intensified it.

Count on them to wheel out the odd, solitary success – the aberrations of the system - and to ignore the large scrap heap of failures. Any business operating at such a high level of failure would very quickly have gone bankrupt. Senior Managers would have been called into account! Their feeble excuses would not have been tolerated long. Their claim that it was the "workers fault" would have been derided.

In business, there would be very real consequences for those who would rightly bear responsibility for the failure. Not so with these Oralists. They continue to do just fine, thank you. They continue to bask in the false light of societal approval and to receive their significant government subsidies. They continue to be rewarded for failure!

And the Deaf children continue to pay the highest price!

Naturally, the Oralists would quibble with my use of the term "failure". They would likely suggest that their anaemic programme has actually been a success! How? By pointing to a Deaf person's ability to say a few words and to lipread some? If we objectively examine the extent of these oralist 'successes' involvement in society, we would see that these poor 'successes' are effectively isolated from meaningful human contact.

With generally imperfect speech and hearing, they can only function on a one-to-one basis and are heavily reliant on members of their family. They

114

cannot participate at meetings or in social situations where there is more than one other person or where they need to communicate with someone who is more than ten feet away!

Some success! So much for the philosophy of normalisation!

Oralism operates just as a chimpanzee's tea party in the zoo. Dressed in our clothes and taught to act as human beings, they pour and drink tea out of teacups. How clever the chimps are! How "human-like!" It's cute, isn't it? But, of course, these chimps are hardly human-like. It's a farce. A charade. They can never be like us.

If only these chimps could only be seen by their primate friends in the jungle! Then this charade would become less comical. It would be revolting and degrading.

Oralism reduces Deaf children to the same level as these poor chimps!

There is no way a Deaf child can ever hear like hearing people. Their imperfect speech marks them out as "odd". Their lack of comprehension marks them out for ridicule. As hearing people they are deformed and abnormal. This is what oralism accomplishes! It reduces Deaf children to being less than their hearing counterparts. To being second rate hearing people.

But Deaf children are NOT less than hearing children. They are simply different. And unless this difference is acknowledged and respected, they will always be at a crueller disadvantage than any God or nature presented them with.

"Normalisation"? As if Deaf children are 'normal' only if they can speak.

Let us consider the situation of the so called normalised 'speaking and lipreading' Deaf person. That person would require the other people around them to face them and to use exaggerated mouthing so communication could take place. It means that hearing people around that person have to become abnormal with turning to face each other with exaggerated mouthing. A full "aquarium" of goldfish like creatures.

What is normal about that?

Contrast this with a BSL using Deaf person. Hearing people instinctively react more appropriately, as they would with a foreign language speaking person.

If they cannot sign, they try other visual means to communicate. And they are generally successful. Those hearing people remain throughout this process as normal hearing people.

The point here is that it is the oralist Deaf person that is abnormal. Not the signing Deaf person!

Furthermore, it is possible to have full participation and inclusion for Deaf people through BSL. Not through oralism.

Stepping aside from the debate on oralism and 'normalisation', the success of a Deaf child's education should not be in terms of how well they can speak or in terms of how well they can use their residual hearing. It should not even be on how well they can sign. It should be the extent to which they are able to *really* participate in society. On the basis of that criteria, oralism as a method of educating Deaf children is clearly failing miserably.

There is no clearer indictment of the system than the fact that Local Authority specialist Social Workers are required to deal with many of these Deaf people after they have left school. Children from ethnic and linguistic minority groups whose languages and cultures differ from the white English speaking population are not perceived as Social Services caseloads just because of their ethnic or linguistic differences.

I am not quibbling with the theory behind oralism. It's as good as any other system – in theory. Unfortunately, the reality of a Deaf child's life isn't lived "in theory". It is lived in the real world. And in the real world, oralism has proven to be an abysmal failure. It has no intuitive logic! Tell a lay person that Deaf children are forbidden to use sign language and they'll look at you as if you've grown a second head.

"What? That's crazy!"

"Then how can they communicate?"

"How can Deaf children be educated if they can't hear what's being taught?"

"How can the teachers respond to their requests if their poor speech limits understanding of what they're trying to say?"

116

Good questions.

A lay person will recognise immediately the common sense failure of oralism. Common sense points directly to sign language for Deaf children and adults. My God! How could anyone fail to see that?

In a 'normal' educational setting, teachers begin with an aim to educate and then use a variety of means to teach - speech, hearing, books, television, etc. In a Deaf setting, there is a topsy-turvy world in which educators begin with working on the Deaf children to enable them to be able to operate with the means used by hearing children (i.e. hearing) before they even begin to educate them. Years are wasted in teaching Deaf children to 'hear' and to 'speak', years during which their *actual* education is delayed.

Most never catch up.

Placing primacy on the acquisition of speech and hearing denies Deaf children their rights to education and to ready access to necessary information.

The system is failing Deaf children! Worse still, these failed processes continue to be perpetuated.

I should point out here that oralism is actually not the only game in town. Some schools have reverted to the use of sign language. Both as an admission of the failure of the oralist system and in facing up to the reality of the situation.

However, in most schools Deaf children don't have a real chance because they usually have a mix of deaf and Deaf children. The "signing" is then biased towards English rather than BSL, which means that Deaf children are still at a disadvantage when it comes to comprehension. Their education, although far better than in the pure oralist setting, is still not what it could and ought be.

Deaf children who "have to use signing" are still seen as the poor cousins of those who manage to 'speak' and 'hear'. However, there are two or three schools that have hit the right note. The Deaf children in those schools are fast catching up. They are likely to be overtaking those in the oralist establishments at some point in the future.

117

No issue has greater urgency than establishing the human and civil right of Deaf children to a successful education. We must review the various means and methods for achieving this right without being blinded by prejudice and self-defence, without the taint of tradition or the influence of people who have everything to gain by maintaining the status quo.

Acquiring speech and utilising whatever residual hearing the child has should occur separately and parallel to his education, taking place under the rubric of social skills development. In this regard, the National Curriculum is good news for Deaf children. For the first time, we shall be able to measure a Deaf child's progress in education against national standards. Schools and Authorities should now be forced to experiment with a variety of methods until they find one that enables Deaf children to meet the Curriculum targets in the same way as any other children.

I'm willing to wager that the successful methods will be based on visual methods of communication like sign language? Any takers?

Unfortunately, there is little sign that such an examination of methods will take place unencumbered by prejudice and the stench of failed tradition. Even today, 'hearing' seems to be the primary goal in working with Deaf children. Surgical implantation of electrodes inside the cochlea of the Deaf child's ear is the new oralist grail. These Cochlear Implants as they are called have become their sacrament.

Implants will save the oralist philosophies!

The Deaf shall hear again!

Saints be praised!

And we Deaf people shake our heads in anger and frustration as we watch the very same patterns developing as with earlier varieties of oralism. Cochlear Implants involve the same principles as oralism, get the child to hear and speak and then we can educate them. Education, if we ever reach that point is conditional on the child being able to 'hear' well enough – a largely futile exercise.

Deaf people and some organisations have registered their objections to implantation on children, which they see as experimentation. However, given the rapid spread of this phenomenon, some Deaf people argue that implanted

118

children should be allowed to use sign so that they can begin to be educated immediately. Parallel and at the same time as this, they would learn to 'hear' by identifying the electrical stimuli that are evoked by the implants. If they eventually do manage to 'hear' well enough then the signing could be phased out. If not, then they have not lost out in their education.

Simple isn't it? But, the Oralists, no doubt fearing that signing would be so successful that the Deaf child will never want to abandon it, reject such arguments out of hand.

There is no need to change methods!" the Oralists cry out. "Let us change the child and then our methods will be proven sound!"

Again and always, the "flaw" is with the Deaf child. Fix the child and the method will prove successful.

The arrogance of these Oralists! It is astounding that they are touting the same, tired arguments! It would be only distasteful if not for the fact that real people, Deaf children, continue to suffer. Deaf children continue to be reduced to fodder in their educational "cannon".

There are those who might suggest that I am too harsh in my condemnation of oralism. But I make no apology for attacking oralism. It is a prime cause of suffering for many Deaf children and people. Ask any Deaf person. There is no greater condemnation possible than that from the actual participants of a system.

If you want hard statistics, there is the national comprehensive research on the oral skills of Deaf children carried out in 1976 by Dr Reuben Conrad from Oxford. He summarised the results in a speech:

"When Deaf children leave school, half of them have a reading age of less than 7.6; half of them lipread worse than the average hearing child, untrained and inexperienced; 70% of them have speech which on the whole is too difficult to be understood, and only 10% have speech which their own teachers consider fairly easy."

The average reading age for the whole population of Deaf children was eight and three quarters. Similar results have been found in the USA, Japan and Europe. As oralism dominates in those countries, it is then a standard pattern for the outcomes of that philosophy of education.

119

What Conrad did not say but is implicit with those figures is that those Deaf children were not getting educated. How could they - if they couldn't lipread their teachers to understand what they were saying? They were not even even able to read their way round this communication debacle.

That was in 1976. What did the Educators do? Ignore these statistics and carry on using the same failed methods that produced such appalling results. Of course, "It is the Deaf children's fault."

Twnty five years on, guess what? Those figures have hardly changed! And guess what? The meyhods that produced these results are still being used!

Time for a change? You bet!

One of the greatest cruelties is the oralist exhortation to parents that they must not sign to their Deaf children. Imagine the mindset of these people who would erase the ability of a mother to communicate with her son? To reduce the communication of a father with his daughter to a level of mutual idiocy? And for what?

How many Deaf adults must ruefully remember the sadness of not being able to communicate with their own parents before this cruel abuse is brought to an end? Apparently quite a while. Governments and Local Education Authorities persist in ignoring the views of those who experience and suffer the consequences of the system.

What positive proposals can be made for Deaf children?

Not only do we need to guarantee the fundamental right of every Deaf child to education, we also must guarantee that they have the two-way access to information that this requires. These rights must be established immediately. There is real urgency at stake. Every day of delay is another day of unnecessary suffering by a Deaf child.

I do not wish to deny Deaf children the opportunity to learn to speak and to use whatever residual hearing they have. What I am saying, however is that speech and the benefit of residual hearing should not be a criterion for the Deaf child to be educated. First learn. Then gain the acquisition of these skills to round out an education.

Don't hold Deaf children back until these skills are acquired. Teach the children and then allow them to develop these skills. Give Deaf children ALL the tools they will need to succeed in society.

There are other key factors vital to the development of well-educated Deaf children, who will have every chance to participate to a significant degree in society. Parental awareness and support, Deaf role models and adequate provision in the classroom are all essential, but there are four others, which are of particular significance to Deaf children.

1. The model of Deafness, as generally reflected by the medical and educational system and consequently viewed by many people, is one of undesirability - a problem or imperfection. The general reaction to this is too often to "correct it" and make the child somehow "normal" again. We need to shift to a social model where Deaf children are accepted for what they are and where deafness is seen as part of the rich diversity of society.

2. Education and the development of Deaf children should not be assessed primarily through hearing, speech or even sign language, but through *communication*. Each child has different requirements, but communication is a must. The method is almost irrelevant as long as there is a *fluent* two-way exchange of information.

3. Deaf children must acquire a sense of both individual and social identity. Not as a second-rate hearing person but a first-rate Deaf person. This encourages the development of a sense of self-worth. Social attitudes are affected by this identity, or lack of it.

4. The focus should be on the children's ability – not their inability. Education should not be about what children can't do, but what they can do. Deaf children should be encouraged to adopt a philosophy of "I can do it." This would enable them to develop confidence in themselves and their abilities.

These four, the social model, the primacy of communication, the acquisition of an identity and the focus on ability are the values which must become the foundation of the education of all Deaf children.

There is no excuse to perpetuate the old, flawed philosophy of educating Deaf children especially within our 21st century society where individual differences are accepted, even welcomed as part of the rich and diverse fabric of our society.

It is time to change our approach and attitudes to educating Deaf children. It is time to forget about trying to mould them into 'normal' hearing children, ending up with inferior versions of hearing children. It is time to focus on developing them into first-class persons in their own right as normal Deaf children.

Chapter Seven

A New Dawn

Go confidently in the direction of your dreams. Live the life you have imagined.

Henry David Thoreau

Deaf Education was only one of the important issues that I was hoping to bring into focus when I became the Chief Executive of the RNID – albeit one that others were hoping I would influence!

On my appointment in December 1994, the future looked bright for Deaf people indeed. They had reason to believe that change was in the air.

I am not so full of myself to think that this was all my doing. By the same token, I fully understood the significance of my appointment and the responsibility I had to Deaf people. I saw my role as being the catalyst for more fundamental change.

Of course, most people were unaware of the extent of my goals. As a result, my appointment was met with support from all quarters. Only a very few people were aware that I was anything but a token appointment. Those who knew me knew that I would never have accepted the leadership post of the RNID unless I was convinced that I could use the post to further Deaf people's rights. That was, after all, my ambition.

I had yet to see how such ambitions could be eroded and sabotaged by a handful of individuals in key positions, people with agendas that were very different from my own – or that of the Deaf.

My appointment represented a golden opportunity Deaf people to make political progress towards achieving the goal of equality. We were all inspired by a palpable sense of "We're gonna change the world." I didn't mince words. I stated on the BBC "See Hear" programme and elsewhere, that my appointment was only the first step.

Of course, at this point, all I had was rhetoric and hope. I had yet to deliver. There was still a long way to go before any of us could mark real progress.

However, we could all take solace in the fact that we were moving in the right direction. How could we help but believe that a new era had begun? An era in which Deaf people took control over our own destiny.

I received many cards and messages of goodwill from all quarters, with many of these coming from people outside the Deaf world. I was fortunate to receive very positive and supportive reaction from the media, a reaction which included an in-depth interview by The Times newspaper. I received congratulations from people who normally would not pass the time of the day with a Deaf person.

I recognise that there was an element of sycophancy in much of this. Hell, I was being congratulated by people I knew didn't like me! The delivery of a bouquet of roses from Teletec, the suppliers of text phone equipment for Deaf people, was a bit over the top. Roses! Roses for me? They were a bit embarrassing for a chap like me from a northern coal mining area. They were a bit of an uncomfortable presence in a vase on a table in my office until my Secretary eventually removed them. It was a good job that my old mates from up north didn't visit me in London. They would never have let me live it down!

The RNID staff seemed very positive about my appointment. My well-known aversion of sycophants limited the fawning I received from those who normally cawed and crawled before a CEO.

All in all, I was given a very helpful and supportive welcome. Of course, there was no way I could have responded to the inevitable expectations that many Deaf people had of me as the first Deaf CEO. They had hoped and expected that the doors of the RNID would be suddenly flung open for them and there would be something akin to a Deaf take-over. Likewise, a number of the hearing staff at the RNID feared exactly this eventuality and that their own positions and responsibilities would be affected.

I needed to communicate to everyone the very realistic limits and timetables for moving forward. I also needed to ensure that deaf people knew that I would respect their own agendas.

People also needed to be aware that I had been appointed as a CEO of an established organisation. As such, my priority had to be the effective management of that organisation in achieving its objectives. My being Deaf was, and ought to have been, incidental on this count. I didn't want my Deafness to be a management issue. My Deafness would come into play when it was time to chart the direction of the organisation and in building up Deaf affinity with the RNID.

Not that I was or had ever deluded myself in thinking that I was the Deaf equivalent of Sir John Harvey Jones, who used to manage ICI. Nor did the Board. I was appointed for the qualities I had. They happened to fit in with what they were looking for. They must have been impressed with my explanation during my interview, of where I thought the RNID should be going. And how I would do it.

Now we all know, there's no such thing as a perfect Manager. We all have our weak points. Both Whitlam and Etherington had them but generally compensated for them.

While I have strengths in most aspects of management, I was not a specialist in financial management or the ways of the City. Nor did I believe that it was necessary for me to be involved with the tiniest details of all the plans. Communication was another bugbear for me. Oh yes, I can't help being a Deaf BSL user, but I was operating as a CEO in a sound based environment. That has to be a "weakness" in terms of making smooth progress. Against that, I was unmatched in the breadth and depth of my knowledge and experience of Deaf issues. Very few in our field could touch the scope of my CV.

Initially, as I did when I was managing a professional Football club, I planned to appoint a Deputy. John Taylor was the one I had in mind. We had complementary qualities. He was Director of Finance and had an eye for detail. We decided early on to hold that off for a while as it could send the wrong messages to the three Directors who had failed in their bids for the CEO post. It would have seemed like I was "rewarding" the one Director who hadn't applied!

I fully recognised the valuable contributions most of the hearing members of staff had to make in moving the organisation towards equality for Deaf people. That was a message I wanted everyone to understand. In order to deliver it, I personally went to every RNID establishment in the UK to reassure the staff that there was a future for them in the RNID. I wanted them to know that furthering the cause of Deaf people did not mean a reduction of the rights of hearing people.

"This is not about a Deaf take over," I told them. "It is about gearing the whole organisation to work together better than ever to achieve our common vision."

For me, it was about building on the progress that the RNID had made over the previous eight years.

I was also keenly aware of the importance of the partnership between all the organisations in our field. I paid visits to key people in the other organisations to state my commitment to working together. I understood that those who were deafened or hard-of-hearing were suspicious of my motives. I wanted to re-assure them. I proposed that we set up joint projects on issues of concern to them. While I had direct experience on Deaf issues, I was not - nor did I have any intention of ever - neglecting or denying the rights and problems of other deaf people.

But, after eight years of fighting to get Deaf issues placed on the public and political agenda, and developing itself into a strong and stable organisation, it was time for the RNID to move closer to Deaf people and to get them on board. In addition to this, the time was right for the RNID to review its position in relation to the external environment and the likely future needs of d/Deaf people.

A climate of consumerism existed in the outside world. The most successful commercial companies were listening and responding to their customers. Statutory agencies, like the Local Authorities, were compelled to consult with people when they drafted their policies and plans. Many authorities were granting contracts for services to those providers who had mechanisms for consulting with the service users and for obtaining feedback from them. In this context, the principle of the RNID working closer to Deaf people and their needs was particularly appropriate. What's more, the absence of BDA leadership in this area made RNID leadership even more compelling.

The BDA was by now languishing under weak leadership. There was no vision, no stated goals. The vacuum created by the BDA's inadequacy provided a tremendous opportunity for the RNID to move to establish bonds with Deaf people, to change Deaf people's perceptions of it, and to gain Deaf people's trust.

Given this climate, I articulated three key challenges for the RNID: to get d/Deaf people to identify with us and to move the RNID closer to the communities; to achieve a balance between the business and the voluntary ethos and; to be innovative and forward looking, keeping the RNID at the leading edge in all aspects of our work.

The key issues for the RNID as I saw them were: to realign its vision and objectives; to strengthen and improve its current activities; to examine the depth of its relationship with d/Deaf people; to explore new opportunities and; to prepare for the future. Given these issues, the RNID needed to establish a new, or modified vision, a new plan and an amended organisational structure in order to implement the goals implicit in these challenges and issues.

Any organisation's vision is its definition of why it exists and what it hopes to achieve. The RNID had always been concerned with the deaf person in society, and with the barriers that prevented their full involvement in all aspects of the community. Given that focus, a re-alignment of the RNID's vision needed to reflect a determination to do all that could be done to realise the organisation's goals.

The modified vision was set as:

"d/Deaf people have the right: to realise their full potential as individuals, enjoying respect, dignity and freedom from discrimination; to fully participate in, and share responsibility for, social, political and economic structures of society, with equal access to goods and services.

The RNID holds these to be the rights to full citizenship, to be exercised by d/Deaf people using the communication of their choice."

This vision contained two main elements: the first had to do with the d/Deaf having rights as individuals and the other with the d/Deaf having rights pertaining to participation in society. The RNID was determined to achieve this vision through two main avenues: Campaigning to challenge society's attitudes and to influence policies and; Providing services, which enable the achievement of the vision.

None of us were deluded into thinking that this vision could be achieved in the immediate future. It represented our long-term goals. We established shorter range aims, aims that could be attained in a approximately two to three years. These were spelled out in the RNID's mission statement:

"The RNID will earn the recognition of d/Deaf people as the key organisation promoting their access to society by campaigning for equal rights and by delivering services."

This mission statement was of particular significance because it was by the terms of this statement that the RNID would be measuring itself and its achievements. For the first time, the RNID would actually evaluate itself by reference d/Deaf people themselves rather than the previous internal assessments, which amounted to little more than patting ourselves on our back. The other key point in that statement is the fact that the RNID sought to *earn* the recognition of d/Deaf people, meaning that we were determined to measure our progress according to terms which d/Deaf people themselves defined. This was quite a challenge, one unheard of previously.

Although it might seem strange that an organisation as long-standing as the RNID might need to revisit its mission statement, or even to rethink its vision, the fact of the matter was that, after so many years of existence, the RNID had reached a profound crossroads. My appointment as CEO spoke to that reality as clearly as anything else. The time had come to rethink the entire thrust of the philosophies and issues, which affected d/Deaf people. Everything about the RNID had to be reconsidered and rethought.

This did not in any way suggest that the RNID would completely change. There was a great deal to admire about the RNID (even if that was not always evident to Deaf people). There were many staff members who were doing excellent jobs. The RNID had access to resources that needed to be maintained. There was absolutely no desire to throw out the baby with the bath water. However, it was equally clear that changes needed to be made. The RNID needed to be more responsive to the political and cultural realities in the world insofar as they affected Deaf people.

To that end, in addition to rethinking its vision and mission statement, the RNID needed to re-evaluate how we were going to behave as an organisation in achieving our objectives. There was no room for "cowboys" on the staff. If we were going to be effective in achieving our goals, each and every member of the staff had to know the characteristics and behaviour they were expected to exhibit.

I wanted to elevate every aspect of the RNID. While this often meant addressing issues of policy and philosophy, ultimately it meant addressing how

127

people – our staff – best represented the RNID and the needs of the people we were dedicated to serving. Re-educating the staff about what was expected of them and how to behave in trying to achieve our goals was fundamental to being successful.

The appropriate actions and behaviour of our staff were determined by a small number of values. I was certain that these would be what distinguished us from others organisations. Six values were identified and articulated as being key to the RNID and all it did:

1. **A Commitment to d/Deaf people**. *The RNID will measure all its decisions and actions by the degree to which they meet the needs of d/Deaf people.*

2. **A Commitment to staff.** *The RNID will value its staff and be committed to developing their potential at individual, team and organisational level. The RNID will strive to be a model employer of d/Deaf people.*

3. **Integrity**. *The RNID will display honesty in dealing with others and with itself.*

4. **Innovation**. *The RNID will develop and adopt new ways of meeting d/Deaf people's needs and will be open to adapting innovation developed elsewhere. The RNID will achieve this by making the best use of knowledge, experience and understanding wherever they lie. The RNID will devote its energies to anticipating the future as much as addressing the present.*

5. **Competence**. *The RNID will operate with efficiency and effectiveness to ensure a tight and reliable organisation.*

6. **Quality**. *The RNID will strive for continuous improvement in all it does to ensure it meets and exceeds the expectations of its customers.*

There was a feeling amongst the staff that we were setting very high standards for ourselves. We were! And were confident that we could meet them in spite of the obvious challenges before us.

However, as impressive as drafting philosophies and policies might be, it doesn't necessarily accomplish what needs to be accomplished. After all, the oralists had been leaving quite an impressive paper trail over the years. The only problem was... their methods and philosophies didn't work! They looked good on paper, but not in the real Deaf world. So, in order not to fall victim to that same failing, we determined that we needed to be in consultation with Deaf people so that we could carry out our work in a manner that suited Deaf people.

This was such a revolutionary concept that it astonished people! Consult the Deaf? About Deaf policy and practice?

Were we mad?

No, we were only just finally coming to our senses. The RNID had never consulted with Deaf, or even deaf people, in any serious and meaningful manner! A Deaf consultation group had been set up in the pre-Whitlam era but it was so clearly tokenistic that it was offensive to members of that group – its intent was to get d/Deaf people to "rubber stamp" the existing policies and practices of the RNID. The group disintegrated after only two meetings when the insulted Deaf people refused to take any further part in it.

Clearly, they weren't missed by the predominately hearing Board of Trustees who had always made their decisions without referring to Deaf people or their views anyway.

Clearly, I believed that all that must change.

I set about developing a mechanism by which the RNID could obtain the views of Deaf people at different levels, views that would then actually influence how we set policies and delivered services.

The mechanism I came up with operated on three main levels. First, at the top policy making level, where the views of d/Deaf people would be considered as policies or direction for the RNID. Second, there would be local user groups. These would consist of eight to ten local d/Deaf people with whom the regional staff would consult on RNID services. We had a model for these already in place. Such groups had been operating under the Community Services Department when I was the Director for about two years with varying degrees of success. They had been used to monitor our performance under Local Authority service contracts. Third, there would be a mechanism for obtaining individual feedback, such as customer satisfaction cards, which Deaf people would fill in their comments about whatever service they had utilised. (Again, Community Services had initiated a similar mechanism about a year previously, a mechanism which was then absorbed into a wider Customer Care programme.)

The two lower levels of communication had been in place for a period of time. These needed only to be strengthened and improved. It was at the first, or highest, level that we had the most work to do.

The Board had never had a problem with the local feedback mechanisms because, frankly, those mechanisms had little, if any, impact on it. However, I was determined to bring that very same dynamic right into the Boardroom. That was not going to be easy!

Not only was there going to be possible resistance on the part of Board members, the reality was that the different categories of d/Deaf people had never worked together very well in the past. Their feedback was often contradictory, leaving the Board with the same degree of control that existed prior to a mechanism of feedback.

The political climate in the country was in dramatic flux. Rights issues were looming on the horizon. The various groups had to respect one another and work together in order to aid one another in their different - and very legitimate - needs. I was determined that we create a win-win situation for all our service groups. The ascendancy of Deaf rights should not ever be a reason for deaf people to lose services or rights.

I confronted the task of bringing the various groups the RNID served together by first determining three separate categories of deaf people: Deaf, hard-of-hearing and the deafened. I then set about bringing together a representative group for each category consisting of a maximum of twelve people and led by someone who had a reputation for being a strong campaigner on behalf of their own particular group of d/Deaf people.

Stephen Lloyd agreed to lead the hard-of-hearing group. Ross Trotter led the group of deafened people. Paddy Ladd led the Deaf group. Ladd's agreement to participate was a remarkable step forward. His intense dislike of the RNID and all it stood for was well known. That he was willing to give this a shot spoke volumes of the hopefulness that Deaf people embraced at that time.

130

The membership of each group consisted of very strong-willed and fairly determined people. To their credit, they had taken full note of the RNID's history. They would only agree to be involved when it was made clear that they were not token groups and that this was not an academic exercise. It took some doing to convince them that we were serious about listening to them and that we would implement as many of their recommendations as we possibly could.

Even so, they were taking things one step at a time. As we all agreed, the "proof of the pudding was in the eating". We'd all been led down the garden path before. We weren't anxious to have it happen again.

The meetings followed a three-level structure. At the first level, each group met separately with only a RNID note taker to record the minutes of their meetings. The groups had two topics to discuss at these meetings: What they thought of the RNID and what they thought the RNID should be doing over the next ten years.

The second level of meetings repeated the first level save for one significant difference. Each group would have the notes taken during the meetings of the other two groups. Their agenda for the second level of meetings was to comment on the views of the other two groups. Again, minutes of these were taken by an RNID staff member and circulated to the other groups.

The third and final level of meetings brought four representatives from each group coming together in my presence. Our discussion was in-depth and defined by candour. We all had the minutes from the previous meetings before us. No one was pulling punches. By the same token, everyone had come to understand and respect the needs and goals of the other groups.

One of my goals in this meeting was to identify a few key issues shared by everyone as well as a few key issues particular to one group or another, which could be recognized as worthy of the support of the other groups.

That final meeting was remarkable in the way everyone pulled together and supported each other. They agreed on six or seven issues, the top three being: Education, Employment and Hearing Aids. Right under those was the recognition of BSL! Each of the representatives - Deaf, deaf, and hard-of-hearing - agreed that even if BSL only impacted Deaf people it was of such importance that they all would support it.

Everyone involved with this group and this series of meetings had nothing but the highest praise for the participants and for the content of the discussions. As indeed one might have hoped for. This was the first time in British history that such an achievement had been attempted, let alone attained! There was unanimous agreement that this format should be on-going.

My intent had always been to maintain this representative group as a source of advice and consultation for the Board and also the Senior Management Team. (Needless to say that the group and the format died when I left the RNID two years later.)

Clearly, the various changes we were undertaking required that there be some adjustments in the principles that defined how we operated our services and also in the way we delivered these services. They also demanded a gradual shift in the style of management throughout the organisation.

Some of the consequences of our change in principles included taking away the charity income subsidies for contracted services. The principle of equality dictated that we could not allow the statutory agencies to get "off the hook" by providing services through charitable income.

If, for example, a Deaf person contacted the RNID for help to obtain housing or with some complaint about local services, he or she would be referred to the appropriate Local Authority. It was not the role of charities like the RNID to find houses for Deaf people. Or to make a complaint on behalf of the Deaf person. We would, however follow up the referral by contacting the relevant Local Authority to make sure that they would deal with it.

Although this change required a difficult adjustment for a number of individuals, ultimately it meant that Deaf people would have equal access to the Local Authority Departments.

The same was true of interpreting services. These services should never be provided for from charity funds. Access to an Interpreter for Deaf people should be as of right, not charity. If an organisation or company refuses to provide an Interpreter for a Deaf person, the role of the RNID should be to apply moral and political pressure for them to do so – not to relieve them of the moral responsibility to do what is right by using charity income to provide the service that the organisation or company should be providing.

132

Likewise, contracts for residential care in the RNID Homes, Interpreting or other services on behalf of statutory agencies had to cover the real costs and then be managed within those costs.

All of us who worked for charities were well aware of these principles and we were fully supportive of them but we tended to drift towards the easy option of subsidising services. We tended, like most people, to take the path of least resistance. In addition, fundraisers always had targets to meet. Getting money for communication issues like interpreting was a relatively simple task. So, the fundraisers meet their targets but with money that is earmarked for interpreting provision, which should by right be paid for by the various statutory and community agencies!

However, it is possible to legitimately use charity money for things like "interpreting services" without abusing the rights issue. For example, charity money could be used for things like training of Interpreters, research into interpreting provision, pump priming new ventures in interpreting and so on – just not in the actual service delivery.

As I noted, I understood the tendency to take the path of least resistance in this context. However, I insisted from the outset that no charity money be used in areas of provision that relate to Deaf people's rights (e.g. Interpreting). Nor was charity money to be used in subsidising contracted services. This was an extremely unpopular decision with the Regional Services. I understood that it would be. However, if we were ever going to make real progress on rights issues, there would be some bitter pills to swallow along the way.

Sola, the Director of Operations, was unhappy about my decision. And with good cause. At the time, the RNID subsidised interpreting services in the region of £500,000 a year. I insisted that they reach a break-even point within two years. Unfortunately, this did not improve my already strained relationship with Sola. Since she was one of the RNID Directors who had applied for the CEO post. My difficult relationship with her was just one of the personnel prices I had to pay for having been given the job.

Although my two year limit to remove the service subsidies was a set one, I wanted to include incentives that would convince the Regional Managers to devise plans to achieve this goal. I established a scheme in which the money saved as a result of this would be used to finance new developments in the Regions.

Even with the incentive, I continued to meet with resistance in some of the Regions. However, it is interesting to note that while my enforcement of this principle upset some of the regional staff not one single Deaf person (staff or service user) objected to it. Not one! And these were the people who suffered when no Interpreter was provided by the RNID in those instances when an external agency refused to pay for one.

Deaf people, who knew only too well the humiliations of being denied basic rights, were more than prepared to suffer a little in the interests of longer-term achievements.

In addition to removing some services from receiving charity subsidies, adjustment needed to be made to the way some of the other services like Sound Advantage (the trading arm of the RNID involved in the commercial sales of assistive devises for deaf people, like visual flashing alarms) and Typetalk (the telephone relay service which the RNID ran under contract from BT) were run. These needed to be run as purely commercial concerns with the aim of making a profit. They required an analytical and hard-nosed marketing approach in order to survive in a competitive commercial environment. Others, like community development work and residential care, required a very different approach and ethos, an approach, which fostered relationships and community spirit.

Under the previous CEO, these various services all fell under the same Operations Department. With the development of the community-oriented ethos in the Regional Services, it made sense to move the Typetalk and Sound Advantage Divisions from the Operations Department to Public Affairs with its marketing orientation. After all, the Director of Public Affairs had a background in marketing. That renamed Department of Public Affairs and National Services then had two branches: Public Affairs, which covered media relations, political campaigning, fund-raising and publications and National Services with Sound Advantage and Typetalk.

In this new scheme, the Operations Department was more appropriately re-named Regional Services Department.

Community services were now free to move towards a more community-related operational ethos (albeit according to the principles outlined above). Unfortunately, Sola perceived this very logical and pragmatic institutional move as a threat to her power base. Although she continued to head the largest department in the RNID (in both staff and budget), she was beginning to react in negative ways to my leadership. She mounted an emotional campaign to persuade the other Directors to back her in her call for maintenance of the status quo.

I rejected the status quo on every level. Not only had it failed to meet the needs of the Deaf, but also it could not function institutionally in an efficient and effective manner. From my perspective, there was nothing personal about it. From her perspective, clearly everything about it appeared personal. She linked it to her having applied for the CEO job, which was far from true.

We could not go back or even stand still. A community-oriented ethos was not compatible with a hard-nose marketing ethos. Separating the two was the right thing to do.

But Sola did not seem to be weighing things from that perspective. She was embodying all that had been wrong with the leadership of d/Deaf organisations for years and years. She had turned everything around so that it was about her. Unfortunately, other Directors were agreeing with her for the wrong reasons. They were acting either out of sympathy to her woes or in fear of her wrath if they disagreed with her.

I could not allow what I perceived as a petty and personal power struggle damage the progress the RNID was set to make. I took personal responsibility for moving the changes forward. By executive order, I enforced the new structural modifications. As it happened, it all worked well and Sola herself later begrudgingly admitted as much.

Because our mission now depended on a new ethos and called for a new understanding d/Deaf people and our other customers, issues regarding the management of quality became a priority. In line with the principles I had already set when I was a Director with responsibility for Quality, "quality" was defined as meeting customer requirements. The staff therefore had to seek out the opinions of d/Deaf people and other customers about our services. They then had to adapt and adjust the service or mode of operation as a result of the feedback they received. An organisation-wide Customer Care programme was set up which included training for all staff on the meaning of quality and the importance of our customers.

Following the successful phases of first, the entrepreneurial manageralism of Whitlam and, second, the commercialism of Etherington, the time was right to move towards what I hoped would be the thing that would define my leadership – "ethical commercialism".

I hoped to lead the RNID in retaining our sense of commercialism - with its foundation of efficiency, effectiveness and economy – while at the same time expressing and responding to a real concern for the needs of Deaf people. It also implied operating in an organisational culture that put Deaf people at the centre of all that we did.

Ethical commercialism required a participative style of management throughout the organisation. Managers needed to be encouraged to open up and take more responsibility in how they operated. They had to have the freedom to adjust the service delivery directly as a result of feedback from the users. They had to be encouraged be open to new ideas and developments. In fact, Etherington had recognised the need for this shift in style, and had begun to think along such lines, in spite of the fact that his personal style tended to be more of a command and control approach to management.

Accomplishing all these aims depended upon a stellar SMT, on a team that would evolve and implement strategic and business plans to enable progress towards achieving the vision we had established. Underlying the success of the SMT would be its attitude toward having a Deaf person – and someone who had come from within their own ranks – as their leader. More to the point, this potential for success would be coloured by the reality that three of the members of the SMT had unsuccessfully applied for the CEO job.

Initially, the SMT seemed to be under the impression that my appointment was not much more than a "token gesture" - that it would run the RNID and I would simply tag along as a "figurehead". They were in for quite a rude awakening when they learned that I was actually going to take lead of the organisation as Whitlam and Etherington had done before me.

A new vision to bring the organisation closer to d/Deaf people didn't exactly suit one or two of the members at first flush. However, after we had worked together on it during a few away days where everyone made excellent contributions, they became more enthused. The Board approved of the new vision, mission and values in the spring of 1995.

Even with their intellectual and emotive support, there was some resistance when it came time to put our new vision and ideas into practice. Changing the management culture at the top of the any organisation is never easy and it was no different at the RNID. The former culture of command and control was one that top management had been comfortable with. It is so easy to order people to do what you want them to do and then to check up if they had done it. Participation, where staff had a say in how things got done is so much more difficult even if it pays off at the end.

It just happens to be the style required for our ethical commercialism to work well.

Of all the members of the SMT, the changes were probably easiest to implement for John Taylor, the Director of Finance. After all, other than becoming a bit comfortable with adjusting some of the practices of the finance department to take into account comments from the staff throughout the organisation who interacted with his staff, finance is finance. However, I believe he would have been just as supportive of me and my ideas that first year, even if they would have required him to make significant adjustments.

My relationship with Taylor was so successful that I originally wanted him to be my assistant/deputy. I felt that he would have been an outstanding choice. We had complementary skills. Where I was eager to get things done, he was cautious. Where I looked at the big picture, he had concern for the details. However, in spite of these benefits, we both agreed that the timing was not right. In those first days, when Sola was still seething, any move that would have raised the profile of another Department leader would have been perceived as a slight and would have been met with resistance. As a result, she would have become even more bitter and the Senior Management Team would have been divided. Taylor and I agreed that it was best for the Senior Management Team to remain united even if one of them remained somewhat displeased with me.

Brian Hindson, the Director of Administration, in addition to completing his MBA and facing the stress of final examinations, had responsibility for administration and personnel. His key role in the new set up was to bring to the RNID a new vision of organisational development, a new concept in the charity world. Rather than undertaking personnel management and staff training on an ad hoc basis, as was common among charities, we would have a planned staff and organisational development programme, just as most of the successful

137

commercial companies had. It included the responsibility for the development of quality and organisational culture.

This was both radical and innovatory. Normally "quality" would be attached to the end product or service and be the responsibility of the Department that is delivering the service. Here we were turning it round and placing "quality" as a core personnel and organisational development issue. It made sense in that if every member of staff inherited and operated a quality culture in all they did, it would add up to high quality end of the line services.

Included within the organisational development would be strategies for the training and support of Deaf people into becoming Managers. There was concern at the relative scarcity of Deaf Senior Managers. This was to be tackled by first undertaking an audit of all the Deaf staff to determine the exact reasons for this. An action programme would then emerge.

Unfortunately, our moving forward in this regard was delayed by his degree course. When he had finally completed his MBA and prepared his Department, Hindson moved up to a post as a Director at the British Red Cross! As a result, our entire concept of a planned organisational development strategy never really got off the ground. It was unfortunate as this would have had a major impact on how the organisation performed and at the same time geared it for whatever emerged in the future.

Karl Holweger, the Director for Public Affairs, was the "kid on the block". It was clear from the outset that he was destined to move on to greater things. Despite his considerable responsibilities - and additional workload with the inclusion of Typetalk and Sound Advantage into his brief - he never shirked from the load. He achieved far more than any of us had any right to expect.

It was a pleasure to work with him. He was eager to get things moving. His marketing background made him ideal to drive through Typetalk and Sound Advantage. He made a big difference to the performance of both of these units. His Campaigns, Fundraising and Publications Groups were staffed mainly by yuppie types and they made things "sing". His strong personal sense of rights and justice made him ideal to oversee the campaigning work.

Holweger formulated the "Equal Citizenship for Deaf People" project, a project which incorporated five key interlocking elements:

138

1. Parliamentary and media work to press for full civil rights for d/ Deaf people;

2. An extension of the successful "Louder than Words" Campaign to include a Chartermark award for companies and organisations which met the ten point criteria for their organisations to be fully accessible by d/Deaf people;

3. A Louder than Words service that included an audit of any company to determine their needs in ensuring access for d/Deaf customers;

4. The Louder than Words advances would be supported by the Regional Trainers in providing awareness training, Sound Advantage in installing the necessary equipment and the provision of Interpreters where required;

5. This would be monitored and supported by local user groups who would act as mystery customers and undertake evaluations of services. Chartermark Companies that had slipped behind would be given the opportunity to remedy or else have their Chartermark revoked;

It was to be a major and wide sweeping Campaign, beyond the purely commercial objectives of the original Louder than Words Campaign.

This was to be put before the Board for approval sometime during 1995 but got delayed until January 1996 when the new Chair was in office. Holweger was impatient with the delays during 1995 and the apparent lack of interest from the Community Services people (where it all had to happen). The delays were primarily due to Sola saying that they had other priorities to sort out first and that they required additional resources in the Department before they could undertake their role in this campaign.

Sola nursed her bitterness at me for a very long time. Not only did she seem to be angry about my getting the Chief Executive post but she was also resistant to all aspects of the restructuring. Even when Holweger made it all happen and she accepted that he was the best person to direct Typetalk and Sound Advantage, she could not bring herself to forgive me.

"It's more to do with how you did it than what you did," she claimed. She seemed determined to take offence at every turn.

In spite of her feelings toward me, I could easily appreciate her strengths. She was not particularly creative, so she was weak at thinking up new ways to accomplish a task. However, she was a good manager. If she was given a set of rules and requirements, she would make it happen in an efficient manner. The "new ways" seemed to stymie her. For example, when instructed to "move closer to the community", she was simply unable to progress. She was unable to come up with ideas like user groups, consultation forums, local co-operation, initiatives or whatever. She wanted me to spell it out for her.

To my mind, this inability points directly to the difference between a Director and a Divisional Manager. A Director should have the ability to come up with ideas and strategies to achieve objectives while the Manager must have the ability to implement the plans within the given budget.

She maintained her resentment for a long time in spite of the fact that she did do her job competently. Others in my position might have seen fit to move her out but, for better or worse, it is more of my style to try to work with people and develop their strengths rather than to cut them off because they are resistant to change. Although my approach often reaped benefits, in hindsight, it was a big mistake in this particular case.

However, the Regional Services Department did pursue, among other things; the highly successful Louder than Words Campaign. A charter of residents rights was drawn up for all the RNID Homes. A Customer Care programme, which included giving out customer satisfaction questionnaire forms after each Interpreting assignment. She also managed to cut down on service subsidies and was well on track to eliminating them in the following year.

Keith Fishenden the Head of Technical Services took over my old department, the Department of Research and Development, on a temporary basis. Towards the end of 1995, Jim Edwards, who had previously been the Regional Director for the Southwest, was appointed as the Director.

The rest of the team that enabled me to be an effective CEO included Adam Gaines, the Head of Campaigns and PR, and Jim Toohill, the Strategic Planner (an innovative and most valuable post that was established by Stuart Etherington). Gaines was very loyal, supportive and gave useful advice on my campaigning and PR roles. He was the main architect of the "Louder than

140

Words" Campaign that achieved a lot and could have made very real impact had it not been subsequently watered down and sidetracked. His departure, to join Etherington at the National Council of Voluntary Organisations, was a great blow for me. His replacement never exhibited his same loyalty, vision or inventiveness.

As an honest Yorkshire man with socialist tendencies and without any pretensions, Toohill was a man I could confide in. His value to me and the organisation could not be measured. However, my ability to fully confide in him was later tempered when he entered into a personal relationship with Sola. At that point, the line between the personal and the professional became a bit more difficult to establish. However, even taking those new considerations into account, he continued to be a valuable asset and supporter.

After the first, difficult initial months, the SMT began to change for the better. We all became familiar with new procedures and new expectations. We began to see successes (which always improve the general morale!) And we came to learn that participatory methods would not undermine our various roles and responsibilities.

In spite of constantly working with people, the role of CEO is very isolated, from both staff and the Deaf world. Therefore, the backing I got from the Chair (and Board) was vital. During the first year, support from the Chair, Jim Grear was very positive. I received excellent co-operation from him and, consequently, the Board. They were generally very pleased with the external reactions to my appointment and really wanted it to work.

Grear had a clear view on the role of the Board vis a vis the staff. He was anxious to stress the distinction between governance, that of setting organisational policy, direction and objectives and management, the actual implementation of the objectives. He set the ground rules on governance and management, which went a long way from preventing some of the more ignorant Trustees from interfering with a Deaf CEO. His view was, "We set the objectives and Doug is responsible for making it all happen." He never interfered in the running of the organisation, as long as all was well and our objectives were being achieved.

Despite some significant difficulties (not least of which was having three members of the management team who had coveted my position), these objectives were, in fact, achieved and, in some cases, exceeded. In addition, there was a drop in legacies to all charities during that year, most likely the result of the recession. In our case we got £500,000 less than our anticipated £4 million income from that source.

141

These difficulties created very real obstacles to our goals but they did not stop us.

All the objectives and targets were achieved within the reduced income by managing things like staff recruitment, cutting down on non-essentials, managing down expenditures, reducing the service subsidies, and so on. We even managed to retain the 10% ear marked for new initiatives and actually use it on development work.

With the finances, we introduced improved controls and better risk management. Over the two previous years, despite the effects of the recession the total income had increased to nearly £25 million. There were plans to increase it to £35 million over next two years.

A new headquarters building in central London had been purchased during 1995 and modified to suit us. We were ready to move into it early in 1996 with an official royal opening lined up for June of that year. The reception area was furnished with quotations extracted from my own collection, built up over several years, relating to equality, citizenship and rights. These visuals spoke volumes about the vision and leadership of the RNID. They reflected our ethos and the trend for the future. No longer paternalistic, but foursquare for rights and empowerment of Deaf people.

The scene was set for a bold and positive move into the future, a future defined by Deaf people's rights. However, a black cloud formed on the horizon before the end of 1995.

During the summer of 1994, when Etherington was still the CEO, moves were made quietly and with the knowledge of only a very small handful of people, to ease Grear out of the Chair. He was talked to by both Etherington and Tumim, who was by now an honorary RNID Vice-President. It was felt by these people that someone like David Livermore, a recently co-opted member of the Board who was the Managing Director at the RAC would be a more suitable Chair. The reasoning was that he would be more in tune with the organisation's more commercial orientation.

Livermore had been introduced to the RNID Board by Tumim. Having a d/Deaf daughter and the experience of raising a lot of money for the Mary Hare Grammar School, of which he was a Governor, were seen to be additional factors in his favour. Although he was interested in becoming the Chair, he did not feel able to devote the time to it while he was still at the RAC.

Interesting that, (whether or not by coincidence), Tumim was also involved in the co-option of James Strachan onto the RNID Board. A deaf photo journalist for the past five years or so. Previous to that he had been employed for just over ten years as an investment banker at Merrill Lynch. Was it also coincidence that these two *non-elected* Trustees would eventually move into positions of power at the RNID?

Livermore quit the RAC in 1995 and Grear was persuaded to stand down as Chair. It is not clear why Grear "had to go". I am not sure who said what to him. Whatever was said to him behind the scenes, he was true to his calling as a soldier. He had been led to believe that the right thing to do was to stand down. And stand down he did.

His farewell to the RNID was heart wrenching. It was clear that he didn't want to go. His departure closed a chapter in the history of the RNID and opened a new and more ominous one.

Livermore's nomination and election at the December 1995 Board meeting was queried by the only two Deaf Trustees.

It is interesting that although I could see the benefit of Livermore as Chair, both these Deaf Trustees had the same "gut reaction" to him - that there was "something not right about him"...and both are women. With hindsight, I should have known better. But things were moving so well that I could not see anything preventing our positive progress.

Ah, hindsight. Blessed hindsight.

Chapter Eight

Nemesis

It is nauseating to see Mr. Gandhi, a seditious Middle Temple lawyer, now posing as a fakir of a type well known in the East, striding half naked up the steps of the Vice regal Palace, while he is still organising and conducting a defiant campaign of civil disobedience, to parley on equal terms with the representative of the King Emperor.

Winston Churchill

If you can't abuse power, why bother to hold it?

Austin Mitchell M.P.

What a year that first year was! In spite of the obstacles that had to be overcome, I was quite satisfied that my first year as CEO of the RNID had been a tremendous success. Not only had many objectives been realised but also there was every indication of the hopefulness that many Deaf people felt in a brighter future was well-founded. Little did I realise that my first year was merely a prelude to what was to become something akin to a Shakespearean tragedy. My second year became a witches brew of Macbeth and Julius Caesar, filled with plots and culminating in a shocking assassination. As in Macbeth, a shadowy lady played a significant role and, like Julius Caesar, after the first unexpected knife several others followed in rapid succession.

David Livermore was officially elected as Chair of the RNID in early December 1995; however, he did not assume responsibility until January 1996 when he came to my office in the old RNID Headquarters on Gower Street to meet with me. The stated purpose of this meeting was as direct as it was appropriate – to become better acquainted with one another and to discuss my personal performance measures for the year.

Having supported Livermore's election, I was surprised at how differently he appeared to me in my office than he had as a candidate for the Chair. How I wish I had taken more to heart the insights of some of the others who came away from their meetings with him with deep distrust! As he entered my office, he paused and viewed me for several seconds. He was all smiles, he was. The palm of one hand clasped over the back of the other hand at chest level, just like a salesman in a car showroom, or a mortician selling coffins to the still-living.

144

For a parent who had raised a d/Deaf daughter with the oral method, it was sad and ironic that he was notoriously difficult to lipread. Like many Deaf people, I found myself struggling just to make out what he was saying, let alone understanding the deeper meaning and context of his words.

I did not want to be in a position of needing an Interpreter for every meeting with Livermore so I chose to have our first meeting without one. I thought that would set a very positive tone to our relationship. I knew that our first meeting would be more awkward without an Interpreter than with one. When I first worked with Grear, I struggled a little at the very beginning as he did. But it became quite easy once we both were accustomed to each other. I had no reason to believe it would be otherwise with Livermore. Indeed, I had every reason to expect that it would be a good deal easier. After all, Livermore was an oralist with the d/Deaf daughter. Surely, he, of all people, would be easy to lipread. I had managed to successfully lipread many people when I was at ICI, people who hadn't had any experience with the Deaf or deaf.

Certainly, Livermore should be easy to lipread.

He was not.

We did enjoy certain areas of agreement. Like me, Livermore wanted to see things happen through the RNID. Our perspectives in coming to this overarching goal could not have been any more different. I was driven by my negative experiences as a Deaf person trying to make way in the world. He was driven by his experience as a parent of a d/Deaf child.

Our different life experiences had given us differing views regarding the best educational methods for deaf and Deaf children. Even so, we were in complete agreement as to the need to improve education for Deaf children. And, like everyone else, he was appalled at the employment situation for Deaf people and wanted to see some improvement (his daughter had not been able to get a job since graduating with an arts degree).

My reasons for becoming CEO of the RNID were clear to me and those who knew me. I had spent a lifetime in activism for Deaf causes. Livermore's motives for becoming the Chair were not so readily known. There were those who believed that he was motivated by personal ambition, that he was anxious to obtain some honours to compensate for having been pushed out at IBM, where apparently he had been the victim of cutbacks in the Company. He suffered a similar fate at the RAC where as the Managing Director he'd had problems with the Chair. Both of these events would have hit his pride very hard. As it would anyone else. Together, they could have been an enormous blow to his sense of his standing in the world.

Added to this was the fact that he now had a lot of time on his hands.

A man of standing and wealth with too much time on his hands is often a very negative force to deal with. He tends to become involved in things to address his personal boredom, not to accomplish things. Or he could dive deep into some work.

These possible aspects did concern me. My experience had been that people in his situation tended to see and use Deaf people as mere playing pieces on a board game in their minds. They never managed to recognise our capabilities and full humanity. I hoped he was not one of these.

However, in spite of all this, I believed that my achievements in the past nine years at the RNID, along with a friendly Board, would help things to work out just fine.

Sometimes I pinch myself when I think back to that time. What in my experience had made me such an optimist? Hope, yes. But what evidence did I have then for a successful outcome? As it turned out, not much more than my hopes.

I prepared for my first meeting with Livermore by going over my various concerns, one of which was that our respective roles should not conflict with one another. My desire was to make my mark as a Deaf CEO. I believed that I was well on the way to succeeding in realising that desire. I certainly wanted to continue without interference from the Chair. I knew that Livermore could be a bit pushy in his manner. As an ex-Managing Director of large commercial concerns over a CEO of a mere Charity.

However, I reasoned that we could work through such personality issues. I was more concerned with his being a Governor of Mary Hare Grammar School. This suggested that he was likely to have a less than desirable attitude about Deaf people who use BSL

So, I went into the meeting girded with hope and good intentions. I overlooked how damaging it might be to the likes of Livermore and the ideology of the school where he was a Governor in having a signing Deaf person as CEO. My very existence undermined his assertion of the superiority of the

146

oralist methods of education. He could have had subconscious - and not so subconscious - difficulties in accepting that I, as a Deaf person, was capable of doing the job.

Had I been hearing, I am sure that Livermore would never have had these kinds of reservations.

Perhaps I could have minimised his visceral reaction had I simply refused to use BSL and stuck to speaking and lip-reading. But, of course, I did not. After all, I would never have got to where I was without BSL.

All these things were swirling just beneath the surface as he stepped into my office and struck his car dealership pose. And me, all professional pride as I tried to lipread him, thinking that if he simply followed Grear's principles, concentrating on managing the Board and leaving me to manage the organisation as I was appointed to do, we could achieve good results.

Several times throughout that one hour-long meeting, Livermore put his hand on my arm and said, "Trust me".

Trust me. I have forgotten at which point in the hour his exhortation began to ring as hollow as a politician's.

He stressed that he cared about supporting me as CEO. "I want to do what is best for you. To help you to build a strong Senior Management Team". I should have paid more attention to what he *didn't* say. He said nothing about a strong RNID or about achieving things for Deaf people. He emphasised over and over that he was there to support me, to promote me. But I wasn't really interested in that philosophy per se.

His words didn't ring true but I couldn't quite get a handle on why. After all, it wasn't unreasonable for me to presume that, by supporting me, he was supporting what I stood for and what I hoped to accomplish. In the continuation of the progress made by the RNID over the past nine years. Was it?

I reasoned that it was probably his sales background that made him sound the way he did. Wasn't that a key tenet of convincing the prospective buyer to make a purchase – spell out the benefits that the product would bring to the buyer? The merits of the product itself became secondary. The sale was a dance between people. It wasn't about things.

I got the impression that he was trying to do the same at that meeting. However, he was obviously unaware of the fact that I was not there for personal glory. I was more interested in seeing things happen to improve the situation for Deaf people.

The glib techniques of the skilled salesman did little to convince me. However, I was still slow to heed the warning bells that sounded at that meeting.

Damn. I knew better than to trust anyone who said, "Trust me".

Actually, I didn't trust Livermore but it did not occur to me that I would not be able to work with him. Over the years, I had acquired the habit of working through problems in a pragmatic manner. I did not think he represented an insurmountable problem. I never dreamt that my position could be threatened, not with things moving forward so well. Livermore's background. His obsession with his daughter's oralist education. His pompous manner. These were disturbing realities. But I always thought we would be able to pull together in order to achieve our goals.

I reckoned that his daughter would adjust to the reality of her situation like many d/Deaf people have done and begin to use sign language, even if she avoided it in front of her father. And like many parents in such situations, he would come later to see the importance of BSL as the only route to true equality for people like his daughter. Many hearing people who champion sign language are such parents, people who in loving and caring about their children realise the inadequacies of the oralist methods.

Unfortunately, there are also many parents who, believing too strongly in the oralist method, "kill the messenger" rather than the message. They blame their children, accusing them of "not trying hard enough" or they blame the teachers, charging that they "hadn't been up to it". They simply can't bring themselves to question the very method itself. As a result, they then press even harder for more stringent oralism to prove that they weren't wrong in opting for that route in the first place.

I would never presume to speak for Livermore, but I for one did want it to work between us as Chair and CEO. I was keen to prove that a Deaf person could be a CEO, to open up avenues for other Deaf people to move upwards. I wanted to seize the opportunity to achieve the vision that I had for so long, that of equal citizenship for Deaf people. I thought that with his daughter's emerging frustration with the barriers she was facing, he would empathise with this aim.

148

After that first meeting with the new Chair, I was still prepared to do what I could to make it work. I minimised the negatives. I thought once he got the aggravation of the RAC out of his system, he would settle down and let me get on with my job. How blind I was! No one gets to be a senior player in organisations like IBM and RAC without a lot of smooth talking and ruthlessness – behaviour the Charity world was unaccustomed to. The Charity world, up to that point, was still primarily about goodwill and achieving the charitable objectives. The cold-blooded ruthlessness of the city and the commercial sectors, the ethos of crushing or brushing aside anything and anybody that might get in your way was not yet part of the picture.

After our meeting, Livermore met with each Director. This was a fair and sound thing to do. However, he never bothered to meet with me again to discuss the feelings and perspectives of those Directors. He never bothered to try to understand the whole picture. He never asked me why I felt it necessary to do certain things. Instead, he built his judgments based on what he heard from the Directors, apparently ignoring the fact that three of them had failed in their desire to be CEO and that one was particularly bitter.

That this was troubling is an understatement. However, in hindsight this behaviour is typical of hearing people who just can't believe in Deaf people. Needless to say, the "good Senior Management Team" never materialised. Not while I was the CEO.

However, from the outset, I tolerated what I viewed as Livermore's shortcomings. I was ever conscious of the importance of the Chair/CEO relationship if, as in any successful charity or enterprise, the RNID was to continue to move forward. I continued to tell myself that our relationship – both professional and personal - would stabilise sooner rather than later. I was depending on Livermore's experience at IBM and RAC to make the RNID's financial progress more certain. Unfortunately, I had taken too optimistic a view. I had depended on his clear strengths, never fully reckoning on the negative aspects of his perceptions and personality.

There were other clues that Livermore would be a difficult Chair. It is normal practice for the Chair and Trustees of a charity to receive reimbursement for "reasonable expenses" incurred on behalf of the charity. However, few if any ever receive amounts that rival a salary. In stark contrast, Livermore demanded standards of expense and hospitality equal to what he was accustomed to at the RAC. He demanded that the RNID pay first-class fare for him to travel from his home at Winchester. No matter that the rest of us, including the other members of the Board, travelled standard fare.

Since he was at the RNID Head Office almost daily of his own choice, the expense was not inconsiderable. Then there was the expense account for hospitality lunches and dinners.

He also demanded his own office rather than use the Board room as none of the previous Chairs had done.

From the outset of his tenure, Livermore compounded his strategy of discussing things with the Directors without my knowledge by actually instructing them in what he wanted them to do. Discussions were one thing. Directives were quite another. This behaviour undermined my position as Chief Executive. Even with my understanding of his psychological state at being removed from the RAC, I could not be comfortable with this behaviour. I was willing to be "understanding" regarding his familiarity with being a CEO rather than a Chair. However, understanding or not, I had no desire to be undermined. If he was truly still thinking like a CEO, he would have respected my position and would have backed off.

Given all this, it was particularly ironic that the rumoured reason he'd been removed from the RAC was because he did not get on with his Chair and resented the interference as undermining his role as the Managing Director!

Still, I believed that if I kept my cool, Livermore would settle down after some reasonable amount of time start behaving as a normal Chair.

Mind you, I was not alone in being troubled by Livermore's methods. Directors Holweger and Hindson wanted very much to respect my position as CEO. However, doing so was complicated by the reality that saying no to the Chair is no easy task for Senior Managers.

"Just hang on," I reassured them. "Let Livermore vent his spleen over the RAC and things will settle down."

Unfortunately, things did not "settle down". When Hindson left the RNID later that year one of the reasons he gave was his concern at the way Livermore was operating. He foresaw a grim future for me and the RNID.

Not only did things "not settle down", they got worse. Livermore began to deal directly with some of the Managers, who were below the Directors. Not only was he undermining my authority, he had gone on to undermine the authority of the Directors! Even worse, he often behaved in an autocratic manner, a style that his salesman's smile did little to soften. His manner was not only distasteful to me but also to those who bore the brunt of his demands. More to the point, such a management style ran counter to everything that was being taught by the country's top business schools. That such a method was being employed by someone who had, during an early meeting, preached his faith and belief in "Total Quality Management" - something the RNID had been trying to practise over the past three years with varying degrees of success - was more than a little troubling.

As a result of Livermore's unsettling methods, I was forced to waste a ridiculous amount of my time on internal issues – "chasing" after Directors and Managers to learn what Livermore had told them to do and then to tell them differently when necessary. Less and less of my time was spent on external issues.

With the Chair in the office almost every day, this off-balanced situation was destined to get worse.

As bad as the situation had become within the RNID, the situation with the Board had become even worse. Livermore was just as dictatorial with the Board, but he – the consummate salesman – adjusted his pitch to his customers. With the Board, he devoted time outside meetings in one-on-one discussions designed to establish prearranged consensus for his policies. It might not have been democratic but it was damned effective.

As a result of Livermore's methods and practices, I was quite literally cut "out of the loop" when it came to Board discussions. With Livermore regularly referring to Directors Taylor and Hindson on management-related issues, I was in effect neutered as an effective CEO.

Nothing like this had ever happened when Whitlam or Etherington were CEOs. Nor did I suffer such exclusion when Grear chaired the Board meetings.

It seemed to me that Livermore was either determined to cut me out for personal reasons or he was determined to cut me out because of his attitude towards Deaf people. Or he was ignorant of the issues faced by the Deaf. My gut feeling was that, in his mind, they were all one and the same.

I tried many times to negotiate some change in his behaviour. However, he remained deaf to my protests. To be clear regarding how specific I was in communicating these issues to him, I am including the following extract from a note I sent to him following a Board Meeting:

1.   I was effectively cut out of the meeting

*2.   There were occasions when I wanted to say something but could not
      get the opportunity to do so. What made this worse was the fact that
      everyone round the table could see me indicating to you (which you
      probably didn't notice) and apparently getting "ignored". This gives
      the impression that I was deliberately being shut out.*

*3.   All the dialogue on management issues was between you and the
      Directors.*

*4.   This led to Directors agreeing to undertake some action points without
      my involvement.*

*5.   Directors were being given directions to do work and take action
      without my involvement. (In some cases the action would better be
      done by some other person.)*

6.   Trustees then addressed everything to yourself and the Directors only.

*The effect of this is damaging my credibility in the eyes of the Trustees.
This is reflected by the fact that during the early months after my appointment,
several of the Trustees would talk to me, ask me things or refer things to me but
now, none of them talk to me. This is partly due to their difficulty and discomfort
at talking to a Deaf person but mainly due to the perceived irrelevance of
addressing anything to me. The sole exception so far is Owen Tudor who at
least does refer items to me via letter.*

*All this was against the agreed procedure when we first opened up the
Board meetings to the SMT. It was agreed that issues would be referred to me
and I would incorporate/redirect to the appropriate Director if appropriate to
do so.*

*We are in danger of firming up the concept that you are an "Executive
Chairman" and I am just the token CEO!*

Livermore's conduct had a chilling effect on the Trustees. Already
uncomfortable with a Deaf person and taking their lead from him, many ceased
communicating with me. Some preferred to go directly to the Directors rather
than talk to me. The situation worsened when new members were elected or
co-opted onto the Board. Some were nominated by Livermore, but three
nominations came from me.

I hoped to persuade a couple of Deaf people to come onto the Board but they could not make it for daytime meetings so had to decline. The three (hearing people) I did get co-opted onto the Board were Mike Bishop, an ex-Director of Social Services, Owen Tudor, an official at the TUC, and Stephen Lloyd, an active hard-of-hearing person whom I had cultivated through the Reference Group of d/Deaf people.

I hoped that they would stand up for principles and, when necessary, have the courage to face up to Livermore.

How very wrong I was!

I was under no illusion that I needed the Chair's support. There is no magic or secret involved here. It is commonly understood that the success of any CEO is, to a great measure, contingent on the support of the Chair. During my first year as CEO, Grear's support enabled me to move forward and to develop with confidence. But Livermore, ironically, the parent of a d/Deaf daughter, was truly horrific. As is often the case, the Chair's personality set the tone for the rest of the Board. That was certainly the case with Livermore. Grear's Board supported me as a Deaf CEO. Livermore's Board often acted as if I didn't exist. Most of these people never went near Deaf people except at Board meetings. They enforced their own blind ignorance regarding the very people they were nominally responsible for reaching out to 'help'! They refused to try to have a clue as to what it was like for Deaf people. In fact, they were actually uncomfortable in the presence of a Deaf person!

What were these people doing on the Board of the RNID?

Livermore rewrote Grear's proposals for a modified Board remit. Grear's document included clarification of the respective remits of the Chair and the CEO. Generally, as is normal with most organisations, the Board had overall responsibility for policy decisions and the CEO had full responsibility for the management function in ensuring that the policy objectives as set by the Board were achieved. Livermore however, insisted that a clause be inserted that the responsibility for the appointment of Directors was to be shared equally between the Chair and the CEO. This blatant power play was designed to deny me my own selected team of Senior Managers. As a result, the team had to be one the Chair approved of - even though ultimate responsibility for delivering on the targets still remained with me.

This clause was as insidious as it was stealthful. It alone was to become the lever by which Livermore finally obtained extensive control of the management function. For me, it proved to be a very clear indication of his desire for control and to get things done his way.

Throughout these various political machinations, I remained painfully conscious of the fact that, for the sake of Deaf people everywhere, it was vital that a Deaf person in a senior position at the RNID succeeded. What was the message that would go forth if a Deaf person was unable to manage at the RNID? How could anyone make the argument for Deaf Managers in mainstream organisations if Deaf Managers were unsuccessful in an organisation supposedly dedicated to their success? No one is an island. Success is never an individual enterprise. This is particularly true for a Deaf person.

Certainly, the Chair of the RNID would be expected to be sensitive to such a reality. (That the Deaf person in question happened to be me was beside the point.) The Chair should have been aware of the importance of my succeeding as part of the validation of Deaf people everywhere. Of course, should I prove to be incompetent, then that would be a different matter. My competence had never been an issue.

With Livermore as Chair, the reality was the opposite. His constant interference and its consequent effect on the Senior Managers, resulted in my becoming completely isolated.

Rather than enjoying any support from the Chair and the Board, I found myself in free fall, with little real support from anyone.

Even as this painful isolation was deepening, I had to make great efforts to ensure that no one saw what was happening. I could not allow these events to have me be perceived as either a Deaf failure or worse, a Deaf whiner. I would not allow Deaf people to know of my isolation or my difficulties. They and some others rightly had high expectations of me, particularly as this was the RNID.

Even more, I would not allow the Chair or the Board to know the damage they were wreaking. If I gave the impression of weakness, I would open the door for them to consider me incapable, incompetent or both.

154

As a result, I was trapped in a surreal world where many people expected me to succeed beyond their wildest expectation whilst a few seemed to be working diligently to ensure that I would be nothing more than an abject failure. Given these circumstances, the external mentors that I relied upon were particularly valued.

Life was difficult enough when I was just a Deaf person trying to do a CEO job in a hearing environment, but with Livermore's interference, the burden became nearly unbearable. It was so much more difficult than it had been through the previous year – and it was getting worse day by day.

I'm sure that this degradation would not have happened to Whitlam or Etherington. I'm equally certain that it would not have happened to me if I had not been Deaf. In fact it did not happen with Grear in the Chair. This would probably be true for many other potential Chairs.

Livermore showed little sensitivity of the issues faced by Deaf Managers. If he was aware how easily certain actions would put them at a disadvantage, he didn't seem to do much to ensure a level playing field. He treated the Deaf Board member with equal disregard. Whatever benefit he should have gained by having a d/Deaf daughter seemed to be completely squandered in this environment.

Although Livermore spoke constantly to the Directors and Managers over the telephone, he never once phoned me directly. The reason was that he "did not have a textphone at home". Did not have a textphone at home? For goodness sake! He had a d/Deaf daughter! Either he *had* a textphone at home and lied about it or he kept his daughter at an unfair disadvantage. In either case, this behaviour was inexcusable. The RNID sold the things!

So, he and I were unable to communicate directly over the telephone. Neither of us were comfortable using Typetalk. Although its operatives were under oath to maintain confidentiality, we did not feel able to trust them enough! Most voice calls were made via my Personal Assistant. Anything private and confidential was sent by fax.

There is no question that it was easier for him to phone the Directors. That was true of Grear as well. However, by contrast Grear had made a determined effort to aid my success. Livermore seemed to behave in the opposite manner. His refusal to find an effective way to communicate with me, along with his tendency to by-pass me in his discussions with the Directors, had the very real effect of undermining my position as CEO.

None of these things were taking place in a vacuum. There was tension within the SMT as each member was, in effect, reporting to two people - the CEO and the Chair. I was losing my influence on the SMT, which had been so painstakingly built up over the previous year. Certain Directors – particularly Taylor because of his affinity with Livermore and Sola who still harboured her smouldering resentment over the restructure that I implemented soon after my appointment – seemed to do little to stem my slipping influence.

I then began to find that there were Managers who were doing work as instructed by Livermore. I was never made aware of what he said to the staff unless the staff took the trouble to inform me. Or unless I found out by accident.

As a result, I was very often at cross-purposes with my own staff! Either that or they found themselves "having to work around me". It wasn't long before the Directors, Managers and Trustees began to go directly to the Chair on management and operational issues instead of coming to the CEO, as they should have done.

Sadly, my Deafness, which required additional effort from them to achieve successful communication, contributed as much to this situation once Livermore set the pattern.

The SMT, which had made such wonderful strides the year before (even Sola was coming around, going so far as acknowledging that Holweger was doing a great job with Typetalk and Sound Advantage) was falling apart in the face of Livermore's actions behind my back. Hindson and Holweger expressed their concerns on this count, as did Toohill who, as the Strategic Planner, had a key role in the SMT. Hindson and Holweger resented the interference. I never heard such protests from either Taylor or Sola. Instead, Taylor did all he could to extol the merits of Livermore. Sola was not quite so blatant in her support of the Chair.

It didn't take a fortune teller reading tea leaves to see where all this was heading. I was at risk of becoming nothing but a token CEO while Livermore took over the entire running of the RNID.

This was an eventuality that I refused to allow. I have been a great many things in my life. A token had never been one of them. I wasn't about to become one now.

I took the initiative by requesting a meeting with Livermore. It was my intent to deal with all these issues with absolute candour. If Livermore was going to try to undermine me and behave as CEO then he would have to take full and open responsibility for his actions.

In this meeting, I explained that most of what he was doing day by day was plainly within the written remit of the CEO.

I sent him a memo prior to the meeting. It included an example of what I was talking about.

"My concerns relate to your recent visit to Sound Advantage. You requested a report from Carolyn Perkins and followed this request with a letter in which you asked her to take some action.

Three key and relevant points to note here:

1. *Carolyn drafted the report you requested and then sent copies to Directors and some Managers without sending same to me (the attached copy of her covering memo is self-evident).*

2. *You requested that she prioritise her projects and let you have her report on this. Surely, such prioritisation is a management task for which I should be responsible. I feel that it would have been preferable if you had directed such requests and advice to me rather than to demand it from Carolyn.*

3. *Your intercession in this matter has had the intentional or unintentional effect of undermining my position, which then required me to take action with the Managers to attempt to re-establish my appropriate position.*

These actions tend to create tensions between the Directors and myself as it leads to the development of a situation where Directors are looking to you for instructions rather than to me. My appropriate authority as the CEO and my ability to manage the RNID's activities are undermined by your actions.

At the moment this is a relatively minor concern, but if left unchecked and other equally minor issues cropped up, they could all accumulate into a real tension between us, which neither of us would want.

I hope you take this note in the spirit intended."

157

It was quite evident that Livermore was none too pleased with my bringing all this to his attention. However, I was successful insofar as he seemed to know what ought to have been happening. He said he would adjust his approach and be more sensitive to my position.

I was very gratified by these words. I thought that, perhaps, I had managed to get through to him... until I learned that within an hour of our meeting, Livermore was on the phone to Taylor, giving him instructions! I only learned of this when I asked Taylor to do something and he informed me that Livermore had already asked him to do the same thing half an hour earlier.

So much for "getting through to him"!

Livermore sought to influence my leadership in other ways as well. Often he made suggestions on all sorts of management-related issues, many of them quite minor. I always listened to his advice but after weighing up the pros and cons, I made the decision as to what I would do based on what I believed was the best for the organisation. This was, after all, exactly what I should have been doing. Ultimate responsibility for any failure was mine. I had no problem accepting that responsibility – if I had made the decision. But I would be damned if I was going to be blamed for a problem if someone else had imposed the problem on me.

There were times that my decisions were in agreement with Livermore's suggestions. There were other times when they were not. Whenever I disagreed with him, I was able to lay out my reasoning. However, regardless of my reasons, he won't have been too pleased that I took a different tack than his.

His "Napoleonic" complex climaxed early on when he went so far as to phone my mentor in an effort to get him to influence me to do things the way that he wanted. My mentor, being a man of principle, was outraged at this attempt to manipulate me through him. As his company could be doing business with the RNID, he felt compromised.

"I'm sorry, Doug," he told me. "But I can't have this sort or meddling. It's not right. It compromises me. And it compromises you."

As a result of Livermore's attempt to interfere with a confidential mentoring process, my mentor regretfully told me that he could no longer fulfill his role. He referred me to another person who had no ties whatsoever with the RNID.

You can be sure that I was careful not to give away the name of my new mentor, even though I knew that she would have given Livermore short shrift if he had tried to nobble her.

Can you imagine the gall of someone going to such unprofessional lengths in order to get his own way? I was outraged.

As with the usual practice, the annual plans for the RNID's work and associated budget are set during the previous financial year. They are agreed by the Board and become the objectives by which the work of the organisation is measured. At the December 1995 Board meeting, when Livermore took over the Chair, the plans for 1996/7, to commence on 1st April 1996 were approved. My objectives for the year, as agreed jointly with Livermore in January 1996, against which my performance would be measured, were broadly based on these, along with a few others that related to the RNID's relationship with the Deaf community and with other organisations.

The work program for the year 1996 was designed primarily as a continuation of the developments of the past ten years. The Board was keen to consolidate and build on what we had established. In addition, we were on track with improving the organisational ethos and to moving closer to Deaf people. We were also on track to reach the break-even point with more of our contracted services, such as Interpreting.

A comprehensive campaign was to be built around the "Louder than Words" work, to include the introduction of a LTW Charter mark, as explained in the previous Chapter. Many of these advances were to proceed under the "Equal Citizenship" banner. Unfortunately, this strategy was quickly aborted by Livermore and Jane Wilmot the Vice-Chair at a Board meeting in early 1996. It is hard to underestimate just how troubled I was by this action. The extent of their short-sightedness astonished and distressed me.

How could they not see how vital these programs were to d/Deaf people? Was Livermore, who I rightly or wrongly, took to be the prime mover behind these machinations, being malicious or was he simply blind to the needs of the d/Deaf - and deaf to the perspective I was there to provide?

This behaviour forced me to become something of a "Pollyanna" within the very organisation I had been hired to run! I was determined to ensure that this particular work was to continue unabated. If I needed to, I would find some other route to marshal the RNID behind a rights direction. Wasn't it our stated Vision?

159

It was such a shame that the Equal Citizenship Project was not fully up and running before Livermore arrived. As it was, it was formally ended at a February 1996 Board meeting by Wilmot. I was furious since it was to be a major plank in an organisation-wide drive for rights of d/Deaf people. Some elements of the campaign remained, but the wind had been taken from the sails. To make matters worse, Holweger, the main driver of this campaign left the RNID before I could re-submit it to the Board later that year.

He moved on, as he wanted to "run his own show". In a debriefing session with Livermore before he departed, Holweger expressed his concerns at the way he operated. Naturally, it did not make one iota of difference to Livermore's conduct.

In the end, the "Equal Citizenship" plan never again saw the light of the day. In hindsight I am sure that there was no way that Livermore or certain members of the Board would have moved forward with it. They had other priorities in mind.

Looking back at this Chapter, you may have got the impression that the whole year was spent in fencing with Livermore. Far from it.

Even while the centre was "ceasing to hold", the nearly £30 million worth of work was being successfully implemented. The cause of the RNID and the Deaf was progressing in the external environment. The image and credibility of the RNID had grown steadily, particularly in the eyes of Deaf people. The organisation was beginning to look ahead to the millennium and beyond. To expanding its work to reach greater numbers in greater depth and with more relevance to the needs of d/Deaf people. Plans were developed during the year towards achieving such ambitious goals.

The work out in the Regions continued through the year on a more or less steady course. With the reduction of service subsidies, extra resources had been created to enable some development work. The regional staff had been encouraged to think of innovative schemes. These included the possibility of using our residential establishments as day centres for local Deaf people who needed this facility (rather than go to the usual day centre with hearing disabled people). Outreach projects were set up to use the expertise gained in our residential homes, out in the community itself in the homes of local Deaf people.

There were plans to run experiments in remote interpreting via Typetalk. This was to have a microphone in the meeting room that transmits speech through a telephone connection to Typetalk. The operator's typing of the speech would appear as text on a screen in the meeting room for the deaf person(s) to read. This would be a forerunner for the eventual use of sign language interpreting on a screen in the meeting room using a similar method.

With the likelihood of the need for relay services changing through advances in technology, there were considerations on extending Typetalk into a national communications centre to cover all the various mainstream helplines. Instead of the helplines (for battered women or whatever) having their own equipment, which are expensive, they would use that at one central location (i.e. Typetalk). The adviser or counsellor based at Typetalk would take the calls.

Plans for the 1996/7 financial year also laid the foundation for the goals of the following year. After a period of establishing a solid framework for the organisation and then bringing it closer to d/Deaf people, it was now time to look ahead to what the RNID should be doing over the course of the next five years. The 1996/7 budget would give us the opportunity to plan for that period. The Futures Group, set up by Etherington some two years previously had produced their report. The Deaf Reference Group, which I had set up early in the previous year, had also made their recommendations. The Group had singled out Education, Employment and Hearing Aids as being the issues that needed to be dealt with most urgently. Some attention now needed to be given to those consumer priorities. The Group's fourth placed priority, recognition of BSL, did not get an airing. For one thing, three major priorities were enough to be going on with at any one time. For another, I doubted if the Board was ready for such a challenge.

The education of Deaf children in the UK had always been and continued to be an appalling mess. Hearing people who purported to know it all still squabbled over the best way to educate the Deaf. They clutched their little bits of meaningless statistics to "prove" their case. In the meantime, the mountain of failures generated by the system continued to grow. The professionals and the various Government Ministers continued to ignore the failures.

Clearly, something needed to be done. The first step was to establish accurate and objective information on the educational attainments of Deaf children in all types of educational settings. This alone would provide some guidelines to evaluate the reasons schools were failing to meet standards. This information would also highlight the successes and give us some insight into how these were achieved.

Any thorough evaluation of the education of the Deaf in the UK needed to be the joint effort of a number of organisations – those concerned with the Deaf and those concerned with education. To this end, a steering group comprised of representatives from those organisations was established under my chairmanship. This steering group would establish the guidelines for the subsequent research work as well as to consider bids from the various research bodies willing to undertake it.

Our fundamental question was, "Why were Deaf children failing to achieve at the same level as hearing children?" Our next was to identify ways to level the field when it came to academic achievement. In evaluating "achievement", a broad spectrum was considered, one that took into account the personal, psychological and social development of the individual students, as well as the national curriculum scores. The former was a new development. Little interest seemed to have been taken in the past on those three qualities.

In addition to the quality of Deaf education, we were anxious to turn our attention to the crisis of Deaf employment. Why did Deaf people have twice the national rate of unemployment? Why had the initiatives to get Deaf people fully employed not succeeded?

None of us was anxious to continue "throwing money at the problem" or wasting any more time with ad hoc schemes which were obviously not being successful at solving this problem. We needed something that was thoroughly considered and well-executed, something that would tackle the root of the problem.

Just as with education, our first step was to gain genuinely useful information, information that was objective and accurate. Obtaining this information would require research into the employment situation of Deaf people. We needed the full range of information, from how many Deaf people were employed or unemployed to the type of employment, career progression, etc. We also needed to examine such factors as employers' general reluctance to employ Deaf people.

162

This information would be invaluable in getting to the root of the Deaf employment problem. The research would also give us some idea on the causes for the poor employment of Deaf people, apart from that of poor education. It would give us a solid base from which to address the causes.

Another issue that had to be dealt with was the hearing aids service whether they were obtained privately or through the National Health Service. This had long been a bone of contention among deaf people. Those who were hard-of-hearing had strong views about the inadequacy of the Health Service when it came to the diagnosis and provision of aids. Research was required to evaluate the levels of the service all over the country to give us a baseline from which to mount improvement campaigns.

Another issue that we wanted to consider for 1997 was membership of the RNID. At the time, the actual number of members was around 350. Although no one seemed to know why, the Board had set it at a maximum of 500 members for some years. Traditionally, these consisted of "subscribers" to the Charity. Hearing people who joined to "do good". People who had a deaf relative. Plus some professionals. Even some deaf people. Deaf members were relatively scarce. Usually mavericks from the Deafworld.

For their subscription, apart from "feeling good at supporting the cause", they got a monthly magazine on deaf issues and the right to attend the AGM. Generally, around 40 or 50 would turn up at the AGMs. Just over 100 in total would bother to vote in the postal ballot to elect Trustees onto the Board.

Over the recent years, the number of Deaf members had increased steadily. No doubt as a result of the new direction of the RNID, my presence and the increasing number of Deaf employees. The subject of opening up the membership had first been discussed the previous year when Grear was the Chair. He had frozen any new applications for membership pending a review of the system itself. To see how best to use them and what could be offered for membership.

It should come as no surprise that Livermore, with his commercial upbringing, was obsessed with numbers. He reckoned that if there were 8.7 million deaf people in the UK then the RNID should have at least one million members. He later scaled down the target to 100,000.

It was "a bit on the low side," he contended. But he was still convinced that membership could be built up from there. He wanted to use it as a bargaining tool for political purposes.

Part of his strategy for 'building up" membership was to draw on the 7,500 existing subscribers to the RNID's "See Hear!" magazine. He fancied that if each of these subscribers were to become members that we could easily recruit another 90,000 from somewhere.

An agency was commissioned to undertake research into the feasibility of such a membership proposal and what people would expect from it. The research showed that we would not get that many and that it would be a very costly process. True to his nature, Livermore decided to forge ahead with his plan despite these findings. However, the researchers were eventually proved to be right.

Currently, after a long and intensive recruitment drive, the RNID has a grand total of 12,000 members. Not particularly impressive when you consider that they started with 7,500 subscribers to their See Hear magazine – subscribers who automatically became members with their subscription.

Livermore's "over-reckoning" with numbers extended far beyond membership. According to his reasoning, if the RNIB received £30 million in voluntary income then the RNID ought get substantially more than the £5 million it was receiving at that time. According to him, the RNID should have been bringing in nearer to £20 million.

As you can imagine, having Livermore as Chair, with his brutish style of leadership and his willingness to disregard the advice of researchers, moving all these plans forward was not a smooth process. The various projects that we'd considered in our five-year plan were very ambitious.

However, we agreed that rather than bumble along as most organisations (including the RNID) had been doing, operating bits and pieces of various projects that never really tackled the problems, it was better to do this properly and comprehensively once and for all. We were determined to gain solid evidence to justify whatever course of action we settled on. I was convinced that the results of our work, produced in a definitive document, could be used in a wide range of political agendas to obtain real and more permanent benefits for Deaf people.

Of course, all this new research was not without cost. The estimate for it was £1 million. Since I was determined not to draw resources away from existing services for these purposes, the £1 million would need to be found from some other sources. I had no doubt that it could be done.

So did Livermore. He was equally certain that he could get the money. After all, as he had been quick to remind everyone that he had raised £4 million for Mary Hare Grammar School.

The Board approved all our plans, including the mega membership scheme.

I needed to make some changes in the organisation's structure if the new money for these plans was to be found. Not only did we need to give a higher profile to fundraising but also to increase the profile of the organisation and to gear it to accommodate new elements like the increased membership. I could also see potential for raising more income through existing services, particularly Sound Advantage and Typetalk.

With Livermore's agreement in my pocket on this restructuring to enable implementation of these ambitious new plans, I wanted to get on post-haste with the appointment of the new Directors, so that I could start building up a new SMT and have it fully operational by the start of the next financial year in April 1997. I was also keen to begin some of the work in preparation for the new developments during the current financial year, so that we would hit the ground running after April 1997. Livermore was generally agreeable to this.

Or so he seemed to be.

In actuality, rather than the strong beginning to a promising five-year plan, we were at the cusp of a wave intended to drown the Deaf dream.

Given the conditions that existed at that time, what happened next was almost predictable.

Chapter Nine

The Smiling Executioner

As some day it may happen that a victim must be found
I've got a little list - I've got a little list
Of society offenders who might well be underground,
And who never would be missed - who never would be missed!

Ko-Ko – The Lord High Executioner
Gilbert and Sullivan – The Mikado

My downfall as CEO could be traced back to the moment that Livermore was named Chair of the RNID. However, it began in earnest with the organisational restructure which had been anticipated and which was necessary to achieve the ambitious new plans to be implemented during the financial year commencing in April 1997. Even so, it is very difficult to pinpoint the exact moment the moves to oust me from my position as CEO began.

True to form, this "Palace coup" took place behind my back. I had no inkling of what was going on. It wasn't until the beginning of 1997 that I heard the first clear indication of my undoing. It was then that more supportive members of staff informed me that apparently, Livermore's daughter was telling some Deaf people at a party in August 1996 that "my father does not like Doug Alker". August 1996. Almost seven months earlier! August 1996. I still believed that Livermore and I were working well together. Certainly he was doing everything he could to give me the impression that he was my "best friend"!

There were some members of staff who told me in February 1997 that they knew as far back as September 1996 that I was to be replaced by Strachan. I suppose the exact date is unimportant. What is clear is that at some point around mid-1996 Livermore initiated moves to oust me as CEO.

The first clear sign that Livermore's smiles were a sham came soon after the official opening of the new building. Looking back, maybe that event was the straw that broke the camel's back. Maybe he just could not abide the sight of the Duke of Edinburgh being escorted round the building by a signing Deaf person.

Livermore must have been squirming! What with all our VIP guests, including Ivan Tucker, the Head of Mary Hare Grammar School. It must have caused him terrible grief to be forced to acknowledge a signing Deaf person in the top spot. My very existence was a threat to their oralist philosophy.

Of course, it could have been nothing more than my insistence on doing my job my way. After all, the only thing worse than a signing Deaf person is a proud, competent Deaf person.

Maybe it was just everything together. Whatever.

Sometime that year, after the summer 1996, Livermore's façade began to show signs of cracking. He continued to give me the "all smiles, all thumbs up" mask but the reality was that behind my back he was undermining me, especially with certain more pliable members of the Board. There is a great deal that I can criticise about Livermore. However, I must acknowledge his ruthless brilliance when it came to strategy. He picked off the weak first and then, when consensus was his, he went after the strong.

He held off on the more determined members of the Board. He would save them for later when he felt it was the right time to work on them.

His more overt moves coincided with the departures of the two Directors who were the most supportive of me, Hindson and Holweger. Once they had gone, I was even more isolated. It seemed I was without any staunch supporters who could stand up to Livermore.

Once things began to go downhill, things began to accelerate. Starting around late Summer of 1996, the SMT unity was effectively scuppered. Apparently it was clear to Sola and others that Livermore wanted me out. Early on, they seemed to know they only had to bide their time.

Their behaviour toward me, of course, changed.

The screws were beginning to tighten. The first area of conflict was the year's plans, including the very substantive pieces of research work, which would point the direction of the RNID over the next five years and beyond.

The vacancies left by the departures of the two Directors, and the need to incorporate the new work created by the ambitious plans, presented the opportunity to modify the management structure during the current financial year so that by April 1997, we would be well geared for the way forward.

One area of restructuring was the Fundraising Division. Up to that point, the Fundraising Division had been a section within the Public Affairs Department. With 80% of RNID income earned through contract work, that hierarchy seemed appropriate. However, with the stated goal of raising an additional £1 million through new avenues, we needed major fund-raising initiatives. It made sense to separate the fundraising function from the Public Affairs Department. That fundraising would be led by a Director on the Senior Management Team which would give it a much higher profile throughout the organisation.

The existing Public Affairs Department would then become a Department for Communications (Public Relations, parliamentary work, publications etc). A new Marketing Department was planned, with a Director of Marketing to be recruited from the commercial sector. The development of Typetalk, Sound Advantage and the proposed membership scheme required a marketing and sales approach; this marketing drive would also have benefits for other services like Interpreting.

Finance and Administration would become a Resources Department. Community Services, encompassing all the regional work, was to include residential care, community services and any developments in the areas of Education and Employment that may arise out of the forthcoming research work.

The Research and Development Department was to be kept as it was pending a review of the role that the RNID could have. We were cognisant of the fast-emerging, competitive innovations in that field. It was likely that we would need a new Technical Director to oversee these developments. That would give us six Departments and six Directors – an appropriate number for an organisation of our size.

In August, at a day-long meeting at his house near Winchester, Livermore carried out a six-month review of my progress in achieving my annual objectives. We had agreed to this review the previous January. My progress at this meeting was deemed to be satisfactory, particularly in view of the emasculated SMT. The set targets were either achieved or on track for achievement before the end of that year. In some cases the targets had been exceeded.

Further, Livermore agreed that the modified structure I outlined made sense. We therefore needed to recruit four new Directors to add to our remaining two. Three were to be advertised for immediately and the fourth, the Technical Director, would be put on hold until we had an assessment by external technical experts of the RNID's future role in that field.

All quite rosy. All smiles. Good work, lad. Pat on the back. Well done.

Then the first knife in the back.

As explained in the previous chapter, the new remits for the Chair and CEO, remits that Livermore had drafted a few months previously, determined that he and I had joint responsibility for appointing Directors. Strategically, this was a crazy situation. A direct consequence of this plan was that I would lose control over who my key colleagues would be.

Anxious to set up the new SMT and get moving with the new plans, I didn't protest. I just wanted to get the recruitment process moving. In no time, we'd managed to get Board approval for the adjustments in the Budget to cover these new appointments. We agreed to use a recruitment agency to organise the advertising and the headhunting for suitable candidates. I didn't make much of the fact that the Consultant hired to do this was an old ex-IBM colleague of Livermore's.

Livermore was generally agreeable to everything moving forward. Adverts were placed and interview dates set.

However, out of the blue he suddenly balked at the Director of Fundraising post. He contended that we needed to explore this change further before going forward. He proposed that Strachan, a co-opted Board Trustee, be employed as a paid Consultant for six months at a salary level that rivalled that of the CEO. His remit would be to examine the fundraising situation and propose a strategy. It was to lead to the appointment of a new Director for Fundraising. How that could be a full time job for six months, I don't know. But that was the proposal.

I protested against this plan. I argued that there were experienced Fundraising Consultants around that could do this job for us. In less than six months too. But Livermore was adamant. He wanted Strachan. I felt that this was inappropriate and I put my feelings in a memo to Livermore expressing my negative views on this suggestion.

I am not sure that this (employing Strachan as a Fundraising Consultant) is the best option – nor would I be comfortable with it.

1.   To start with he is more of an investment banker than a fundraiser.

2. *It would create problems with the governance / management situations in respect of the Board and SMT.*

3. *He has shown no sign of being innovatory.*

4. *From what I have been seen of him, he would be a disruptive element in the management framework.*

5. *It would not be good for staff morale.*

6. *It would be difficult for me to work with him – especially when he reports to you. The Directors have enough of a split in responding to your interventions whilst trying to work with me as CEO. This would make things more difficult for them and lead them towards reporting to you more than ever.*

7. *The Directors and other Managers would not wish for this arrangement.*

8. *It could lead to other similar arrangements where there are a number of people in various parts of the organisation doing tasks and reporting to you.*

9. *It would make my position, which is not easy, even more difficult*

I also have other concerns over this development:-

1. *It appears that some moves have taken place – e.g. James (Strachan) knows about this and also Jenny White yet nothing was said to me until last Monday night (effectively at the last minute).*

2. *There have been meetings between yourself, James and Jack Shapiro on these developments and I was not even included.*

3. *It indicates a general lack of respect for me as I am quite sure that this would not have happened with either of the previous two CEOs or any hearing CEO.*

4. *It also indicates a lack of confidence in me – and not helpful to me when I am trying to establish how a Deaf person can effectively operate at a senior level.*

The whole issue is indicative of an issue in the Reserve Powers, which needs examining.

As CEO, I have the responsibility for implementing the strategy as approved by the Board. I have to deliver and do have clear ideas (aided by your useful advice) as to how this can be achieved. An essential part of this is the recruitment of key Directors.

Yet, I am held back from progressing due to a disagreement on the appointment of a Director. This is having a negative effect on my ability to deliver the targets set by the Business plans – unless I use existing staff to do so.

I would prefer to go ahead and appoint a Director of Fundraising despite your reservations; I believe we can find someone suitable. We have nothing to lose.

(Editorial note: "Reserve Powers" refer to the criteria for Governance and Management at the RNID, where the responsibility for appointment of Directors was shared between the Chair and the CEO)

In spite of my protests, Livermore continued to press for Strachan's appointment. He was so determined that he suggested a meeting between himself, myself and Strachan to explore the situation. I have never refused to meet with anyone to discuss and air ideas. I certainly wasn't going to refuse this meeting. After all, it was important that I present an open mind to any suggestion that the Chair and a Board Trustee presented.

My goal was to decide on the best option for the organisation. To that end, I was happy to discuss anything and everything.

It was at this meeting that I had my first serious rift with Livermore.

The meeting got off to an ominous beginning when Strachan's hearing aid battery failed at the beginning of the meeting. He refused to carry on unless we found him a battery from somewhere, which we eventually did.

At the meeting, Strachan was adamant that as "Fundraising Consultant" he would only report to the Chair and not to me, the CEO. On this point, Livermore was backing him one hundred percent.

I was more than a bit miffed at the suggestion that any Consultant or Director should by-pass me. It was also clear to me that Strachan had some serious problems when it came to working for a Deaf person. In hindsight, it appears that these two had conspired on their position prior to the meeting.

171

I fought Strachan's appointment because I saw nothing but serious problems with it. As a result of my refusal to concede the appointment, progress in the appointment of the other Directors was being unnecessarily held up. Livermore absolutely refused to go forward on the other appointments without first "sorting this out". Of course, had they gone ahead and my choices of Directors installed it would have been infinitely harder to shift me!

I felt so strongly about my position that I was considering putting my own position on the line. This was the opportunity that Livermore seemed to be waiting for. Rather than "sort things out", Livermore actually said that I could go if that is what I wanted to do.

I couldn't believe it! So that was the game! Okay, now that I saw the cards on the table, I was going to dig in as well. I could not let them win. I had come to the RNID to do a job and I had every intention of doing it! I certainly was not going to crawl away with my tail between my legs. But it was clear that it wasn't going to be easy – or pleasant. I was determined to see it through. I reasoned that the rough period would only last about six months, after which time things would be back to where they should be.

Ah, blessed hindsight! I should have refused to go along with Livermore's plan. However, unlike him, I just couldn't continue having the RNID taken hostage to his bullying. I wanted things to get moving again. It had been four months during which we had operated with two or three Directors and a couple of acting Directors. I was also confident of my position and of being able to deal with Strachan. I never dreamt that they would later jointly resort to so many underhand and dirty tactics behind my back. Maybe the world of business operated by dirty tricks and back-stabbing tactics but things like that just did not happen in the Charity world. At least for me, they didn't.

Even during my worst thoughts about Livermore, I always believed that the Board would serve as a steadying presence. How could the Board, which I trusted to do things honourably, agree to such a move, which had obvious moral and practical implications?

Equally importantly, I wanted to avoid an open fight with Livermore in front of the Board. Such a fight would only further sour our working relationship, which I still hoped would improve once I had a full SMT.

How could people fail to see the conflict of Strachan's position? How could a Board member also function as a paid staff person without problems? I suggested that he could stand down from the Board for the six months of his service, but my suggestion was fiercely resisted by Strachan. He was determined to remain on the Board.

Did the Board do the honourable thing? Did they respond to the ethical issues presented before them?

No.

The Board agreed to everything Livermore wanted.

Only the solitary Deaf Board member resisted on ethical grounds. She argued that Board members should not directly benefit financially from the Charity. Even the Treasurer was not paid. She found herself completely isolated as the other members of the Board. Even those I thought had strong moral fibre, capitulated. With the aid of a legal adviser on the Board, Livermore stated that this principle of not paying a Board member could be circumvented by using a little known or used clause in Charity Law which states that a Board member could be paid for doing work for the Charity if it can be shown that there is no other option. In spite of the fact that there were clearly many other options - and that Strachan had absolutely no experience in the area of fundraising, the Board went meekly along with the proposal, subject to the Charity Commissioner's agreement. It raised many eyebrows both within the Deaf field and outside.

Fortunately, the Charity Commissioner was not nearly as meek as the Board. He refused to approve the arrangement. He stated that he could not see why Strachan could not resign from the Board in order to do this paid work. Strachan eventually did resign from the Board but even then he insisted that he remain on the Board as an "Advisor". I couldn't understand why he was so insistent in remaining on the Board. As scheduled, he would only have missed two Board meetings and could have got copies of the minutes easily enough.

In his highly paid consultancy role to look into the best way to fundraise, Strachan reported directly to Livermore. His written remit was purely fundraising – to consider the best way to move forward successfully while, at the same time, maintaining current fundraising levels. During this entire period, he never worked with me. He preferred to deal with Livermore only.

173

Although his brief was strictly fundraising, he wasted no time in broadening his role. He took to interviewing all Directors, ostensively to get a feel of what was being done.

These interviews gave Sola the opportunity to inject poison into the process, including what she felt about my restructuring soon after my appointment. (It is ironic that Strachan took issue with my "executive action", viewing it as a flaw on my part and using it to discredit me. When he later became the CEO he imposed an autocratic style on everything he did! (I take only minimal satisfaction in my belief that Sola must have ended up kicking herself.)

Even as Strachan was exceeding his remit, Livermore was beginning to make subtle moves to discredit me. He even hinted to others at my replacement by Strachan. Of course, all this was unknown to me and done behind my back. Some individuals did try to warn me of this but, to my discredit, I did not realise the extent of the danger. I was complacently confident that I could handle this challenge as I had so many others. I naively thought that once Strachan's report was delivered, he would return to being a Board member and we could all get back to normal.

This became increasingly unlikely as he began to upset nearly everyone he had contact with. The Head of Fundraising, Clare O'Brien was so upset that she sought advice from Personnel and Taylor. Of course, her concerns got back to Strachan who then proceeded to criticise her in a wholly inappropriate manner.

I stepped into this fray and informed him that his behaviour was not acceptable. If he had any cause for complaint, we had an established procedures to follow. Of course, by then it was already too late. Clare O'Brien left the RNID as a result of Strachan's harassment.

Meanwhile, we had to move forward on the new Directors. The interviews were to be conducted through three different panels for each post. Livermore and I were on all three along with one different Trustee for each post. Jack Shapiro, Owen Tudor and Strachan. Because of the time restrictions in getting free dates, the interviews for the three took place on the same day with the panels changing for each post.

As with the other Trustees, Strachan was to be involved in interviews for one post only. However, it quickly became apparent that he had other plans, plans that clearly meshed with Livermore's. After we had interviewed the first candidate, the panel changed and Shapiro came in. I looked at Strachan, expecting him to leave. But he remained in the room as the next candidate for another post came into the room. I called this strange behaviour into question but Livermore, the Chair of the panels, refused to pay attention.

As a result, Strachan, contrary to what was agreed, remained for all interviews. All very smooth and easy. As if this entire scenario had been pre-arranged.

Two of the candidates won over the panel – including Livermore and me. Everyone was quite pleased that we were able to reach a consensus on this important decision so quickly. I was particularly pleased that Livermore and I were seeing eye to eye on this matter. It made me think that perhaps things were getting better.

My optimism was short-lived. The following morning, after "sleeping on it" Livermore changed his mind outside of the panel interviews. By fiat he over-ruled the decisions of the panels, panels which had included sitting Trustees.

"Why?" I wanted to know.

His answer was vague at best. The decisions simply hadn't "set well" with him. Rather than go forward with the panel's decision, he had agreed to allow Strachan to talk to some people he knew, people he felt would be better than those we had seen.

"Look, it's certainly worth exploring these avenues before we lock ourselves in a final decision we might regret. No harm done."

No harm indeed! What about the harm to the trust that had to exist within any organisation?

However, I had no option but to go along with him. Our joint remit made it impossible for me to veto his plan. More to the point, if I challenged his suggestion, the entire process would be held up again – and that was something that we could ill afford if we were to progress on any of our goals. I was also aware of the in-house political reality. If I did not go along with Livermore, the whole thing would be thrashed out at the next Board meeting, a forum when Livermore held all the cards. The chances of the Board siding with me and against his smooth-talking approach were slim. A conflict between me and Livermore in front of the Board would only benefit Livermore. Not me. And not the RNID.

So, beyond the witness of any other person at the RNID, Strachan interviewed the people he knew and persuaded them to take the posts. No one else was an active participant in this process. Certainly, I was kept completely at arm's length. Of these people he arranged to have appointed, one had actually applied previously for one of the posts but had failed to make the short-list.

Livermore was one hundred percent in agreement with Strachan's choices. However, he was too clever to completely cut me out of the process. He had Strachan set up "interviews" between me and the two he wanted to appoint. Strachan didn't resist. However, he insisted on being present at these "interviews".

You can imagine my sensibility regarding this whole sordid affair. However, even at my most cynical I would never have imagined how far things had gone. When one of these "candidates" was leaving the room after our interview, he turned and said to me, "I look forward to working with you."

To him, this interview was simply a formality. In his mind – and in reality – he already had the position. What an amazing set of leaps to power for Strachan, brought in by the Chair as a Consultant on a short term contract!

And where did this leave me? With every day we delayed, our goals were lying fallow. I needed a full team if we were going to realise any of the far-reaching goals we'd established. I was anxious to move forward. If I had protested about this foul process, it would have meant a lot of hassle at the Board meeting and then a delay of a few more months as we began the entire process again.

So, as Christmas time approached, we moved forward. During that season of charity and forgiveness, the final plans to push me out must have been put in place.

It was clear that Strachan had exceeded his fundraising remit. He was into many other areas of the RNID. In these and all other matters, he reported directly – and only – to Livermore.

Livermore was no longer operating alone in trying to undermine me. Now, he and Strachan worked as a team to foment unrest and dissatisfaction with me inside the RNID. They became bolder in their inappropriate behaviour. Unknown to me, word had been leaked to a Government Department that I would not be around much longer!

Meanwhile, Strachan was actually failing miserably with his fundraising remit. Over that period of six months the fundraising targets crashed.

Since Mike Whitlam had begun the tradition some nine years earlier, the Directors had enjoyed their own Christmas Dinner. This particular year, it was held in an Italian Restaurant near the Headquarters. Without the courtesy of asking me, and breaking with tradition Sola invited Strachan to join us. How were they able to eat and joke, knowing full well what was going on behind my back? Had they enjoyed watching me in that awkward situation, knowing I was fighting to hold on?

As was always the case, my job performance was to be reviewed in January. I was comfortable facing this review, knowing that I had more than exceeded the targets of the previous year. So, I was not overly concerned when I came into the meeting on the first Monday in January, a time when people were still wishing each other "A Happy New Year".

Based on my performance of the previous year, I had set some targets for the coming year. However, Livermore did not seem at all interested in hearing these objectives. He seemed distracted. I was defining a particular target when he, out of the blue, stated that he wanted me to move up to a "prestigious position" and vacate the CEO post.

In effect, he was offering to kick me upstairs!

I was stunned to silence. Our meeting was taking place in the Catholic chaplaincy in Gower Street - Livermore had suggested it as a "neutral venue". Even in my shock, I couldn't help but sense the irony of the site. Livermore could not have picked a venue more at odds with the morality of what he had lined up. Such Christian values!

The only thing 'Christian' about this entire chapter was my eventual crucifixion!

Why? Why was he suggesting that I move up?

Nominally, his reasoning was that he lacked confidence that I could achieve the "Opening Doors" aspect of the new Operational Plans approved by the Board. That was the title we gave to the £1 million research work in education, employment and hearing aid provision.

177

"Of course I can," I argued.

But he was adamant against my getting the chance to do so.

What was particularly galling about his position was that there had *never been any mention as regards my competency by him or anyone else.* Further, an examination of my record over the previous two years would show that all the specifications had been met and indeed exceeded. Even more, I had achieved things that were beyond the scope of my remit, such as the identification of Deaf people with the RNID.

"Where is this coming from?" I demanded.

Livermore responded by arguing that the CEO role had two aspects, the executive and the political. He felt that I should focus on the political – where even he could not dismiss my strength – and allow someone else to take care of the executive.

"You cannot separate the two," I pointed out. I felt very strongly that, in addition to my political skills and the network I'd honed through years of Deaf activism, my political advances were actually the result of the executive position. He strongly disagreed. "Rubbish" was the word he actually used.

It is interesting that, in retrospect, these two aspects of the CEO role were not split for Strachan. Nor had they been considered for any CEO previous to me.

However, I am getting ahead of myself. From my meeting in the Catholic chaplaincy, Livermore's behaviour made it clear to me that the die was cast. He'd committed himself to the next step. He had left himself no room to manoeuvre. Certain members of Board had already been nobbled on my removal.

He had no choice but to reject any protest from me. It was as if he'd been setting up his chess pieces dutifully from that time. Now, as he prepared his endgame, he certainly wasn't going to be swayed by anything I could say or do.

He was not interested in whatever I offered. The only option he would consider was my moving "upwards" out of the CEO post.

I had the distinct impression that, even if I presented a compelling argument that could have convinced him, he could not change his mind. At that point, everything was set up. Other people were clearly involved. Seemingly above or behind him, or "lurking behind curtains". Unelected. Unseen. But still powerful. He could not back out.

It was only later that I learned of the extent of Livermore's preparations. Even while our discussions were underway, he had secretly set the scene for my removal and replacement by Strachan. He had even met with the PR staff and instructed them to prepare the appropriate press releases.

Even the Board was ignorant of the extent of his preparations. I was caught in a Palace coup. I was cornered!

Cornered, perhaps. But not cowed. I argued that I'd been hired to be the CEO of the RNID and that I would not accept any other post.

"If you and the Board are not satisfied with my performance, then say so outright. Fire me if you can demonstrate that I've failed in the job. But don't insult me with this plan of yours!"

Livermore devoted a great deal of time and selling expertise trying to convince me that his plan was the best option for me. But he was selling to the wrong customer. I was not to be budged.

The message and the method of Livermore's intrigue had other consequences as well. Out of the blue, Jim Toohill the Head of Strategic Planning with whom I had been working closely resigned. His letter of resignation dated 29th January 1997 is reproduced here:

Dear Doug,

There have recently been various rumours circulating RNID concerning your future and your replacement. I have myself received scantily veiled threats from the individual expected to be your successor. This expectation is not groundless; I understand the Department for Health, for example, has been briefed.

This has made my own position barely tenable in the short term. Not surprisingly, therefore, I have given some thought over recent weeks to the attraction or otherwise of remaining within the RNID in the medium term. My conclusion is that there is none, and for the following reasons.

179

It was clear at the time of your appointment that the Board was unambiguously signalling its desire to move away from the "managerialsim" of your predecessor. That was a point you yourself made in a number of media interviews at the time. No one, yourself included, was under any illusion that your strengths are not primarily managerial. At the time of your appointment, you were well known to the Board - there were no surprises. The Board had made its choice and many people within RNID set to make it work, myself included. The Board now seeks to reverse its choice in a way, which may well do damage to the organisation and to yourself. It seeks to do so with impunity. It is a measure of the unaccountability of charity Boards that no one will take responsibility for that reversal. Ultimately, you alone will pay the price. Nor will the Board accept responsibility for the past two years and the debilitating stresses the organisation has been subjected to by the various manoeuvrings towards this point. I do not wish to belong to such an organisation.

The likelihood is that you will be replaced by James Strachan. James is an individual with a considerable intellect, albeit a very selective and obsessive one, and is capable of much charm. However, there is little in his background to prepare him for this role. It is unclear to me what being a "Managing Director" of a merchant bank entails. My friends in the city tell me that terms such as that, or Director or Associate Director are generally given to denote volumes of business handled rather than management of resources and have a prime purpose of impressing clients. Specifically, James' deficiencies in managing people have already made themselves well manifest to those with whom he has close contact. I doubt that Clare O'Brien's departure will be the last. Certainly, I have no wish to work for James.

There is a wider issue. James joined the Board as a co-opted member from a coterie associated with a former chair. He subsequently stepped down from the Board to undertake a well-paid RNID assignment. It is now likely that he will become Chief Executive without any open competition. This has all happened, as power has steadily been concentrated within the Board and in the Chair (the removal of Committees, the dual role of Chair and Chair of the Audit Committee and the absence of a Treasurer).

The most valuable asset charities have is the trust they hold; it should not be put at risk even by the appearance of impropriety if not the substance. RNID carries responsibility for some £30m of public money in one form or another, almost £6m freely given. Many large charities have sought to move away from drawing Trustees from the networks of "old pals" by advertising vacancies and recruiting against published job specifications. For RNID to allow patronage to spill over from governance into management would be to invite opprobrium, not least amongst staff, whose respect senior managers must earn.

We might also note the irony that RNID declares itself to be striving for Equal Opportunities and an organisation, which is "honest with others and with itself". I for one would find it very hard to convince staff that the publicly held values of the organisation are other than sham.

It is for these reasons that I tender my resignation. I do not believe that RNID is a place in which to do a honourable day's work, and is unlikely to be for some time. I am sad to have to do so. I have put much effort and time into RNID, which has had. I believe, good effect.

This may appear peremptory, and for that reason, I am sharing this letter with immediate colleagues in strict confidence. I shall write separately setting out what I believe to be the most productive way for me to spend my time remaining with RNID, which I estimate to be about one month, allowing for holidays.

Please accept my genuine good wishes for the future for yourself and for RNID. You both need them.

Yours faithfully,

James Toohill

That this letter came as a great shock to me is a gross understatement. More than Toohill' resignation, which I viewed to be terribly detrimental to the RNID, was the final confirmation that all this intrigue had been going on behind my back, was well known to the key staff.

Toohill's letter of resignation, along with my appraisal interview with Livermore, made it clear to me that what was going on was more than a personality conflict or a difference of opinion about how things needed to be done. It was abundantly clear that there was a plot by Livermore and probably Strachan to get rid of me.

For nearly six weeks from that fateful meeting in January, Livermore maintained the pressure on me to accept his suggestion of taking a prestigious post. In trying to persuade me, he used his most effective strategy – Dinner meetings! Dinner was his best tactic when he really wanted to get his way. His logic was sound – we are all less likely to resist after a bottle of wine and a fine meal, when the deal we are offered glows in candlelight rather than the harsh light of the day!

Throughout this ordeal, I maintained a cool, professional front. However, on the inside, I was roiling like a volcano. I was angry with many people, none more than with myself. How could I have been so blind and so trusting? After a lifetime of mistrust, I had gained sufficient confidence in the position of CEO to start to open out and trust people more. There is really no other option if one is to be an effective CEO. No one can run an organisation single-handedly.

And what did my openness get me? With arms and eyes wide open I was knifed not through the back like Caesar but in the gut by someone with the gall to smile the entire time! I was reminded of the quote from Shakespeare's play, Henry V1 – *"Why, I can smile, and murder whiles I smile."*

I was furious. The dishonesty and the deviousness of it all burned through me. Yet, I had to maintain a cool appearance in front of everyone. It was only by maintaining a professional demeanour that I could earn myself time to sort this whole situation through and decide how I wanted to proceed.

Meanwhile, Livermore was tightening the screws. Time was, for however briefly, on my side. He wanted the change to happen right away. The longer I delayed, the more unnerved he became. Ideally, from his point of view, I would move "up" to be Vice-Chair or something similar where I would promote the RNID – the RNID he wanted. I finally understood Livermore clearly. Strachan had been dishonest and devious, but without the support of those behind him, not as dangerous as Livermore. He was for the most part a puppet to do Livermore's will. Of course, Strachan had his own ambitions, probably driven by his frustrations in other spheres. Attending an Art College after a spell as "Director" at Merrill Lynch was not exactly a good career move for someone in his early thirties!

My departure would spell the end of the "new" RNID that Deaf people had come to respect. The RNID that Livermore and Strachan directed would most likely regress to a bigger version of the original RNID that we had, thankfully, moved away from some ten years previously, a RNID that Deaf people rightly detested.

So, what was my next move? Become one of those titled posers on full pay? Fight it out? Or quit?

Chapter Ten

Fight or Flight?

To be, or nor to be - that is the question;
Whether 'tis nobler in the mind to suffer
The slings and arrows of outrageous fortune.
Or to take arms against a sea of troubles,
And by opposing end them?

Hamlet - **William Shakespeare**

In spite of - or maybe because of - events that were unfolding around me, I was determined to hold firmly onto my position. I was certain that I could not lose my position simply because Livermore didn't like me. I had exceeded all the objectives that had been set. I had received no complaints about my performance from the Chair or the Board. I could easily document this with the minutes of the Board meetings and the notes of the review sessions with the Chair. In any case, I was convinced that if they had had any cause to question my performance, they would have informed me so that I was able to resolve matters.

Unless, of course, the issue was my Deafness. There could be no adequate resolution for that.

Short of that, I presumed that the Board would follow the same procedure we did with our staff. The RNID Employment Manual sets down clear procedures for dealing with any cause for dissatisfaction with performance.

Why should it be any different for the CEO, who is, after all, an employee of the RNID?

However, given the circumstances, I decided to double check my position. I went to the Trade Union. I had continued with my membership of the Manufacturing, Scientific and Finance Union (MSF) even though technically, they would support the staff side over management in any dispute that may arise. My management position had done nothing to alter my basic beliefs in the rights of worken. I was still a great believer in the principles of trade unionism, of the need to protect the employee's rights against any possible abuse.

I suppose my mindset was that I continued to be an employee, even if I was employed in a management position. So it was something of a rude awakening when I was told by a top MSF Officer, Chris Ball, that the Board could remove me and that I had very little legal recourse.

"Sorry, mate," he said, trying to soften the blow. "You're one of them now."

In short, the Board could do to me what I would never be allowed to do to one of the Directors or any other member of the staff.

If I wanted to remove a Director or any other employee, I would have to go through a process of appraisal and performance measures to justify my action. This, I believe, is appropriate and right. This, I believe, protects the basic rights of employees.

Apparently, CEOs do not share these same basic rights.

In retrospect, my mistake had been not to have insisted on a contract when I was first appointed. A three-year contract was the very thing that had saved the CEO at another Deaf organisation. Due to an oversight by its Executive Council, he did not sign the contract at the commencement of his employment. As a result, at the end of that period when the Executive Council wanted to move him out, they could not do so without incurring financial penalties. They had little alternative but to keep him on.

I had not given much thought to my personal position. At the outset, I was so determined to get things done that I hadn't had time to think about myself. In any case, I had absolute trust in Grear and the Board to do things honourably. If they were in any way dissatisfied with my performance, I believed I would have been told and been given a chance to improve. If I had performed badly, I would have no problem in quitting the job.

It never entered my mind that one day Grear could be gone and replaced by such unscrupulous characters! Nor did I dream that the Board of the RNID could roll over so easily at the beck and call of the Chair.

Ball told me he would speak with Owen Tudor, whom he knew well. He asked me if I wanted him to have a word with Johnny Monks, the TUC General Secretary who was Tudor's boss.

"I'm sure I can get him to lean on Tudor," he said.

"No," I told him. I wasn't anxious to use that kind of influence, even if other people were.

The whole sordid episode took me back thirty years to a situation we had at ICI. I had set up the Association of Scientific Technical and Managerial Staff group to protect the staff from an abusive employer. It was ironic that even as CEO at the RNID, I had encouraged the staff to consider Union membership. Now the MSF was making clear just how limited Union protection really was.

In organisations like the RNID, where the Chair was uninterested in workers' (me) rights and would only do what he was legally obligated to do, the Union was effectively toothless.

Ball basically laid out my two choices - fight it out with Livermore at a Board meeting or quit.

"That's it, huh? Black or white? Up or down? In or out?"

"I'm afraid so, Doug."

In addition to my decision, my future depended on the Board's sense of fairness and decency, and on whether they would insist that standard procedures be followed in querying my performance.

Given my options, I decided to first weigh my chances in front of this Board. If I judged that they would give me a fair run, I would challenge Livermore. If not...

The Board, as explained earlier consisted of a mixture of traditional Paternalists, Educationalists (largely oralist-biased), Audiological professionals, the odd Deaf person and the new breed of Trustees (people who have backgrounds and experience in rights or business issues). I was very much aware that, almost to a person, the Trustees were out of touch with the needs and desires of Deaf people. Some of them were actually uncomfortable with Deaf people.

Ironic that these people were Trustees on the RNID Board to begin with, isn't it? That's the way it has been for over 90 years.

185

As a group, the Board seemed like a tough nut to crack. However, I then considered each individual Trustee. I reckoned that Jane Wilmot would do what Livermore told her to do. The same went for Jack Shapiro. A brief chat with Stephen Lloyd revealed that he was practically in Livermore's pocket, saying the same things to me as Livermore had said to me. Although he was generally reasonably fair, Richard Eldridge, being an Audiologist at Mary Hare Grammar School, would lean more towards Livermore's wishes. Margaret Du Feu seemed mesmerised by Livermore despite her professing to be a "BSL user". Laura Darbyshire, the solitary Deaf person would be on my side, for the right reasons. Catrin Williams, Alison Heath and Morag Turner could go either way, depending on who was doing the best talking and providing the strongest arguments.

In my mind, the key people would be David Adams (an Ear Nose and Throat Consultant who had reasonably good links with the Deaf community in Belfast and generally supported Deaf causes), Mike Bishop (an ex-Director of Social Services, who would surely be aware of employment procedures and rights issues) and Owen Tudor (a full time employee at the TUC where he would presumably be for the rights of the workers). These three would hold sway at any Board meeting to deliberate on my position. All were respected by the other members of the Board and could argue a case well when they needed to. If these members sided with me, sided with justice, rights and fairness, the members in the middle would be won over.

Once again, I allowed my optimism to cloud my thinking. How could these Trustees fail to be swayed by the dynamics at hand? I was so convinced that the issues of rights and morality would prevail that it never occurred to me not to go forward.

At the very least, I believed that any move against me would have to take appropriate procedural routes. If there were grounds for dissatisfaction then they would be spelled out and I would be given the opportunity to do something about them.

After all, my track record was good and I had achieved beyond the set targets with a crippled SMT. That had to count for something.

My strategy was simple. I planned to speak with each of these three Trustees individually to explain what had happened and to ask for their support in ensuring it was all dealt with fairly if the situation was brought before the Board.

186

I visited David Adams in the hospital where he worked. It was located rather appropriately in the heart of the troubled areas of Belfast. He had not yet been nobbled by Livermore and was genuinely troubled that such a thing was taking place. More to the point, he was truly appalled at the thought that Strachan was being lined up to move in as soon as Iwas pushed aside.

He promised to do all he could to ensure fairness.

Mike Bishop, whom I met in a motorway service station at Sandbach, Cheshire claimed he knew nothing about it and had not been approached by anyone. He also promised to ensure that the right things were done. He would get in touch with David Adams and discuss it with him. So far so good, two down, one to go.

The last person and a vital key was Owen Tudor. I felt that if he supported me along with Adams and Bishop, I would have better than a 50/50 chance. These were odds I was willing to deal with. If I had these three, I would initiate a fight against Livermore's plan.

I had little doubt that Tudor would follow principles of rights and equal opportunities as befitted a Trade Union Official.

Ominously, Tudor cancelled our pre-arranged meeting twice before we finally did meet. He waffled on about Norman Willis, a previous General Secretary of the TUC, who had resigned from his post about a year previously, stating that there are times when it would be best to change. I felt my heart sink to my stomach. He was using almost the exact same words that Livermore had used with me. He'd already been talked round by Livermore! He was going to support him. He was not even going to listen to my side of the story first.

I couldn't describe how stunned I was.

It was just like that scene in the Mel Gibson film "Braveheart", based on the story of William Wallace fighting against the English to keep Scotland for the Scots. It was vital that he had the King of Scotland, Robert Bruce, on his side. After all that was what he was fighting for. The scene I am referring to is the one where in the heat of a fierce battle William Wallace realised that he had been betrayed by the King himself. The earlier betrayal by some of the Scottish Chiefs was bad enough but when he found out that the Scottish King had also been bought off by the English it crushed and effectively finished him! The Scottish rebellion for their own independence died there and then.

That a man from a body that represented all I'd stood and fought for throughout my life could simply abandon the principles of justice and fair play did more than leave me stunned. It left me with a feeling of despair that bordered on the physical, a feeling as if the ground had opened up under me. Even when Livermore was doing his bit at the chaplaincy, I was confident enough of being able to fight it through if I had to.

With Tudor's betrayal of principles, the wind was knocked out of my sails. What else could I do? I just gave up. I knew that I was finished.

I harboured a tremendous anger toward the MSF. If it was going to be so toothless, then I didn't see any sense in continuing my membership. I wrote the reasons for my resignation to Roger Lyons, the General Secretary. His perfunctory two-paragraph reply made it clear that he did not give a damn one way or another.

This entire episode caused me to become very disillusioned with the Trade Union movement. The apathy and powerlessness of MSF was so distressing. If people who thought and behaved like Tudor were working at the TUC, then it was no wonder we were witnessing the death throes of the movement in this country. Defenders and champions of the worker's rights? Oh yeah! Like all the other "backroom bosses", they are too focused on their own needs to be bothered with such 'trivial' matters as rights and principles.

Bottom line was bottom line. I had exceeded all objectives set for me. I had never received a single complaint from the Board. Yet I was being dismissed.

All very cut and dried.

With Tudor on Livermore's side, I had no chance in the Boardroom. The deck had been stacked No matter what I said or did, the executioner stood at the ready.

Whatever else might have happened, the driving force that had brought me down was Livermore's introduction of City Boardroom tactics into a Charity environment. My focus was on trying to do my job rather than do battle with Livermore! Foolish me! I was keeping my focus on the needs of those the RNID was dedicated to assisting rather than the politics of the Boardroom. Foolish indeed!

188

Livermore pursued his goal relentlessly. He had already met with people like the RNID President Jack Ashley and briefed him. Had they gone so far as to grant me the courtesy of responding to the poison Livermore had spewed about me, I could have easily and effectively challenged everything he'd said. But they weren't interested in hearing from me.

I was Deaf after all. Communicating with me was awkward. It troubled them. It... it... who knew what it did to them? And who cared? They should have been ashamed, every last one of them.

I tried not to remind myself of the irony that I had a role along with others in bringing Livermore onto the Board and the Chair. It was my idea to revive the defunct RNID Medal of Honour so that it could be awarded to Shapiro. The nominations of Bishop, Tudor and Lloyd came from me. Each and every one of them eventually either assisted Livermore in digging his knife into my back or, just as shamefully, stood by and observed silently as it happened.

Even though I knew my fight was futile, I was not yet without options. I could, of course, fight the Board even though I knew I was doomed to be brought down. Or, I could involve the media.

I knew that the media option would only be effective if there was an outcry from Deaf people. If negative reports began to appear in the media, it would have an effect on the RNID itself, perhaps overriding the Board.

But would Deaf people give me the support I needed? Would they realise the serious implication of Livermore's actions? Or would they view the situation as an unfortunate circumstance in Doug Alker's life?

I knew only too well that this fight was not about me. Unfortunately, I was starting to think clearly and I reasoned that, save for a few of the more politically aware people, I wouldn't find much support.

Some members of the RNID staff organised a meeting with representatives of the MSF Union outside of the RNID. They wanted to discuss what they could do to support me. Tony Poole, a Deaf person, who led this initiative, was threatened in no uncertain terms by his Manager. It was implied that there would be serious consequences for him if he pursued with this staff meeting. She came to "warn" me of Poole's moves, asking me to head him off.

189

Information about this proposed meeting got to Livermore. He spoke to me about this "foolish action". His insinuation was clear. Poole had better watch his step!

I called Poole into my office, "Tony, I strongly advise you, for your own sake, not to go ahead with the Union meeting."

"But some of us are concerned about what is going on. It is our right to discuss it and it is taking place in our own time outside of the RNID!", he protested.

"I know, but you will be setting yourself up as a target. Is it worth sacrificing your career and family for this?"

He cancelled the meeting. But was "marked down" anyway. He suspects to this day that he was sidetracked out of his career as a result of this.

Livermore had gone to great lengths to make clear the personal risks I would be taking if I chose to fight him and lost. I would only get the statutory redundancy money, which would only amount to a few thousand pounds. With no prospect of another job at my age.

Any offer of a deal would be taken from the table.

My choices were stark indeed. Should I fight or should I quit?

My head knew that my thinking was finally no longer clouded by my heart. Determined optimism was no longer colouring my judgment. Cold reasoning indicated that the Board meeting would be little more than a kangaroo court, with Darbyshire standing alone against all the others.

And what if I had won the open fight with Livermore? What then? I would have been crippled by having to work with a largely negative Board. My remaining years would have been burdened by so many conditions that I would have been reduced to little more than a token CEO.

I had not become CEO for my own glory. I had aspired to the post in order to change the world. What benefit to me was the post without the chance to bring about change?

It was not to do with me being a CEO. But the wider fact of being a Deaf CEO in a Deaf world. I was effectively accountable to the Deaf world and also to the wider world in respect of a Deaf person's ability to do such a job. I worried that a dirty fight would reinforce any negative perceptions of Deaf people.

My preliminary discussions with some Board members suggested that it would be unlikely that any dissatisfaction in my performance would be based on clearly stated grounds, so that such dissatisfaction would be worked through the organisation's Disciplinary Procedure where the CEO is offered the opportunity to improve.

Even as my situation grew more dire, I was given some incriminating information about Livermore and Strachan with the promise that there was more to come - for a price. Apparently, there was some interesting information relating to Strachan at Cambridge University. And, Livermore apparently was a Board member of a Company allegedly engaged in dubious practices involving private investigators.

There was a brief moment when information like this seemed to be just the lifeline I needed to survive. However, after discussing the information with a few friends, I decided not to use it.

Whatever else happened, I was not willing to be brought down to their level. I did meet with Stuart Etherington, whose view irespected. His perspective was simple and to the point - the CEO never wins a fight with the Chair.

Never.

As true as this viewpoint might have been, it was only later that I realised that it might have been tainted by the fact that he'd already been drawn into the fray by Livermore and his allies.

I discussed my decision with a very small circle of friends. Being "kicked upstairs" was a common ploy in politics. I knew of several key politicians who had accepted a move up into the House of Lords or similar when the Prime Minister wanted to get rid of them. Still, I had always respected those who refused to be bought out and who chose to go onto the backbenches in respect for those who had voted them into the House of Commons in the first place.

I would never be able to live with myself if I compromised my principles or if I knowingly became a token to be played at Livermore or Strachan's whims.

And of course, I could not imagine even working with either Livermore or Strachan after all this. If had stayed in some fancy position, I would have had to spout a lot of platitudinous crap. It would have been near impossible for me to find the strength - or weakness - to do that. And, in playing the part of this token, I would have hurt Deaf people even more than if I'd never been the CEO.

The "Lord Pander" syndrome had burnt such a deep scar in my mentality that I just could not do it. Livermore badly underestimated me if he really thought that a cushy high position was what I wanted. That I would jump at the opportunity for a well paid easy time. Maybe those were his own aspirations and he expected the same in me but he was very wrong there. How could a man as cold and calculating as he ever fully appreciate that some people really did want to change the world above other considerations?

There were other, practical factors to consider. I was, after all, hardly an old man. I was not yet ready to give up working and be put out to pasture, no matter how lush the grass. I had a unique combination of qualities, expertise, experience and contacts that needed to be utilised for a bit longer.

The decision then, made itself. The only way I could continue to honestly fight for the cause of Deaf people was to quit the RNID completely. I needed to be completely free of Livermore if I was to continue to be effective in areas that needed my involvement.

I was open to the possibilities before me. There was the BDA, which I felt could benefit from what I had to offer. Or it could be elsewhere. Wherever and whatever, I was determined to carry on. What had happened at the RNID was one setback. In view of the fact that I intended to continue the fight for Deaf rights, I was determined to leave with my head held high.

So, the decision was made. I was greatly relieved that I had crossed that difficult bridge.

Once I communicated my decision to Livermore, the process of negotiating a buy-out deal began. I refused point blank to accept any position - prestigious or otherwise - on full pay for the rest of my working life. Livermore was planning to have me fully within his control. He wanted to use me to continue to attract Deaf people to the RNID. He felt the RNID could continue to benefit from some of my political skills.

However, when he realised that I was firm in my refusal of an RNID position, he returned with an offer that would have me doing some paid work for the RNID as a freelance.

Again, I was not interested.

I wanted a clean break. I benefited in my negotiations by having a very good Solicitor. As you can expect, she was not the one offered for free by MSF. I had learned my lesson the hard way. My faith in the Union had been shattered and faith lost is not easily regained.

She and her colleague hammered out a good deal for me and they made sure it was watertight. Livermore was so anxious to get it all signed up before 1st April that he seemed willing to concede just about anything.

Do you suppose it was simply coincidence that April 1st was also the date that Strachan's contract as Consultant would end? Hmmm.

The only caveat in my agreement that Livermore insisted upon was that, in return for the deal, I was not to criticise the RNID for two years. For two full years, I was to be effectively gagged. Oh, I could praise them. That would be welcomed indeed. But I could not so much as utter a negative thought about the organisation.

Rather than find myself in a position where it appeared I supported the RNID, I opted to say nothing whatsoever about it - positive or negative - a silence I have successfully managed for two full years. Until now.

Of course, our agreement still required the approval of the Board. Livermore placed my agreement on the agenda of the Board's annual seminar, which was to be held in February at a hotel in Reading. At this time, there were actually to be two meetings. One, a special meeting to involve the Trustees only. This meeting would be for them to sign off the agreement. The other meeting included the Directors and was designed to look into the future plans of the RNID.

Livermore was surprised that the special meeting set up to discuss my "resignation" turned out to be unexpectedly long and lively. It seemed that the sole Deaf Trustee, Laura Darbyshire, had some profound reservations. However, once that was circumvented, there was a discussion on the composition of the interview panel to be formed to appoint the next CEO. The panel was to include five people. There were four names for the five places, one of them the solitary Deaf Trustee, Darbyshire.

193

Go ahead with four on the panel, with the Deaf Trustee on it? Why not? Oh no! Seeing that no one else was interested in serving on the panel, Livermore called for a break to "allow time for consideration". After the break, miraculously, several other names were added to the list of Trustees who wanted to be on the panel. A vote was held and the Deaf Trustee, predictably, came in last.

So, there would be no Deaf BSL user on the panel. That would effectively remove any possibility of a Deaf CEO. Livermore and possibly others must have had more than their fill of those!

Of course, Livermore - ever the salesman - later claimed that there was a "deaf" BSL user on the panel - Du Feu. Du Feu? She is a late deafened psychiatrist who had recently learned sign language.

Another of those cases where someone is conveniently labelled as "deaf" when it suits political or media purposes.

Once again, Livermore resorted to half-truths and typical feints to sell his strategy.

The only surprise - and it should no longer be a surprise at all - is how readily his statements were accepted as gospel.

When Livermore announced my resignation later at the second meeting, Darbyshire continued to challenge him with questions. She was so persistent that Livermore lost his cool and said, "For God's sake, Laura, shut up!"

Could anything speak more eloquently to his attitude toward Deaf people than his reaction to Darbyshire? He would never... never have spoken to a hearing Trustee in this rude manner.

He would later insult Darbyshire in a similar manner at the final Board meeting, just before I left the RNID at the end of March. Lloyd, from a back seat, signalled for Livermore to calm down. It was an emotional time for the Deaf people present and everyone who cared about their cause. Darbyshire referred to Livermore's daughter, pleading that he should think of her and her future. Of course, Livermore would not see that what he was doing was going to damage the Deaf cause.

194

In his presentation at the seminar, which followed the special meeting, Livermore talked up a non-existent crisis at the RNID to justify his moves and to gain support for whatever action he had up his sleeve.

Significantly, Strachan, the Trustee that would not budge from his position to take on the job as paid Consultant, was absent from both of those meetings yet turned up with his partner at the evening Dinner. It was the first and only time anyone had ever brought his or her partner to a Trustee weekend!

At the Board meeting, which took place on my final day at the RNID, Livermore attacked Darbyshire yet again, for challenging the wording of the minutes of the Reading meeting. It was embarrassing and disturbing for all those who were present.

Curiously, Strachan was also absent from that meeting.

When Livermore prepared to close the meeting, he was apparently ready to do so without so much as referring to me or to my departure. Catrin Williams had to intervene and propose a vote of thanks to me. For me, this was indicative of their collective culpability and guilt. It was a sad day for me that my ten years work and efforts at the RNID had to end in this manner.

The staff farewell took place almost immediately after the Board meeting. Only two Board members remained for this.

I had remained cool and calculated all through those last three months, as I knew I would be fighting on for Deaf rights after I left.

The CEO post was advertised in the Guardian only just before I left strangely (?) nothing about requiring a MBA. Not a word in the Deaf media, as was the normal practice with adverts of such posts. There were fewer than 30 applicants, compared to over 300 when I applied two years previously. This could have been intentional, hence the rapidity of the advert and the tight deadline given. No other post at the RNID had been rushed through before or since that one.

With the panel that was set up, and all that had gone on beforehand, it was inevitable to many people that "I am deaf" Strachan would be appointed. His constant use of the "I am deaf" is significant. No one who is genuine about their dearness makes such a pre-statement or needs to.

It was a great wrench to stop working after 34 years of non-stop employment. I felt physically good and at my prime with plenty of scope to achieve things. The machine had been poised on the runway ready to soar. Then it was not allowed to take off!

I have no excuse. I should have seen it coming. I thought I was safe enough because these things simply didn't happen in a Charity, not when things were done in the appropriate manner.

I was blind to so much of what went on. Oh, of course, I was aware of some of it, those things that were most visible. I thought I could effectively deal with these. There is no question that my Deafness was also a key factor. If I had been hearing, not only would I have picked up more, but also they would not have dared to tty anything. Livermore would have reaped advantage from that fact. In hindsight, I ought have resisted the appointment of Strachan as Consultant, but I had reasoned everything out so carefully. I was just so anxious to move on to make things happen.

There are those who believe I made a terrible mistake by quitting instead of fighting. I respect their perspective. There are times when 1 wonder too.

I wonder if I hadn't been a fool to have listened to advice from establishment types rather than Deaf people before I made my decision.

But the nastiness of the entire episode so shocked and unnerved me that I found myself in strange terrain with no reliable map.

The manner of my ousting was so underhand and capitalised so cruelly on the disadvantages that all Deaf people face that I found myself without the tools to effectively react.

More troubling was the serious damage done to the Deaf people's advance.

Deaf people did not and some still do not realise the magnitude of the implications for them. The very presence of a signing Deaf person at such high levels could be gone for a long time. Oralist supporters and their speaking deaf would regain the territory they had lost, territory that should have been claimed by the signing Deaf long ago.

These events would only make it all the more difficult for future signing Deaf people to regain high positions. It was akin to a mini-Milan 1880. The end sufferers, again, would be the Deaf people.

It does seem sometimes that they - the establishment - had won. They had certainly got rid of the odd gremlin - the signing Deaf person - that challenged all that they stood for and preached. For them, it had to be a deaf person who could speak and not "one of those". The parallel in the hearing world would be if say, someone from Wigan fought his/her way through the establishment despite the snobbery of the old boy network. Tne establishment would not be comfortable with this. Unless they could buy him off.

You can be sure that my heart was broken by all these events.., but my spirit has remained intact. Once I made the decision to quit the RNID, the spirit dictated that it was important to maintain dignity and to survive to fight the war. I had to retain a base upon which to fight on in yet other battles in our field. The heart has now recovered sufficiently to continue with the fight. The mind seems as sharp as ever.

And those members of the Board of Trustees at the RNID... sad, sad people. They should all be hanging their heads in shame - but they were not yet fully aware of the extent of their folly.

They were soon to find out.

Chapter Eleven

The Teflon Man

The only thing necessary for the triumph of evil is for good men to do nothing.

Edmund Burke

Throughout history, it has been the inaction of those who could have acted; the indifference of those who should have known better; the silence of the voice of justice when it mattered most; that has made it possible for evil to triumph.

Haile Selassie

I felt the full frustration of the agreement I had made with the RNID as soon as the announcement of my resignation from the RNID was made public. Deaf people bombarded me with questions that I simply could not answer without breaching its terms. How could I speak the truth without shining a negative light on the RNID?

But I would not lie. I simply remained silent, without comment or response. In some ways, my silence was more devastating to the RNID than my honesty might have been. It served to fan the fire of uncertainty. A BBC "See Hear" programme showed Deaf people raising questions about my resignation and Livermore providing his explanations in such a twitchy and evasive fashion that it was obvious that something was not right.

People reacted to the news of my resignation in very different ways. Some wrote poems. These were circulated first as individual poems and then under the title, "Deaf Drum". Some of these poems were distributed through an informal network, which included people inside the RNID who distributed such material throughout the RNID. The poems spoke creatively of the frustration that Deaf people felt at my resignation.

Those who did not write poetry sent out information and criticism through a "Deaf Beacon" information sheet. Others contacted journalists, leading to articles in various newspapers and journals. Still others wrote to the Deaf media. Someone posted an item on the Internet, which referred to "odd goings on at the RNID". Two prominent Deaf people appeared on the "See Hear" programme to criticise the RNID's conduct.

All this and more was happening at the same time. These expressions of anger and frustration were unplanned. They were the cries of people who were wounded.

There was a small number of members of the RNID who refused to let the matter rest. They gathered to discuss the events surrounding my resignation. They were clearly unimpressed with the official word as it had been delivered to them and they were determined to find out what had actually happened.

Once the picture became clearer to them, they requested an extraordinary general meeting (EGM) in an effort to get to the bottom of things. They'd decided that they would not simply demand Livermore's resignation, but would put forward a motion calling for the resignation of the entire Board.

The request was sent to the Company Secretary – Taylor. The request was immediately and unceremoniously rejected. The group was told it had not followed "correct procedure" in calling for the EGM. Of course, there was no attempt to explain precisely what "correct procedure" was.

They pursued the request, learning only after relentless efforts that the request had to be backed by the signatures of at least 10% of the membership. That did not trouble the group in the least. However, the fact that they were denied access to the membership lists in order to gain these signatures was a significant problem.

They were not even told the number of signatures they needed to satisfy the 10% requirement!

Well, you know the old adage… if at first you don't succeed, try, try again! This group was only steeled in its determination by these ridiculous rebuffs. Their treatment made them even more suspicious that the RNID had something to hide.

"How dare they treat us in such an off-handed manner!"

"We're members!"

They were at such a profound disadvantage, pitted against a mammoth organisation with its tremendous resources and manipulative and unscrupulous leadership. Still, this group did not quake in the face of overwhelming odds. Their reasoning was simple. "David felled Goliath, didn't he? So, what's to stop us?"

They believed that being right was enough to ensure victory. Sadly, they were soon to discover, as so many hearing people have before them, that even right isn't always enough.

The group settled on their strategy. With a Proposer and Seconder (Edith Turner and Sarah Broughton), they drafted a letter to send out to members of the RNID. Somehow, they had got hold of the membership list with its 360 names and addresses. 360 names meant they needed only 36 signatures. So, with their own resources, they sent out the following letter on 29th March 1997, requesting signatures in support of an EGM:

Dear Member of the RNID,

Some recent activities by the RNID Board of Trustees have been cause for concern for many people. They have resulted in disturbance throughout the Deaf community and our hearing supporters. The name of the RNID has been brought into disrepute.

The integrity and the credibility of the Institute has been undermined by the questions around such concerns as:

1. The astonishing "early retirement" of Doug Alker, the Chief Executive who was appointed only two years ago. Many people are unconvinced that this retirement was voluntary in view of the fact that the RNID was doing so well under his management with increases in revenues and improvement in services.

200

2. The sudden resignation of Jim Toohill, a key member of the Senior Management Team, as a result of politics and practice within the RNID which raises questions about the integrity of the Board.

3. The unexpected departure of Claire O'Brien, the respected Head of Corporate and Trust Fundraising after a Trustee was given a contract to work among the fund-raising staff.

4. A co-opted Trustee being offered a lucrative six month contract with the RNID at a higher rate than the Chief Executive's salary. This is clearly a very bad practice and gave rise to suspicion and gossip currently circulating both within and without the RNID.

5. The speed and wording of the advertisement placed in the Guardian for the post of Chief Executive. This advertisement was placed only once and with only a two week deadline for response, which indicates that there was no serious intention to trawl widely for a suitable candidate for such an important post. The fact that no Job Description or person specification was available to anyone implies that the Board already had someone in mind and were merely going through the motions to show "equal opportunities".

6. The panel of six (sic) Trustees set up to interview candidates for this post does not contain any Deaf Trustee who uses sign language. Is this making a statement against Deaf people who use sign language? Is this related to the fact that Doug Alker uses sign language?

7. The two most recent Director appointments, with which the Chief Executive had minimal involvement, were made in contravention of the organisation's employment and equal opportunities practices.

8. The media interest in the happenings at the RNID is growing. Once these and other issues materials are picked up by the networks journalists are likely to start asking difficult questions, which threaten the integrity of the charity.

9. The Deaf community has been outraged by the departure of the Chief Executive. This is divisive at a time when all hearing impaired people were beginning to come together and shows a loss of trust in the RNID.

There are other concerns and questions along these lines, which need to be addressed. As the Board of Trustees is accountable to the membership, we have the right to explanation and clarification. We have a duty to Deaf people to ensure that the organisation is heading in the right direction and properly governed.

In view of this, we are demanding that an Extraordinary General Meeting be held as soon as possible to discuss these issues. A motion has been drafted for that meeting to carry a vote of no confidence in the whole of the present Board of Trustees of the RNID, should there not be a satisfactory response to the concerns.

We need as many supporters as we can to reinforce the demand for a meeting. We would like you to add your support by signing the attached notice for a motion and returning it to us as soon as possible. Please note that supporting the call for a meeting does not bind you to a vote of no confidence. You would still vote at the meeting according to your reaction to the responses to our concerns and questions.

The letter was signed by both Turner and Broughton.

In response to this, the following letter went out 3rd April from Livermore to the members (without the Board's knowledge!):

You will perhaps have received a letter from Ms Edith Turner on the subject of the recent resignation of our Chief Executive Doug Alker and a call for an Extraordinary General Meeting to express a vote of no confidence in the RNID Board of Trustees. I am writing to you to refute the various claims and to ask you not to agree to Ms Turner's requests.

As you will know the RIND represents the interests of all deaf, deafened and hard of hearing people in this country. The Board of Trustees is representative of all sections of deaf people and over half our Trustees have

202

significant or complete hearing loss themselves. We pride ourselves on our commitment to all deaf people.

The people who seem to be instigating this campaign, which you have been asked, to join are a small but vociferous group who do not represent the majority of deaf, deafened and hard of people in this country.

In the letter from Edith Turner of the 22nd of March there is a general implication that the Board lacks integrity and there has been an element of impropriety in the Board's behaviour.

May I reassure you that the Board of Trustees has always taken their responsibility for governance very seriously. Where required, on constitutional issues, the Charity Commission has been fully consulted.

To address each of Edith Turner's points separately:

1. Edith Turner exclaims astonishment at Doug Alker's early retirement and believes that the retirement was not voluntary. This is untrue. Doug Alker's has publicly stated that he achieved his main aim of bringing the RNID closer to deaf people, and that leaving the RNID will give him the freedom and time to tackle issues close to his heart. Doug chose not to stay on at the RNID.

2. The resignation of Jim Toohill was related to matters personal to him.

3. Clare O'Brien's departure as Head of Corporate and Trust Fundraising was not as a result of the appointment of James Strachan as a consultant. Clare had always been interested in the Arts and left to fulfil one of her ambitions by becoming Deputy Director of Development at the National Theatre.

4. James Strachan resigned as a trustee and after obtaining approval from the Charity Commission he was employed as a consultant to review our fund-raising capacity. He was employed at normal consultancy rates on a project basis, which cannot be compared to the remuneration of a Chief Executive.

5. *Turning to concerns about the method of appointment of a new Chief Executive. A job description has been made available to applicants. All candidates will be assessed against that job description and against a standard set of criteria. With regard to the timing of the advertisement itself, we considered in the circumstances that it is clearly in the RNID's best interests to deal expeditiously with the appointment of the new Chief Executive. We do not believe that two weeks was a short timescale for applications to be received, and indeed the large number of responses received suggests to us the time scale allotted was sufficient to allow candidates to submit their applications. We are pleased with the quality of the shortlist.*

6. *The panel of five Trustees was selected by a ballot at a Trustee meeting and contains two partially deaf people, one hard of hearing person and two profoundly deaf people, one of whom is a BSL user.*

7. *The two new Directors appointed both applied for their jobs and after extensive interviewing were selected. Both are very well regarded within the voluntary sector.*

8. *We are happy to answer any questions that the media may have in relation to the RNID.*

There is an implication that Doug Alker's departure from the RNID signals some change in direction of our policy. This is simply untrue. We remain absolutely committed to the support of all deaf people including BSL users, like Edith Turner.

I hope that you can see from the above that we have nothing to hide. All that has happened has been with the overwhelming support of the Trustees. I believe that the RNID is well placed to move forward and significantly improve the quality and scope of our services and to increase the vigour and profile of our campaigning to all deaf people.

I sincerely hope that we will have your support to do this and you will reject Edith Turner's request for an extraordinary general meeting, which can only damage the reputation of the Institute.

204

If you wish to discuss any of the above please do not hesitate to contact our staff on the following phone numbers: They will be happy to speak to you.

It is clear that Livermore's first, second, and third points are simply embellishments of the truth, whilst his fourth and fifth points have been fashioned to "sell" the reader what would be called a "dummy" in rugby or soccer. The sixth point sidesteps the fact that there was no native BSL user on the panel. Calling a mere 30 applicants "large" is certainly stretching it. And when Livermore refers to a "vociferous minority of Deaf people" he circumvented the possibility that hearing people might have been concerned as well.

He also failed to see the fundamental contradiction of his assertions – how could he have the welfare of Deaf people in mind if he tried to prevent them from exercising what was their constitutional and democratic rights? He was the "deaf" one, deaf to the reality of a hearing Chair of a d/Deaf organisation preventing some Deaf members from wanting to express concerns and getting some questions about the running of the organisation answered!

The audacity of his exhorting members, most of whom were hearing, to ignore the group's letter and not to support the request for a motion, is all the more astonishing now when one is able to step back from the passion of the moment!

Of course, it was profoundly difficult for the group or members to know which of Livermore's statements were inaccurate and which were bare-faced lies. Despite Livermore's letter, the response was such that the required number of signatures was easily exceeded.

With a great sense of jubilation, a letter was then sent to Taylor, requesting the EGM. The group attached a document attesting that they'd obtained a sufficient number of signatures to make such a request. But Taylor denied them. He stated that the group's figures were wrong. They needed more than 36 names. It seems the RNID had closer to 450 members! Yet, Taylor would not let the group have the lists so that they could verify whether this was true. His resistance only made the group more suspicious.

Even so, Taylor was playing a blind man's game. The group immediately replied that they actually had over 80 signatures, well in excess of the number of signatures that would have been needed even if the membership was 450. That "victory" over the RNID's blocking tactics gave the group much encouragement for the next stages.

But the dirty tricks were far from over:

The RNID had certain staff to phone members who had signed in support of having an EGM to try and persuade them to withdraw. In these conversations, the staff members presented only Livermore's side of the picture. No matter that his perspective had preceded the members endorsement of the EGM! It is both ironic and interesting (and unfortunately, not surprising) that every member that was phoned was a hearing member. Not one Deaf member was contacted.

Even so, this strategy did not work. Only a very small handful of those who had signed changed their minds!

I can just imagine how frustrated all this made Livermore. He was so annoyed that he contacted me at home via fax to have me issue a statement condemning the group's actions and to publicly dissociate myself from them. One of the Trustees, Jack Shapiro, went so far as to try to convince me and others to persuade the group not to proceed with their action, "in the interests of Deaf people".

In the interests of Deaf people! My God, did neither Livermore nor Shapiro take note of the fact that the majority of this group was Deaf? Had Livermore and Shapiro forgotten that the RNID was supposed to be acting in their best interests, not trying to undermine Deaf people?

Of course, I refused to intercede. I argued that, as members, they had every right to do what they were doing. Besides, I noted, why would Livermore or Shapiro think that the group would do as I suggested?

Livermore must have been steaming! He demanded that I attend a meeting with him to discuss it. He asserted that, under my agreement with the RNID, I could not refuse. Well, indeed, I did refuse. My reading of my agreement (and after consultation with my Solicitor) indicated that that Livermore could not order me to a meeting against my wishes.

Clearly, the legal team of the RNID agreed, because that was the last time I had any contact with Livermore.

The RNID's next move, on 16th May was to send all members the date, venue and time of the EGM – along with arguments in support of their own case only. Not a word to suggest that the other side had a legitimate point to make. Proxy vote forms were included with exhortations to members to sign them in favour of RNID and send them in – without bothering to consider the full story! The option of giving a proxy vote in favour of the motion was not included! Not only that, instead of the democratic practice of employing a neutral vote counting firm, the RNID would count the votes themselves! All this was paid for out of the RNID funds.

Ah, what glorious democracy! With (hearing!) leaders like these, is it any wonder that Deaf people still struggle for basic rights?

These actions forced the group to send out information stating the reasons for the motion and pointing out some inaccuracies in Livermore's statements. The group's "rebuttal statement" included the following extract:

"Following the request of some members for an EGM the Chair has sent out three sets of letters/statements in his efforts to avoid an EGM and to pressurise members to vote against the motion.

These letters are so rife with inaccuracies, misinterpretation and contradiction to the truth that we must issue this rebuttal of some of the points in those letters. Rather than go into full detail on each point, which will be done at the EGM, we will just highlight some examples to give you some indication of how the true picture is being distorted and key concerns brushed aside. Taking each of the three letters in turn:

Response to the letter from Edith Turner (3rd April)

207

Those of us who have seen the documentation and heard evidence from various people were taken aback by the brazenness of some of the Chair's responses to the points raised by Edith Turner.

As for his dismissal of Jim Toohill's letter being personal and emotional, those who know Jim won't go along with that. His letter of resignation is already in the public domain and a copy of that letter is enclosed for you to judge for yourself.

Two new Directors were definitely appointed outside the established mechanism. Two Senior Managers and two Trustees who were involved in the legitimate process can testify that this was so.

Those inside and outside of the RNID who examined the whole process of recruiting the new Chief Executive are left in little doubt that this was a "set up".

Statement from the RNID (16th May)

Disregarding the fact that it is not a "RNID" statement, but one from the Chair alone:

* With one exception, each one of the "new initiatives" listed by David Livermore were actually set up by Doug Alker and in most cases in operation before he left the RNID. The one exception, the Employment service, was already in the pipeline, awaiting results of research into the situation of Deaf people in employment.

* The "credit" for setting up signed Political Party broadcasts `in the past six weeks" is laughable in that the Election was on 1st May and these broadcasts were campaigned for and achieved last March before Doug Alker left so that they went out during the election campaigns!

David Livermore's assertion that "the allegations to be totally without foundation" must be vigorously challenged. We have documentation and evidence to support all we have "alleged". This is more than he can say in his own defence. He has provided no answers for many of our points and brushed others aside. The dictatorial style and stridency of his letters speak volumes.

He also tries to ride roughshod over the members' rights and concerns. His use of the term "sterile recriminations" is indicative of his attempts to sweep wrongdoings under the carpet and whitewash over the cracks in the facade. It is akin to saying that the Nuremberg Trials were sterile recriminations!

If there is any doubt that an EGM is the necessary means to a resolution, the frenetic attempts by the Chair to stop this meeting removed them. It is disturbing to find the Chair pursuing an ill-advised course of interference with the democratic rights of the members. It is alarming that he exerts pressure on members to vote against the motion without first hearing the case for it. It is of grave concern that he will not allow the votes to be collated and counted by an independent body, particularly when he is a direct target of the motion. Such conduct reinforces our points and further shakes our confidence in the Chair and the Board.

The only way the RNID can restore its credibility is for David Livermore to take the honourable course and tender his resignation as Chair of the Board of Trustees. This would terminate further negative speculation and allow us to make a fresh start from a position of strength and integrity."

As with their other mailings, this one was at the group's own expense. They included their own version of a proxy vote form for those who wished to give it in favor of the motion. They also challenged the impartiality of the RNID in counting the votes at the EGM. This resulted in the RNID backtracking and agreeing to let the Electoral Reform Society do the counting.

The RNID staff then mounted a telephone campaign to put pressure on those who either had not voted or who had voted for the motion. People who had supported the motion were pressured to change their minds.

One hearing person was so insulted by these pressures that she complained in writing, stating that she was capable of making up her own mind. The Deaf people in the group could not access others in this way because they could not trust the (RNID operated!) Typetalk service.

Tumim, ex-Chair of the RNID, sent out a letter saying she was not involved even as she made it clear that she supported Livermore. Some opined that as a Vice-President of the RNID, she would have gained more respect and credibility if she had initiated an impartial investigation to the complaints from some Deaf members. At the very least, she should not have feared an EGM with the stated purpose to clarify some concerns.

The group collected well over 80 signatures on their own proxy voting forms. Then the RNID, via Secretary Taylor, wrote to the group to say that these proxy forms were unacceptable at the EGM because the wording was not precise! By this time, the group was so used to the RNID's tactics that they simply sent out modified forms, using the old mailing lists. The group had asked for a copy of the membership lists, but they were refused access to the lists even though it was conceded that *they were legally entitled to a copy*. There was no time to waste in challenging this reluctance to let them have the lists as the date for the EGM was approaching very fast.

The proxy forms in support of the motion were to be collated at the Colne area house of a hearing person who had not been involved in the campaign at all. She was simply allowing her house in the North West to be used as a mailing address. In addition to the proxies, the "RNID Action Group" also invited donations from any supporters to help to offset their costs be sent along. The RNID complained to the Charities Commissioner about the group's use of the term RNID, they were told that the Action Group had done nothing wrong!

Nevertheless, the RNID claimed that this was a misuse of their name to raise money under false pretences. The group claimed that the use of the name was justified in that it was action on the RNID by a group of its members. The group felt it was clear that this was an "Action against the RNID group" and not a group acting on behalf of the RNID. The letters that went out to members of the RNID also made this very clear and the request for donations was clearly specified to be in support of this campaign. No letters went out to non-members. Members who donated money to the group knew full well what it was for. It was all above board with a separate bank account opened up. It might be argued that the group ought have called itself "Action on RNID Group" or something like that. But that would have been more misleading as they weren't acting against the RNID. They were acting against Livermore and trying to save the RNID!

Regardless, none of this stopped the RNID from taking the drastic step, of initiating Police action, claiming illegal use of their name to raise funds! The group had collected 51 proxy forms and were awaiting the other 29 when the RNID sent the police to the Colne house. The Burnley Police went to this address and saw some unopened envelopes addressed to the "RNID Action Group" on a kitchen table. The person had not opened anything and was just passing them on, unsealed to the Action Group. The Police entered the house and removed those unopened envelopes *without having a warrant.* Despite the fact that it is illegal to open mail addressed to someone else, they opened the envelopes at the station and found some contained proxy forms, letters and cheques. *It was all sent to the RNID despite the fact that the original senders would not want the RNID to have receipt of those letters!*

The RNID's involvement of the Police against its own Deaf members had a chilling effect. Deaf people involved with the various groups then realised that the RNID would truly stop at nothing. People both in the group and around them, feared that their own jobs and the services they received would be put in jeopardy.

So this was what the RNID would stoop to when challenged! People were astonished at the lengths they (hearing people, in their eyes remember) were prepared to go to preserve their position and power. It made some people realise what the RNID was capable of if you dared to cross them. Other people who usually stood up for rights decided they did not want to know. One even disappeared for two weeks on a holiday abroad, which was booked at the very last minute!

Coincidentally, at the same time, some Deaf people in the groups noticed quirks in their phones. Faxes seemed to disappear and connections through Typetalk (which they did not trust at the best of times) seemed a bit odd. They began to wonder if their phones had been bugged! Paranoid? Perhaps. But this was the climate that the RNID created, after using the

Police against Deaf people in such an illegal manner. People reacted by going so far as to destroy or hide vital papers. Some were even half expecting to meet up with some accident.

The phone oddities seem to stopped immediately after the EGM. Some people speculated, but of course, nothing could be proved.

One of the co-ordinators of the RNID Action Group, Michael Heldon, was actually interrogated by the Police. After taking legal advice, he was clear on his rights before he met them. The Police, no doubt on the behest of the RNID, tried to get the names of other people involved in the groups from him. Heldon remained resolute and refused to give any names. There was nothing the Police could do. It took some courage, as it would have been so easy for him to give names, thereby destroying the emerging activist structure and the will to fight against the Goliaths. That has to go down in Deaf history as a truly courageous act by a Deaf person who put the cause of Deaf people above himself.

Whatever else these episodes did, it convinced the members of the groups that there was obviously something badly wrong at the RNID. They felt that Livermore had caused irreparable damage. Instead of upholding the rights of Deaf people, particularly those who were members of the RNID, he had trampled them into the ground. That if he had any integrity or principles and truly cared about Deaf people he would resign.

There were actually four or five groups in operation in different parts of the country. Some had overlapping membership and others were independent of anyone else. The one in the North West area focused on distribution of information. They mailed out to RNID members as they had an address list, but they did not do so well with non-members. They had no way of distributing material like the "Deaf Beacon" journal, which was produced by a group in the South West. They were all working people and did not really have the time or resources to do this.

Another group was set up in London to get media interest but they were amateurish and badly organised. A group in the middle of England focused on legal issues. They involved a couple of Solicitors who were appalled at the whole thing, and offered to work for free.

212

Not content with this, the RNID took the amazing step of passing a Board motion that allowed senior members of staff to become members of the RNID. The reason for this was so that they would be able to vote against the motion! Certainly, no matter what their principles were, few members of staff would dare not to vote as instructed by Livermore. They were even asked to recruit friends and relatives into membership.

For paid staff to be members of a charity they work for is unheard of. Imagine that if this was allowed, then all 1,000 staff could become members, far outnumbering the 450 non-staff members. They could then vote themselves pay rises and the Board could not stop them! Such moves seemed to be desperate measures by desperate people. It makes one wonder what they were really afraid of.

Consequently, a spoof letter was sent round to staff in the RNID.

"The RNID Board of Trustees has approved a remarkable and innovative idea. The Chief Executive, all the Directors and most of the Regional Directors have become registered members en masse.

It is a well timed manoeuvre to get more votes at the forthcoming Extraordinary General Meeting against the motion to carry a vote of no confidence in the Board. Obviously, the votes of those members of staff are predetermined. No one would want to risk their jobs by voting in any way other than as directed by the Chair and the Chief Executive. What a wonderful idea!

Perhaps all the staff might want to jump on the bandwagon too. Imagine the power ... .with a thousand staff, any decision made by the mere 400 non-staff members can easily be overcome. Staff can then vote for their own Board and ensure a positive upward influence on the pay rates. If they don't like what the Board is doing they can vote them out subjectively at any time. Why restrict such power and privilege only to the Chief Executive, Directors and Regional Directors? All staff should demand the same rights and the annual subscription will come out of the expense accounts.

The question of morality is irrelevant. That of objective accountability by external nosey parkers becomes a thing of the past. Such a great idea to show that the RNID is at the forefront of innovation ....other charities will surely follow.

It does not have to stop there. The Board could start paying all the registered members a salary too. After all, what's sauce for the goose is sauce for the gander. The old principles around ethos do not apply anymore to a progressive charity like the RNID.

Send in your membership application forms. You should have David Livermore's full approval."

The letter was passed to staff through the RNID's internal mail system using their regular, internal mail envelopes.

Taylor was ordered to conduct an investigation to find out which members of the RNID staff were responsible for this letter and its circulation. He noticed that several envelopes had Belfast marked on them (actually from previous mailings from there to Head Office). He flew over to Belfast and put the poor innocent staff there under the grill but never discovered the culprits and the investigation died out, a victim of its own paranoia.

Another group of people were formed in London to organise a demonstration outside the venue of the EGM. Having had some experience of public demonstrations, they were aware of the need to obtain permission from the police. This was duly given. They then began to try to get people to come and join the picket. However, their network of contacts was very weak and consequently the demonstration was not very well organised. As a result, it was not as effective as it might have been.

No story of this kind is complete without a scene of betrayal. This one is no exception. A leading Deaf activist involved in one of the key groups was called to a meeting with Strachan. She went along to it despite advice from other members of the group not to go. She came away from it in a changed frame of mind.

214

"I need to take care here," She thought. "Our organisation could be doing business with the RNID when all this is over".

Her behaviour changed completely. She was completely torn. She could not remove herself from the battle since she knew that doing so would cause her to lose face among the Deaf world. At the same time, she now seemed anxious not to upset the RNID. From that point onwards, she did all she could to get everyone to "hold fire and just wait and see what the EGM brought."

Even when Livermore sent out erroneous material, material, which contained damaging inaccuracies, she did not want to challenge him or send letters to rectify errors. She did not want the group to have its own proxy votes and so on.

She became a classic case of a "bought off" Deaf person.

She even phoned the RNID to ask if they knew of the proposed demonstration at the EGM and hinted that the group may not have asked police permission (this was only a few days before the event). As the group did not trust her, they had not informed her of the demonstration until at the very last minute. She seemed genuinely put out that there was to be a demonstration. Based on her information, the RNID phoned the police, only to be informed that permission had already been granted to the group!

Meanwhile, back at the campaign, one of the groups prepared a leaflet for the RNID members attending the EGM to inform them of some of the facts that were unlikely to be mentioned at the meeting. It is reproduced here:

Why it is important to support the Motion.

*1. The decision to put forward the motion was not taken lightly. The fundamental reason behind it was that **things have been going on within your organisation, which you need to know about.** You would not get to know about them without a meeting to bring them out into the open.*

2. If you need any further proof of this, you only need to consider the reaction of certain people to the very idea that you should be fully informed. When you received notice of the meeting, instead of getting two sides of the story equally presented, you received one side only!

*3. On top of that, you were asked to send proxy votes **without knowing the other side of the story!!***

*4. When people tried to send you the other side, they were **refused** access to you, even though those people were told 'legally you are **entitled to a copy of the [membership] list!** In other words, someone instructed the RNID staff to behave illegally!*

*5. When people gained partial access to the list in their own way, many of you were then subjected to an intense telephone campaign to persuade you to vote against the motion. **Deaf people of course do not have easy access to such phone communication!***

6. As if this was not enough, someone instructed the staff to conduct their own vote-counting system, instead of using normal independent voting systems from the beginning.

*7. People who were alarmed at this tried to collect their own proxy votes to be handed in at this meeting today. They collected over 50 such votes, but **have been hindered from delivering them.***

8. Not content with this, the Board were then persuaded by someone to pass a motion allowing senior staff to become voting members! The absurdity of this is that if all the 1,000 staff were allowed to do the same, they would take over control of the organization from you, which would also be illegal.

***The point is that these all appear to be the actions of people with something to hide!!** If they believed in democracy and free and equal discussion if the issues, none of the above would be allowed to happen.*

216

*9. The significance of these actions is that they are **executed in the same dubious way that led to the removal of Doug Alker as CEO.** If the motion falls, your organization may well continue to operate with the same apparent contempt for democracy until another scandal finally brings them down,*

*10. It is widely believed that certain people planned to get rid of Doug Alker as CEO **irrespective of his record at the RNID.** The details of the events themselves will, we hope, be explained by others in the meeting. One item that may not be covered is the curious resignation of that honourable man who was the previous chair, Brigadier Jim Grear. We suspect a story lurks behind that event, but that is for RNID members to investigate.*

*11. You should also be aware of the resignation letter of one senior member of staff who saw what was going on, and predicted Strachan's appointment months before it happened. Other people, **including a Government body,** were given to understand that Alker would be out, again, months before it happened! You should ask to see a copy of this letter as a member responsible for overseeing the conduct of your organisation.*

*The tactics above are almost a way of life in City boardrooms. **They have no place in a charity!***

12. A Charity is only as effective as its good name. These actions, and the publicity they have generated, threatens your organisation's public standing, its funding and therefore its future.

*13. If this motion fails, it will be considered to have done so because of the failure to follow democratic process. Some members will then be formally requesting that the Charity Commissioners are called in to investigate the RNID. Others will be formally asking Prince Philip to withdraw Royal status. **Both these events will gain great publicity, and further drag the RNID name into the mire.** Similarly, others will pursue this right through to the next AGM in November.*

The best thing you can do, if you care for your organisation and cannot get straight answers today, is to vote for the motion to show the public that you care about democracy within the RNID. Such a vote will also limit the damage caused by the actions of the people involved.

Finally, we caution you to beware of some of the silvery-tongued responses that you will get today. You are dealing with some very 'smooth operators'. There will no doubt be plenty of slurs cast in the direction of those who are supporting the actions here, but they will probably be cast in sad tones of 'regrettable' and so on. If you get 'yes' answers to points 2-8 above, you should be able to draw your own conclusions about the other events that we contend have happened!

The day of the EGM dawned. As Proposer, Edith Turner, gave a rehash of the original letter of 29th March and remained firmly within what happened up to my departure from the RNID. She refused to refer to the appalling events that took place after 1st April. It seemed she just wanted to do her bit and get out fast. That she did.

The Seconder's proposed presentation *was **supposed to have been***:

"Edith Turner has covered the background and some key issues. I wish to concentrate on additional key issues and matters of conduct that have caused some serious concern:

The way in which some members' original expressions of concern were handled was unacceptable. For example:

(a) Mr Livermore's letter to members of 3rd April was an attempt to deny members their right to hold an EGM.

(b) Following the unsuccessful attempt to prevent the EGM from taking place, there was a catalogue of actions by Mr Livermore to undermine the democratic process. It included the use of RNID staff to make telephone calls to get some members to change their votes.

(c) Some senior staff of the RNID were made registered members with full voting rights at the Board meeting on 26th May 1997. While this is not illegal, it is ethically and morally wrong at such a sensitive time.

(d) The Daily Telegraph of 26th June reported that the RNID had called in the police over the activities of the Action Group. This only invited further adverse publicity, which is damaging to the RNID.

These are a few examples of things that have happened since the request for an EGM was made. Members themselves are aware of several other such negative activities.

All this is disturbing. Even today, members have been asked to produce proof of identity prior to admission to this meeting. We have to ask - if there is nothing to hide, why were all these measures necessary?

As an overall summary, it is important for members to remember the key issues that led to the call for an EGM. There are three main issues here:

1. Unethical methods.

A few examples:

(a) Suspicion surrounding the departure of the first Deaf CEO

(b) The way the second deaf CEO was appointed gave rise to suspicions of a set-up.

(c) The appointment of two new Directors outside the established mechanism

(d) The evidence of staff unrest as outlined in Jim Toohill's letter of resignation.

2. Accountability.

The Board of Trustees is accountable to the membership. They must respect this accountability and it is our responsibility as members to see that they do.

3. Conduct.

The conduct of David Livermore is unacceptable in a Chair of a Charity.

In addition, his statements that concerns have come from "an unrepresentative minority" is disrespectful of both d/Deaf people and members. It is as if members are not allowed to express views of concern.

Nor does it make Deaf people feel confident in the RNID's purpose to protect the rights of Deaf people. The RNID is about Deaf people and we, including the Chair must listen to what they have to say.

It would seem that the situation is mainly the result of the activities of the Chair only, but the Board has responsibility for restraining the actions of the Chair, which is why they are unfortunately included in the vote of no confidence.

In Conclusion.

The Chair has steamrollered over the members rights. He has also succeeded in splitting the Deaf world apart and attracting adverse publicity to the RNID. The only way forward for the RNID to develop out of this mess is for us to have a new Chair and new people on the Board who will ensure that the RNID moves forward in a more acceptable manner.

I, therefore, second the motion to carry a vote of no confidence in the Chair and the Board of Trustees and I ask you to support it."

This speech, however, was never delivered.

A well-meaning, hearing member of one of the groups brought in a Solicitor on the previous evening to advise on how to approach the EGM. The Solicitor advised the Seconder to cut the speech and focus only on what the proposer had outlined - in effect to talk about the events up to 1st April and say nothing about what happened subsequently. It is not clear why he gave that advice. Probably on the principle that the Seconder of a motion should stick to backing up whatever the Proposer had said, and nothing more.

As a result, the impact of the case for the motion was diluted down to next to nothing. It was a pity as the response from the RNID was then able to confine itself to responding to the Proposer's relatively weak points.

Despite the information contained in the handouts, no one at the EGM asked any significant questions. There were Deaf people there at the meeting with all the information but they said nothing. Some hearing people said

220

during and after the meeting that Livermore had not answered the original queries. Yet no one of them queried this. No one asked about the frenetic efforts to prevent members having an EGM! No one asked why the need to resort to extreme measures over an open democratic approach. So much for the members' interest in the RNID and Deaf issues!

Two years later, those questions remain unanswered. Other questions have also come up, questions like, what happened to the 51 proxies that the group collected? Copies still exist..but where are the originals and why, since they were not counted, was the whole vote not declared invalid? And what about the contents of the envelopes the Police opened. If the group had some significant resources, they could have sought legal counsel and considered legal action against both the Police and the RNID.

One of the more depressing aspects of the experience was the extent to which the media was seduced by the RNID and how readily it accepted its version of events. Journalists from the 'respectable' papers attended in response to the groups' press release. All were quickly ushered inside the building where the Deaf group outside could not reach them. When they emerged, their attitude to the group had radically changed.

As the Deaf group made their points, they were met with a particular kind of response. The dialogue went like this:

"RNID are appointing another deaf person aren't they?"

"Well yes and no. They are appointing someone who doesn't sign. And anyway that's not the issue. It's the whole chain of behavior that is important. You've read the Deaf group statements?"

"Well, it looks to me like a squabble between two groups of deaf people about what they want (so I won't be reporting this story to my Editor)".

How easily they'd been nobbled! The RNID's blurring of the distinction between Deaf and deaf has been instrumental in their efforts to put down any dissention. If I can accomplish nothing more with this book than making this distinction clear to those in power outside, it will have been worth it!

221

In the end, the EGM and the demonstration were absolute debacles. Inexperienced, fearful and respectful Deaf people let Livermore get away with everything. Able and knowledgeable hearing people kept quiet.

At the end, the Teflon Man (as Livermore was known at IBM because nothing seemed to "stick to him") had slipped through yet again.

There were lessons from the EGM and demonstration. They were alas typical of the Deaf situation over the years.

1. The lack of a cohesive network of contacts. There was a ready made social network in the Deaf world but it also contained "Uncle Jacks" and "Auntie Janes" who would block off any 'dangerous' political information to Deaf people. There was and is a need for a networked system of local activists.

2. The demonstration showed how reliant Deaf people had been on the same small number of activists and how unreliable Deaf people were in promising to turn up and then never appearing.

3. Deaf activism is relatively new. Deaf people still lacked confidence to stand up for their rights. Many were still not even aware of them or their potential power if they chose to work together to exercise it.

4. Many Deaf people do not have the guts or the skills to speak out, even if they had the confidence.

5. There were a depressingly significant number of 'liberal' hearing 'fellow-travellers', who might make radical noises when the situation was safe, but when their own interests or positions were threatened,would not stick their necks out.

At the Deaf groups' review following the EGM, it was decided not to pursue the matter at the RNID AGM in October or to send a letter to the Royal Patron to ask him to dissociate himself from such goings on. By this time, the groups had no confidence in getting support from the generally passive Deaf people or their hearing allies, who tended to rant and rave in private but do nothing at all when push came to shove. Many were too fearful of the power of the RNID.

These events led to the formation, one year later, of a network of Deaf activists to make sure that if such abuses of rights took place, they would be better able make a vigorous response. It had become clear that it was best to start afresh. To try to reach the younger Deaf who have no missionary culture luggage or fear of the paternalists. The difference now is that there are people around who will act on their beliefs and some youngsters who will do more than just spout out. They have some fire in them and are prepared to act.

They are the Deaf world's hope for the future.

Chapter Twelve

The Aftermath

It's not whether you're knocked down, it's whether you get up again

Vince Lombardi

The ultimate measure of a man is not where he stands in moments of comfort, but where he stands at times of challenge and controversy.

Martin Luther King, Jr.

Sadly, few Deaf people appreciated the implications of my ignoble ousting from the RNID. It was not simply a personal defeat. The reasons why and how it happened spoke painfully about the realities of our ability to move forward as Deaf people determined to earn our rights.

In the previous decade, BSL-using Deaf people had finally begun to make strides in society. We were more self-sufficient. We gained a greater public profile and a presence at increasingly higher levels. We were perceived in a more positive way by society at large – except by those Paternalists and Oralists, of course. Paternalists feared their loss of control while Oralists resisted the increasing credibility of BSL, the use of which had demonstrated clearly that a Deaf person could never make real progress through oralism. All successful Deaf people used sign language for full access. A Deaf CEO at the RNID who had top level access was a role model for others. It also raised the awareness of those at the top that Deaf people were capable of leadership roles. In the process, they were introduced to Interpreters.

Secondarily, my being CEO at the RNID meant that the largest and the most powerful d/Deaf organisation in the UK had its full weight behind the Deaf people. The issues for deaf people benefited in the slipstream created by the media interest in the Deaf.

Livermore had destroyed all that in one stroke. The appointment of Strachan to become the new CEO set the Deaf advance back by a decade or more. After the ice had been broken back in November 1994, there was no way that the RNID could replace me with a hearing person. They did the next best - a "half caste" – a deaf person. It is a 'label of convenience' to use in the media, playing on the d/D confusion to suit oneself.

The "D" issues were once more pushed back in favour of more emphasis on the "d" issues. The oral "Deaf" and deaf people began to take the centre stage.

The very fact that these issues were now articulated by a man who introduced himself as, "I am deaf" Strachan spoke volumes about what had befallen Deaf issues. No Deaf person needs to say anything like that nor do the vast majority of deaf people. Only in a specific context, for example if someone was not speaking loudly enough, would such a statement ever be uttered. Obviously, the Deaf have no need to do this. Their use of sign language broadcasts their status. Clearly, Strachan was trying to create political cover for his crass grab for power.

But cover and power for what?

The changes that began almost immediately were both subtle and telling. The trend among RNID staff to learn BSL faded away like a mist in the afternoon sun. Some of the more hard of hearing "deaf" people, people who had taken to calling themselves "Deaf " began to refer to themselves as partially-deaf or even partially-hearing. Fewer and fewer signing Deaf people functioned in public forums; in places they needed to be *as of right.* Instead, they were reduced once again to the role of tokens when Politicians needed their own cover and to be seen with disabled people. (Of course, the BDA should have been taking care of some of these issues but apart from the odd individual at odd moments, they are largely invisible.)

The handful of Deaf people who appreciated the implications of the RNID's actions at the RNID decried them as akin to Milan 1880. The message was clear: Deaf people did not belong in high places. It was as if *nothing* had progressed in over one hundred years! The ban on sign language and Deaf teachers in education was not as formally expressed, as in 1880, but it was just as damaging. High places were reserved for the "hearing deaf" people and those Deaf people who spoke rather than used BSL.

More than not seeing any signing Deaf people at high levels, there was fundamental damage to Deaf progress. Perhaps most subtle was the injury to their collective confidence. A confidence that had just begun to take form for the first time in a century.

What benefit were Lord Ashley or Strachan as the "role models" for Deaf people. None! Yet these were the very people the rest of the world would now look to and visualise when they thought "Deaf".

Neither could possibly portray Deafness to the world. Neither could possibly change the negative public perceptions of Deaf people and their abilities – even if they had a mind to.

Their conduct in trying to be pseudo-hearing, with a little help from goldfish-mouthed conversation style, would set back the Deaf advance by several years.

Unfortunately, no one else was filling in the vacuum that Livermore's actions created. The BDA and a couple of other organisations should have been ensuring a regular Deaf presence in high places. But they hadn't done anything significant for a long time; there was no reason to hope that they would manage to do so with their current personnel and organisational structures. In fact, they seemed more likely to go the way of the UK Council on Deafness (UKCOD) and land into the pockets of a sweet talking RNID.

Unless some drastic and courageous action was taken, they would be absorbed by the RNID, or at the very least, meekly follow the model the RNID had set for their "partners".

Fortunately for Deaf people, there were a couple of organisations (not Deaf organisations!) that were resisting any RNID take-over of the whole d/ Deaf world.

In this context, it is fascinating to consider an interesting story circulating about the UKCOD and the RNID. In the autumn of 1997, the position of Chair of UKCOD became vacant. Because a number of member organisations of UKCOD were concerned about a RNID take-over, they nominated me for election as the Chair of UKCOD. I agreed to stand for the position. I believed that, with my experience and contacts, I could do a good job there in uniting all the organisations in a push for full civil rights for Deaf people. Only a few days before the closing date for nominations, I was the *only* nominee. Then, out of the blue, the deaf Secretary of the Deaf Broadcasting Council, *without asking her own members,* nominated a d/Deaf person, to stand against me.

That person's nomination offered UKCOD members who were either oralist or afraid to offend the RNID a safe option to me. In other words, it opened the door for effective RNID control of or shunting aside of UKCOD. This is exactly what has happened. The UKCOD is now, for all practical purposes, dead in the water.

Unconfirmed suspicions abounded that the RNID had something to do with all this. It is more likely that some of the member organisations were fearful of what could happen between UKCOD and the RNID if I was their Chair.

Clearly, the issues that surrounded my being ousted from the CEO post at the RNID were complex and deeply felt. Their consequences were also complex and far-reaching. Another significant consequence was the change in direction the organisation would take. My departure marked the end of the era that had begun with Whitlam in 1985.

Ten years of successful operations, ended by the likes of Livermore and Strachan! Ten years that were dismissed as too "pro-Deaf".

Ever the salesman, Livermore allowed a reasonable period of "reassuring" people to pass before moving in a new direction that fitted better with the viewpoint of his coterie. This new direction would cast a very wide net due to the RNID's influence and due to the large number of RNID sycophants who paraded in lockstep with its directives.

Livermore was shameless. He went on television and assured everyone that "the RNID will not change the direction as set by Doug Alker". Nine months later, it changed direction.

Both organisational inertia and being politic demanded no change at first. But the "direction as set by Doug Alker", as we have seen, was doomed.

The shift was subtle at first. The statements I had created which were agreed to on the RNID's vision, mission and values were quietly jettisoned (no earth shattering surprises here). They were replaced by a vision that referred to "improving the quality of life for deaf people". But almost the whole of the disability world has moved away from that "quality of life" concept for some time, in favour of rights oriented mission statements.

Many are of the impression that the RNID's new prime values seem to be more related to the numbers game; to try to widen the reach of the RNID; to try to increase the charity income on par a with that of the RNIB; to get around 100,000 members (that was later toned down to around 60,000 over three years); to persuade everyone that there were 8.4 million "deaf" people (later amended to 8.7 million). The new slogan emerging from this, "One in Seven" is going to stick in their craw sooner or later! When everyone realises the truth behind these grandiose numbers.

227

The changes were even reflected in their colour scheme. They threw out the historic RNID red house colours ...in favour of a new blue logo; one perhaps more in line with their true political leanings. The new colours and logo fit in better with the organisation being run by middle-class white people, people with little idea of the real world of Deaf people. Their Board and Senior Managers rarely, if ever, visit Deaf Centres.

There is a sense of a return to paternalism. The new tone cannot hide the truth of the message. "We speak for you". Hearing people from the RNID are once again making comments on various issues on TV "on behalf of d/Deaf people".

The principles around the use of Charity money and the concept of equal access fell by the wayside. For example, the employment placement scheme, funded by the National Lottery Charities Board, involved specialist RNID staff finding employment for Deaf people rather than boosting the Job Centres to be able to do this.

The hypocrisy! Say one thing (about Deaf people's rights) and practise the opposite (helping them in the manner of the old missioners).

And what of our noble goals? The RNID seems now to be ambling along willy-nilly. What happened to the ambitious plans that were going to be the big breakthrough Deaf people needed? The very "Opening Doors" plans that Livermore used to force me out, arguing that he did not feel I could achieve them.

Let us look at what has actually happened to them:

1. The research into educational attainments of Deaf children? They ended up with a watered down and much cheaper version that could only bring minimal results. Little real action has taken place to improve the education of Deaf children.

2. The research into the employment situation of Deaf people to lead to changes became a National Lottery Charities Board funded project to place a few Deaf people into jobs. Which they would probably have got anyway. Deaf people continue to face the same problems and barriers they always have. Any marginal improvement has been the result of the advent of the Disability Discrimination Act. The unemployment rate for Deaf people is still double the national average. The root causes of the real problems for Deaf people in employment are still there. Nothing is being done about these.

228

3. The research and action on Hearing Aids? A survey was conducted on the hearing aid clinics round the country. A report condemning the service was launched in a big PR exercise. Subsequent action? None! ......well there's no money in this so let's move on to other things.

4. The 100,000, sorry 60,000 new members? In the first year they ended with 12,000 members. When you bear in mind the fact that 7,500 of these were already subscribers of their magazine who were automatically transferred to the membership, you end up with only an additional 4,500. A paltry gain when you consider the intense and expensive advertising campaign, with free pens and all of that kind of paraphernalia. So much for there being 8.7 million deaf people! Their use of the hitherto strictly confidential addresses of Typetalk users to try to get more members is an indication of desperation. It shows an apparently blatant disregard for the Data Protection Act. And for the fact that we had all been reassured that Typetalk was absolutely confidential.

So this is where the RNID has ended up. I can guarantee that it wouldn't have happened had I still been in charge. I would certainly have rejected the methods that have been used. I would have rejected the cheaper and "more practical" ad hoc exercises that did nothing to change the fundamental issues at the end of the day. I would never have sacrificed those issues for transient PR opportunities, opportunities that glorified a handful of individuals and achieved next to nothing for Deaf people.

The golden era of the RNID (for Deaf people) was over. It returns to the discredited medical and audiological model…with some residual bits of the social model from the previous era. Where is the vision? Where is the morality? There does not seem to be any real vision apart from working the numbers, making money and self-promotion.

So, whither Deaf people's rights? As the moves towards rights had already been in progress for a few years and the plans for 1997/8 included such work, the RNID had little option but continue with them. Also they dared not stop this after Livermore's assertion of the continuance of my work.

Few things highlight this reality as much as the Government's appointment of someone like Strachan as a Disability Rights Commissioner! Had Government Ministers like David Blunkett and Margaret Hodge listened to Deaf people rather than organisations this appointment could never have come about. More dishearteningly, the appointment further illustrated their ignorance when it came to Deaf issues and politics. David Blunkett would never have appointed a spectacles wearer to represent the views and needs of blind people. Nor would Bert Massie, the wheelchair-using Chair of the Disability Rights Commission be happy if someone with a slight limp was appointed to represent wheelchair users. Yet when it came to Deaf people, what seems to matter most is the sycophantic posturing of the establishment organisations.

I was not blind to the irony of the RNID and Strachan getting involved with the Disability Discrimination Act and the Disability Rights Task Force after the way he had behaved in the moves to remove me from my position! The nerve!

Obviously New Labour and the New Paternalist were cut from more similar cloth than we realised! The "new" Politicians, as they always had, continued to listen to the RNID and the establishment when it came to "what is best" for Deaf people. Without any contact with real Deaf people, how could they do anything but rely on such organisations? And when the organisations are not particularly interested in Deaf issues? The influence on policies and practices was oriented toward deaf issues. Deaf issues were absorbed as a subset of those. The clear distinctions between the Deaf and the deaf was no longer appreciated. The line between them was blurred and, as a result, the Deaf case was not presented as clearly or as strongly as it ought to have been

With the relative invisibility of the BDA, which had regressed nearly to the pre-Verney era, our issues were in danger of being run entirely by the RNID – on its terms rather than ours.

The BDA had become soft on principles, as demonstrated by the Executive Council's refusal to act on a specially commissioned report and motion passed at their Annual General Meeting about Cochlear Implants for Deaf children. The reason put forward for the inaction was that "it could affect our charity donations"! Charity money before principles?

Without a vision beyond "promoting Deaf culture", the entire organisation became a prisoner of fundraising. Their goal seemed to be to keep things easy and maintain their jobs. No one was willing to rock the boat. Certainly not to ensure that campaigns for Deaf people's rights were at the forefront of policy.

230

Meanwhile, many people both in the Deaf world and outside were wondering what I was going to do post-RNID. To these people, it was inconceivable that I would remain on the sidelines. On the one hand, it would have been so easy for me to go out to pasture and take a well-earned rest. But, that was not my style. I may have many flaws, but being a quitter wasn't one of them. One of my favourite mottos, which went back to my rugby playing days was "It is not that you are knocked down, it is how you get up."

I might have been knocked down but that didn't mean I was going to stay down. I would get up and fight on. The question was when, where and how?

Livermore and Strachan, never really understanding me as a person, assumed I would remain quiet. They must have presumed that, after two years of enforced silence, all would be forgiven and forgotten.

After all, their strategy was to take over the Deaf world in those two years. By doing so, they would render me "toothless".

Like most avaricious people, they had underestimated me and overestimated their attractiveness to Deaf people. They did not realise that my ambitions at the RNID was never about the CEO job itself. They should have realised that was why I could not be bought out by a kick upstairs into some cushy prestige position. Nor could I be at the beck and call of the likes of Livermore and Strachan, promoting their flawed policies and practices, no matter how financially lucrative it could have been for me.

I had been fuelled through the years by rights and discrimination issues. My motivation continued unabated even after the setbacks at the RNID. I could not sit back and do nothing about what I knew would be a threat to Deaf rights.

I had a number of options to consider. I needed some time to assess the situation to see which would be the best one to pursue. I was anxious to use my experience and contacts to best effect.

On leaving the RNID on 31st March 1997, I prepared myself for two years of enforced silence. Not able to move forward without going against the RNID meant that I would have to lie low. The terms of my agreement could be at risk of being breached if I was not careful in what I did or said.

I was under no illusion about what would happen during those two years. I knew I would live in a relative wilderness from my so-called "friends" who were fearful of doing or saying anything that might offend the RNID. This group included those hearing people who ran the larger local associations. I found that the key people at the BDA would be no different.

The fair weather friends and hangers on – and there were too many of them – faded fast. I didn't get so much as a wreath from Teletec! You can imagine how many people's attitude changed toward me overnight. If I wasn't clear about it before, I was surely clear about it now. Many people went by what you are (i.e. your position) and not who you are (i.e. the person with qualities).

However, I also learned who my real friends were. I got a few inspirational messages of encouragement, like the card from a well-wisher with the message "Upwards and Onwards". There were no surprises to me about who remained my friends. What surprised me was the number of new friends I gained over the following few months. The most encouraging thing about these new friends was that most of them were either from the grassroots or young Deaf people. They had a mistrust of the RNID and the BDA and what they stand for (or don't stand for).

My new friends were the very people who would eventually become the foundation of the future developments towards Deaf people's rights. Some disabled allies became friends too. Ironically, it was only on the backs of the more militant disabled people that the Deaf were even kept in the political picture.

In view of what had happened at the RNID and was happening to Deaf people everywhere it was clear that there were things that Deaf people had to do to prevent any future abuses from occurring. They needed to heed the experience of women and Black people in achieving their rights. What was needed were:

1.   A strong and active body to act in influencing the Politicians on Deaf issues.

2.   The lead in taking action to be set by Deaf people themselves in all localities.

3.   Deaf people to be given information on political issues and developments for them to use as tools in their own actions.

4.   A national interlinking network of such Deaf Activists and Advocates and their hearing allies.

5.   The positive aspects of BSL and related issues to be promoted and demonstrated in all forums.

In other words, Deaf people had to take the lead in mobilising themselves and others to fight and support each other. Who or which organisation was going to make this happen? Sadly none. They had their own agendas.

The turning point came in July 1997 at the first "Deaf Nation" Conference in Preston, a conference organised by the University of Central Lancashire. I had been invited as one of the keynote speakers. My talk, "The Realities of Nationhood" referred to the importance of a cultural nation (e.g. Black people, Women, Deaf people, etc) in influencing the geo-political nation to ensure their rights. I made the point that although we had made a lot of effort and noise about our "Deaf culture", we had minimal influence on the policy developments in the external political world. I stressed the need for Deaf people to get into this and to lead on it.

My message struck a powerful chord with those in attendance. The concept of an active campaigning body led and driven by Deaf people in all localities appealed to many. Deaf people needed a voice, needed to be empowered, they needed leadership – in other words, they needed exactly what they were not getting from the RNID or the BDA.

The BDA was so weak and constrained that there had to be another organisation that could stand up to the RNID. This organisation would need to harness the talent that was emerging from grassroots Deaf people and the 'young Turks', but which, had up to that point, found no satisfactory outlet. There were also independent active local Deaf groups that could benefit from becoming part of a national network that would fight to protect and advance Deaf issues. It was now clear that Deaf people had been willing and ready to move for some time. What had been sorely lacking was leadership and initiative. There was also a new breed of hearing people and parents anxious to play a role but unsure where that might be. They were sensitive enough to Deaf people's sensibilities to not want to interfere in Deaf people's efforts without being asked. These supporters also needed an organisation in which they could put their skills to work in support of the cause.

I waited and watched for a few months after the conference. When no one did much of anything, I sounded out several known Deaf activists from around the country to see what they thought. Their reactions were very enthusiastic. I then had long sessions with Paddy Ladd to clarify and frame out the key roles of such an organisation. Then I made the move to set up this new organisation, calling it "The Federation of Deaf People" (FDP). The use of the word "federation" was deliberate so that local action groups and individuals would be independent and encouraged to do what they thought best in the achievement of the organisation's primary objectives.

I had learned enough from the RNID to know that de-centralised power would be the greatest benefit to Deaf people.

To raise consciousness of Deaf people's rights and also to promote the Federation of Deaf People (FDP), I undertook a "Deaf People's Rights" lecture tour covering twenty three locations round the country. Such a tour had, sadly, never been put together before. The turnouts and reactions clearly demonstrated the deep feelings out there and the potential for such a federation to be successful. There were many angry and frustrated Deaf people out there!

So, without any advertising or promotion, the FDP gathered with some 600 members in two years. This number alone was ample evidence of the need, the disillusionment and the deep-set (and well-earned) suspicion of many Deaf people.

I then made the decision to leave London and move back up to the north where I could be closer to the many frustrated Deaf people who were fed up with nothing happening. Up north, all the fancy policies around legislation like the DDA were not having any effect. There was also a personal reason for my move. I also needed to recoup my own resources, rebuild around what was out there and be closer to the real everyday world of Deaf people.

During this time, I had the opportunity to stand for election as the Chair of BDA as some Deaf people wanted to nominate me. But, after discussing it with some of the young Turks in the FDP, I decided not to. I could not let them down by joining an organisation that only posed as active but which, in reality, would only push them aside if they tried to make things happen.

They deserved better. We all did. At any rate, there's a place for both organisations in the struggle for Deaf rights.

Getting a new national organisation like the FDP was going to be an expensive option. Money had to be spent to set it up and to maintain it until there were enough subscribers to keep it going. It is quite unlikely that there would be project funding available to get Deaf people to rebel for their rights! None of this would come free.

It had to come out of my own pocket. In a way, you could say it was subsidised by the RNID. There's a delicious irony to that! Consider it as one of their better services!

All of this planning and hoping and organising is now beginning to come about, with younger Deaf people taking more control in their own areas. Things like high profile national Conferences, regular magazines and a March for BSL through Central London involving 4,000 people were all organised by young Deaf volunteers who had never done anything like these before.

And this is only just the start!

Chapter Thirteen

We are Deaf!

To be nobody-but-myself - in a world which is doing its best, night and day, to make you everybody else - means to fight the hardest battle which any human being can fight, and never stop fighting.

e. e. cummings

The future is the only kind of property that the masters willingly concede to slaves.

Albert Camus. The Rebel

Let us now review and briefly summarise the historical development of Deaf people. This gives a sense of where we are now. And where we go from here.

Deaf people have been around as long as there have been human beings. Attempts to cure us, and the use of sign language by Deaf people have been recorded in writings as far back as 5000 BC. Scrolls suggest that Jesus Christ cured a Deaf man by placing his hands on him. Before then, and since, we have had a motley crew of shamans, Witch Doctors, charlatans, faith healers and medics trying to effect cures. Almost all of which have failed miserably. No doubt, a considerable amount of snake oil has been downed in the quest for a cure. Even today, many Deaf people have memories of being taken by their mother to a faith healer. No one can recall any instances of anyone leaping up screaming "Hallelujah! I can hear!" after such a session.

Plato was the first to write about sign language in ancient Greece. There are references to Deaf people in the Jewish scriptures. The Romans codified deafness by laws and used sign language in their pantomimed performances at amphitheatres such as the one at Pompeii. It is also likely that such gestures were used in everyday communication by Deaf people.

During the renaissance of classical learning, Leonardo Da Vinci advised artists to represent gesture:

236

"By copying the motions of the deaf and dumb, who speak with movements of their hands and eyes and eyebrows and their whole person, in their desire to express that which is in their minds. Do not laugh at me because I propose a teacher without speech to you, for he will teach you better through facts than will all the other masters through words."

In July 1791, at the height of the French Revolution, the National Assembly established the first state-funded education for Deaf children in the world. The radical, Jacobin deputy, Prieur de la Marne, who was later to vote for the execution of Louis XVl, proposed a bill to fund an educational institute for both Deaf and blind children. In so doing, he declared the sign language of Deaf people to be:

"One of the most fortunate discoveries of the human spirit. If one were ever to realise the much desired project of a universal language, this would perhaps be that which would merit preference."

Historians have long debated whether Enlightenment philosophies generated the politics of the French Revolution. Here, a direct connection can be observed. The establishment of the Institute for the Deaf was the culmination of thirty years work by two Catholic priests, the Abbé Charles-Michel de l'Epée (1712-89) and the Abbé Roch-Ambroise Sicard (1742-1822), who had developed a methodical sign language based on the native sign languages used by Deaf people themselves. However, it was the Enlightenment philosophies of Condillac and Rousseau that provided their initial inspiration. Rousseau believed that man's original language was gesture and that certain animals, such as ants and beavers, also communicated by gesture.

When Epée observed two of his Deaf parishioners signing to each other, he was thus prepared to recognise their signs as a language rather than mere pantomime. Consistent with the philosophy of Condillac and Rousseau, Epée believed that the addition of "grammar" to the gestures of Deaf people would make their language the equal of spoken languages. What he didn't know was that these series of gestures that he observed already possessed a grammar of their own. Nevertheless, his work led to the realisation that it was possible to communicate with and to educate Deaf people.

From that point onwards the history of Deaf people went into two separate political strands:

237

One relates to the quest for a fix or failing that, to 'normalise' Deaf people, to make them like hearing people as far as possible. This strand, which is effectively represented by the medical history of deafness, has been driven primarily by professionals, paternalists and wealthy parents. It has created an enormous "normalisation industry" of professionals like medics, aids and equipment manufacturers, educationalists, charities and the like, all making good money out of it. It would be such a shame for these people if a cure was actually found – they'd be out of work!

These people and their industries encourage a generally negative perception of Deaf people. Their behaviour and attitudes around the medical model, influences negative social attitudes to Deaf people. This whole orientation to deafness, no doubt from the key role played by Doctors in mediating it, has become known as the *medical model* of deafness. This model, by focusing disproportionately on the individual physical or mental condition, locates the problem in the individual Deaf person.

The other strand is the Social History of Deaf people, which has evolved from and been nurtured by Deaf people themselves. It charts the progress of Deaf people from being the "village idiots" to becoming educated and developing a flourishing local, regional, national and international community. It also illustrates the movement on Deaf issues from 'in need of help' to the realisation of their identity and their rights.

This strand focuses on the range of influences that come to bear on the Deaf person – the social attitudes, the inaccessible information and other symptoms –illustrates that in reality the problem resides with society. Disability arises not from the circumstances of the individual Deaf person but rather from the inhospitable nature of the physical and social environment in which the individual finds themselves. This is known as the *social model* of Deafness, which emphasises the rights, normality and humanity of Deaf people and points out the role that social factors play in the genesis of Deafness.

This social history begins with oralism's failure to make good on its promise to deliver academic achievements. It traces the consequent social exclusion of Deaf people as second-rate hearing people directly to the *failing of oralism, not the failing of Deaf people*. This was followed by the rescue operations set up by the Church "Missions to the Deaf", where the Deaf down and outs were shepherded and given skills in various manual trades such as carpentry.

The move to challenge the abuse of oralism and the yoke of dependency that its consequences brought about was led by a small number of Deaf and hearing pioneers.

Black people's battle for emancipation was initially driven by little known individuals who faced up to extreme hardship, brutalisation and even death. They paved the way for the 'glory leaders' like Martin Luther King and Malcolm X.

Similarly, the advance of rights for Deaf people has involved such people as Paddy Ladd, Raymond Lee, Tony Boyce, Maggie Woolley, Arthur Dimmock and even hearing people like Arthur Verney.

It is important to come to terms with their courage in fighting without any real support from others. Some got burnt out as a result of their battles, whilst others ended up on the wrong side, having been bought off (as was a common tactic in those days, and is still happening even today). However, regardless of their individual choices, we would not have got where we are without them. Contemporary Deaf people with a relatively easier route in a more positive climate get all the glory. We must never forget these pioneers. We owe them a great deal.

The slow and steady movement for rights has, as is always the case, been met with strong resistance from those in power, mainly the hearing Paternalists and Professionals who did not want their comfortable boats rocked. They were aided and abetted by the Deaf elders who were mostly Officers of the Deaf social groups. This sad conspiracy made it very difficult to mobilise the mass of Deaf people. The strong sense of dependency that these elders felt was difficult to shake off. This sense was exacerbated by a real fear of losing services and patronage. Over the years, many prospective campaigners were bought off and others became the token "House Deaf".

As a result of the corrosive effects of their poor education, social situation and paternalistic entrapment Deaf people had acquired a sense of inferiority and worthlessness.

This began to be challenged by a small number of Deaf people and their hearing allies. They began to take to rebel at the way they were being treated and the negative attitudes around them. They made deafness into a political issue.

At around the same time, linguistic Researchers at Universities confirmed that British Sign Language (BSL) was a different – but equally legitimate – language from spoken English. This had considerable implications in how the Deaf were perceived. It forced major re-thinks on some policies on service provision.

Then the book, "When the Mind Hears" by Harlan Lane, landed in the UK. It pointed to the 'normalcy' of the Deaf identity. The NUD fostered this awareness and self-pride by bringing Harlan Lane to speak in the UK in 1984. Key Deaf activists began to wear their Deaf identity on their sleeves. Their example rubbed off on many others.

In 1981, Arthur Verney, became the General Secretary of the British Deaf Association (BDA). He used it as a vehicle to politicise Deaf issues. A series of campaigns to raise public and political awareness were launched. This had a crucial bearing on the wider masses of the Deaf "grassroots". Up to that point, the noises had been made by the tiny NUD whom many saw as "rebellious mavericks". The BDA's actions gave respectability to the rights issues. It gave legitimacy to challenges to the established bodies. Bodies that had contributed to the low esteem for the Deaf. Educationalists. Authorities. Politicians.

Under Verney's leadership the BDA's challenges were primarily aimed at the top. Governments. He never put himself at the front of any advance. He ensured that Deaf people were there to face the Politicians. At this early stage, the number of Deaf people involved was very small.

These initiatives coincided with the pressure exerted by disabled people's movement for their rights. The Deaf rode on the slipstream of that drive. Many were uncomfortable with this association with the disabled.

As it turned out, quite a number of Deaf people did like it and supported these new movements and developments. However, the majority did not have access to all this new information and developments. They continued with their apathetic ways under the yoke of paternalists who had no intention of enlightening them on such issues, which would mean the end of their control.

Recent developments, such as the generic concept of social inclusion, have given added stimulus to Deaf people. "Social Inclusion" is the philosophy that accepts a person as part of a 'normal' society *as they are* rather than forcing

240

some modification upon them in order to fit in with the majority culture. For example, people from the Asian community were accepted as they are, speaking their own language and dressing according to their own religion and culture instead of having to conform to the mainstream culture. The implication here was clear for Deaf people. It meant that it was OK to be Deaf and use BSL. We were then seen as part of a normal diverse community, who could be who they were, and not have to be 'normalised' as pseudo hearing people.

Other important new developments which reinforced Deaf people's rights to their own identity arose as several Universities set up specific Departments for Deaf Studies. These gave added status and credibility to Deaf issues.

However, in spite of all this, Deaf people remained at a great disadvantage. Their education remained as fragmented and piecemeal as ever. Paternalists modified their approaches so that they gave the impression of encouraging empowerment of Deaf people while at the same time holding onto the reins of power and decision-making. Clearly, Deaf people still had a fight on their hands to achieve real equality and full participation. Fortunately, the number of Deaf people who were prepared to fight has grown steadily.

Nevertheless, their biggest obstacles in achieving rights and progress remain the Establishment and a large number of organisations in the field of Deafness.

The Establishment continues to be influenced by the upper and the upper-middle classes, those classes with their general sense of stigma and shame around being deaf or having a Deaf child. These classes remain strongly oriented to cure and normalisation. This perspective is fine for those who are deaf, for hearing people who have lost or are losing their hearing, whose needs and rights issues are quite different from that of Deaf people. Cure and normalisation has *never* worked for Deaf people, nor will it ever. That philosophy had caused such terrible pain and suffering to Deaf people in the past, just as it continues to do today.

It is possible, even likely, that the Establishment confuses deaf and Deaf issues, assuming that they are the same thing. Maybe, if they could realise the difference, they would focus their energies appropriately and ease off from resisting all that Deaf people have demanded.

Organisations, both of and for Deaf people, represent big hurdles for three main reasons. Putting aside the fact that they are hardly ever seen in the right places to try to influence national and local policies, there is the fact that all are charities. Whether or not we like it, the fact that there are charities is going to get the public and Politicians perceiving Deaf people as in need of help rather than as citizens with rights.

Then, we have the problem with those who run these organisations. We either have the hearing Paternalists with their own motives for being there, motives which are little to do with empowerment of Deaf people, or else they wouldn't be where they are.

Or there is the new development in the late 1990's, once Deaf people had achieved some of the top posts in their field, was that we have new Deaf people running things for the wrong reasons and in the wrong directions – if there was a direction in the first place. Many organisations don't have a clear direction other than raising money from wherever they can get it simply to keep the organisation and the jobs going. Often they have taken on the example, practices and attitudes of the paternalists who were originally there. They like their positions so much that they resent anyone trying to rock their boat for whatever reason.

Because the hearing Paternalists see Deaf people who want to press for rights as trouble-makers, they distance themselves from those Deaf Campaigners. They align themselves with Deaf people who prefer to be sycophantic and act out of their own self-interest rather than the needs of the Deaf people out in the community. The list of names of such Deaf people runs far longer than that of Deaf rights Campaigners.

We have finally entered a new phase in the social history of Deaf people. The demise of the Deaf Centres along with their paternalistic controllers and largely tokenistic Deaf Officials has led to the emergence of a new breed of young Deaf leaders who, no longer based at the traditional Centres or organisations, are more independent. They are doing things that have never happened before in UK Deaf history. They are producing radical magazines, organising mass marches for recognition of their identity and rights, visiting the European Parliament to press for rights, organising petitions, demanding and getting meetings with the politicians, setting up pickets and other activities.

They are doing all this from outside of the traditional organisations, organisations that would certainly have forbidden them to do any of these things. They are talking in a different and more radical language than those who are holding onto the traditional organisations. This strand of Deaf history shows promise of exciting developments over the next decade as the younger Deaf people begin to demand and take more control of their own destinies.

242

Chapter Fourteen

Faith, Hope and Sod the Charity

I have long felt that the trouble with discrimination is not discrimination per se, but rather that the people who are discriminated against think of themselves as second-class.

Rosalyn Sussman Yalow

Every body continues in its state of rest or uniform motion in a straight line unless it is compelled to change that state by forces impressed upon it.

Sir Isaac Newton

Do you remember Albert Pringle? He was the gentleman who appeared in the prologue, introduced to provide leadership of the The National Organisation of Minority Women. He was, of course, a fictional character. Almost comical, actually. If not for the lesson his appearance taught us about the Deaf world, he would have been a useless fiction.

However, let us continue our fiction a bit longer now.

What would Mr. Pringle have said as he took the podium? What *could* he have said? He was, after all, wholly unsuitable for the task at hand. He was not unsuitable due to lack of intelligence or lack of concern. He was wholly unsuitable because of the reality of his life experience.

Albert Pringle, good or bad as an individual, should have been booed from the podium.

Mr. Pringle, whatever his intentions, could have said only one thing that would have made sense – that he was stepping aside to allow a strong, intelligent, minority woman to take command. *That* would have been a heroic gesture. A noble gesture. But even in our strange fiction, it could never have happened.

No one relinquishes power for the right reasons.

That being the case, the question, "Where do we go from here?" takes on greater meaning. The Mr. Pringles of the world (the Livermores and Strachans) will never relinquish their power, no matter how destructive it is to the people they give lip service to helping.

For if we have learned anything in our experiences as human beings, as *Deaf* human beings, it is that no one is going to do for us what we must do for ourselves. To think otherwise is to delude ourselves and to risk sinking back into the bog of history.

So, we the Deaf must claim that power as our own. In doing so, we ask for the support and understanding of hearing people. Not their sympathy and not their pity.

The first thing we must do is to learn, learn from our history and learn from our experience. These events at the RNID may anger many Deaf people. They surely will not surprise them. My experiences were particularly intense – but so were Icarus' as he soared closer to the sun. I rose too high, that's all. The lesson is the same to all of us. The intensity of my experiences may be shocking to some readers but the reality is that many of the issues I was forced to confront are the very same issues that Deaf people experience every day in one way or another.

If you substitute the "Royal National Institute for Deaf People" with the name of many other organisations, national and local, many of the same attitudes, prejudices and oppressive practices would be replicated. My experiences show clearly how Deaf people are perceived and treated, not only by the various agencies in the Deaf world, agencies established to *benefit* Deaf people, but, as a consequence of the attitudes of these agencies, in the wider society as well.

It has truly been a case of "really not interested in the Deaf"!

My story should make painfully clear the steep barriers Deaf people face in their own world and in their own organisations, by the very people who purport to help them. It calls to mind the saying, "With friends like these, who needs enemies." The 'help' provided by these types of organisations and people that is foisted on Deaf people, whether they like it or not. It is 'help' that hearing Paternalists deem that the Deaf need

It is help that fails to lift them up. Instead, it is instrumental in maintaining their state of disadvantage.

It should be apparent by now that, in the main, these organisations are controlled by hearing people who have a need for power. By people who presume to know what is best for Deaf people. And what do they deem to be best for us? Cure or normalisation with policies and practices that have their roots in oralism. Anyone who doubts this assertion need only review the desperate measures taken by certain hearing people at the RNID to cling to power, come what may.

244

Helping the Deaf? Really? Please! The very suggestion that these actions benefit the Deaf is as insulting as it is erroneous.

How horrible these things are in the context of the world that all Deaf people must inhabit! Yet it is made even worse by the insidious and overwhelming contribution these attitudes and behaviours have on what Deaf people must confront in the external environment.

The real story behind my experiences at the RNID is the impact of these attitudes and behaviours in the wider society. This is my real concern. The RNID, as troubling as it is, is only a relatively small group of people. It is the influence it exerts in the wider world that creates the real stumbling block for Deaf people.

It is out there, in the real world beyond the d/Deaf organisations that Deaf people face physical barriers to access and participation; out there that we are isolated from a world that relies on sound as one of its founding principles.

Deaf people are expected to adjust themselves into this world of sound without being able to hear. As a consequence of this expectation, the effectiveness of our education is compromised. Our employment opportunities are limited. And our social interactions are stunted.

Behind the physical barriers are the psychological ones. Having lived a life in which negative perceptions deem us to be defective and in need of "fixing", we begin to internalise those perceptions. We fight it but we might as well be fighting the tides! When those who do not 'speak' or 'hear' are deemed to be intellectually deficient and incapable of taking care of themselves, they begin to think of themselves as deficient and incapable.

We struggle in an environment where the perception is that we are unable to conduct our own affairs and that we must be reliant on charity and sympathy... until we believe it too. Until we rely on charity and sympathy.

And who is to blame? While it might be cathartic to blame society in general, the finger of blame must point first to many organisations in our Deaf world like the RNID. When organisations established to benefit the Deaf treat us like defectives, and charity causes. When they propagate many failed policies how can one expect society in general to treat Deaf people any differently?

If organisations give primacy to the medical model of deafness and encourage oralist education. If they create confusions between "deaf" and "Deaf". If they beg for charitable donations. Should anyone be surprised that the wider society behaves in the same way?

The oppression of Deaf people occurs at all levels and in all areas of society. Governments, even the supposedly "social" Labour Party, which claims to "listen to the people", ignores Deaf people's views and experiences in favour of the Establishment's petty posturing. And in reaction to buying into the posturing of the Deaf organisations, national policies are developed. National polices that produce inappropriate education services that consistently produce inferior outcomes and unfortunate appointments to the new Disability Rights Commission, where the Deaf perspective will be effectively pushed aside.

Key Ministers rarely confront real Deaf people. Home Secretary, Jack Straw, had a sobering experience at a recent Conference of the Federation of Deaf People. Straw, who has a hearing loss in one ear, faced blunt questioning by Deaf people, questioning for which no amount of briefing from his Department could have prepared him. This questioning was in stark contrast to the fawning usually paid to Ministers at events set up by the establishment organisations.

It is a sad and unfortunate fact that such fawning is more likely to get results with these Politicians.

At local level, the Education Authorities continue to blunder their way about as they try to provide for Deaf children on the basis of "normalisation". Even with consistently bad results they, relying on the advice of hearing 'experts' and establishment organisations, continue to flounder about – to the detriment of the poor, Deaf children. The views and experiences of Deaf people are not considered, or even desired.

And who do they blame for these pathetic results? Why, the Deaf children themselves, who "are not up to it", "didn't try hard enough" or whatever!

How cruel and deluded can these people be?

As a result, we suffer in the soul crushing situation where the medical model of normalisation predominates, reinforced by the attitudes and behaviour of the organisations and the people who run them. The exclusion of Deaf people from the decision-making processes renders them second class citizens.

What has become of basic human rights? Is it not the case that every person regardless of race, gender, religion, disability or whatever deserves the opportunity to be independent, to participate and be full citizens of this society?

Are human rights for everyone but the Deaf?

No!

Unless you are willing to suggest that being Deaf renders a person something less than human, then you must acknowledge that we deserve these same basic rights as every other person. So, what needs to be done to assure us our rights?

At this time, the thrust of policy developments and treatment of Deaf people is cure, normalisation and support. But if we are fully human and not "less than" then we do not need to be "cured". We need to be acknowledged and celebrated.

The thrust of policy and treatment should therefore become identity, rights and access!

Our demands are less "demands" than sensible responses to the realities of the world. They include:

1. The Deaf/deaf Distinction.

The differences between Deaf and deaf need to be clearly identified and understood. The confusion between two clearly distinct groups is not helping the Deaf. It leads to inappropriate policies and practices.

The two distinct groups of people require very different approaches. Remember the distinction made in Chapter Two between spectacle wearers and blind people.

2. Normalcy.

The acceptance of the Deaf identity as normal is an absolute must. Can anyone continue to justify the current practice that must, by definition, make a Deaf person "abnormal"?

247

Where is the dignity in forcing people to behave like pantomime clowns or chimpanzees at a tea party? And for what purpose? To maintain a status quo that has failed Deaf people for generations?

The acceptance of a Deaf identity would correctly allow everyone to remain what and who they are – both hearing people and Deaf people. We can all acknowledge that Deaf people have very different, and sometimes difficult, communication needs. But these differences and difficulties are no different than a foreign-language speaker might have in the heart of London!

3. *British Sign Language.*

BSL should be recognised as an official language on par with others like the Welsh language.

BSL is a real language, with a full vocabulary and grammar. It is no more or less a language than French, Arabic, Hebrew, German or English! If hearing people have learned BSL as a second language, then they will communicate normally in sign. If not they can use interpreters for formal meetings and pen and paper plus gestures for others.

This is the United Nations approach. In it, everyone maintains their differences and their similarities. Everyone maintains their dignity and *everyone* is normal within their own framework.

Not only will the recognition of BSL guarantee access but also it will have the profound benefit of legitimatising the reality of being Deaf. It will change attitudes toward Deaf people. BSL will cease to be perceived as merely a tool to "help those poor Deaf people" and would gain the stature of any other foreign language, with the consequent effects on the perception of its native users.

4. *Listen to us!*

Government and local agencies need to listen to the views of Deaf people rather than organisations, unless the organisations have management bodies consisting of at least 75% Deaf people.

Only then can the Government appropriately respond to the true needs of Deaf people. Only then can they devise the appropriate policies and practices.

To continue to flog this horse, access begins with communication. There can be no true access unless and until there is an official recognition of BSL for what it is – a true and legitimate language.

5. *The right to access.*

The right to information access should dominate educational issues for Deaf children. Measures of the success and relevance of any method of communication should be based on the percentage of information exchanged and not the number of words recognised.

This exchange of information should be ensured immediately, whatever the method used. Not when the child can 'hear' and 'speak'. By then the education will have slipped past.

6. *Inclusive Society.*

There must be a proactive move towards the social inclusion of Deaf people. The term "inclusion" as opposed to the commonly used term "integration" is deliberate. The term "integration" allies itself with the concept of "normalcy". It has acquired very wide and emotive connotations. It usually means the assimilation of minorities and of differences into the mainstream. It signifies a melting point, incorporation into the mainstream but not necessarily recognising choice and difference.

"Inclusion" better describes equality and access. Inclusion means acceptance of difference and incorporates choice (e.g. choice of schools, etc). It suggests the full participation of minorities - linguistic, ethnic, religious, etc - in all aspects of life in a pluralistic society, on equal terms. It implies a society in which there is mutual respect for each other's language, culture and customs; and where there is full opportunity for minorities to maintain and foster the development of their language, culture and history, while retaining the right to participate fully in the social, cultural, economic and political life of the country.

In short, the Deaf would be accepted and included fully into society as they are – normal Deaf people.

7. *Organisational Models.*

And, of course, underlying all these "demands" is the demand that the organisations in the Deaf world get their own houses in order. They need to set a model of Deaf independence and control of their own lives. Deaf people should have full control of the Deaf organisations. They should have real influence on the wider policies that affect Deaf people. These organisations should amend their Constitutions to insist that their governing bodies are made up of a minimum of 51% Deaf people.

Deaf Chairs are an absolute must. Remember our parallel with ethnic women.

This is not to demean hearing people. Hearing people belong on such bodies as long as they discard a paternalistic approach to Deaf people. Their presence is to support Deaf people, not to determine their lives. Not to seek glory for themselves on the backs of the Deaf.

These are our demands. How are they to be brought about? And who will carry the banner?

I have begun each chapter with quotations that I believe are relevant to the content of that chapter. It has been particularly so in this chapter.

We have found ourselves in a rut because we have continued along the path that was hewed many generations ago. Because of the traditional approaches and culture of dependency, Deaf people's perception of themselves is not positive.

Also, what is true of physics is true of people – we will continue to travel the path we have been travelling unless something compelling turns us a different way.

That "something compelling" won't come from the existing organisations. They have a vested interest in maintaining the status quo. Nor will it come through a Government that will only listen to the establishment views, no matter how dismal the failure of the Establishment record.

The bottom line is that change will not come about through the 'kindness' of hearing people. It will not come about by Paternalists nicely handing over the reins of power. Or Educationalists accepting that their methods are flawed. Or Organisations eschewing their charity image and status.

At the end of the day, it will only come about when I stand up to be counted. It will only come about when every Deaf person stands up to be counted.

Deaf people need to break out of this "state of uniform motion". Not by arguing among ourselves or by trying to convert the converted. We have to turn round and confront the outside world. Frightening, yes. But we must do this. We have to convince the general public that we are here and we are staying! We must focus our efforts on action and persuasion where people are more likely to listen to us.

It will only come about when we Deaf ourselves enforce these changes in every part of the country. This battle is primarily a local one. It has to take place in our own localities. That is where our problems are – and where they are not being addressed. We need to influence local Councillors and local Members of Parliaments.

They need to see real Deaf people in the real world. They can make changes out there that really affect the lives of Deaf people as opposed to the hollow kudos the top people seem to thrive on. They are more likely to listen to and respond to the Deaf in a way that Ministers rarely will. As the Establishment enforces the absence of Deaf people, Ministers assume we are incapable.

For too long Deaf people have put up with this negative situation. We have made lofty statements about rights. We have demanded access.

And we have waited for someone to do something.

But no one has done anything.

Waiting is not enough. It is time to act.

Deaf people need to take more control of the situation. We have to stand up and challenge current policies, practices and attitudes. We have to take the lead in seizing hold of our own destinies.

But we cannot do it alone. Our hearing allies must have a major role. Just as white allies had a role in supporting the Black people in South Africa. Support by getting behind Deaf people, rather than in front of them. By querying existing policies and attitudes. By demanding changes.

For too long, Deaf people have suffered in humiliating silence.

We can no longer allow that to happen.

We must shout it out.

We are Deaf!

We only ask that you hear us.

251

Epilogue

Poetry is an orphan of silence. The words never quite equal the experience behind them.

Charles Simic

A number of poems were circulated between March and June 1997 under the banner of "Deaf Drum". They were written by various people one coming after another once the first two went out. Because of the absence of an established mailing network they failed to reached many people. Two of the collection of 24 are included here as an important element in the development of Deaf political consciousness. It is impressive that the authors are still unknown, and that all, being sign language users, show excellent command of English!

Betrayal

It's a mighty sad world
When sleaze enters charities
In the guise of the upright.
On the backs of the disabled
Ride the hungry for power.
Under cover of caring
Come egos just raving
To wreck the careers of those
They purport to serve.

In an unwary world
It's the wicked who win,
With all the right words
And the old school tie kin.
A background of money
With contacts to match
Form the right requirements
Of accent, style and class
To manipulate the mass.

252

No law can prevent them
The rules are differnt here.
The Chair of a charity
Has powers beyond compare
With a Board quite unaware
He offers a payoff
To keep his victim quiet
Or calls a Board meeting
To have the poor sod fired.

He does this with impunity
His plans are well in place.
With insidious moves
Canvassing goes apace.
So when the Board does meet,
Key people take their seat
And vote the way he points
So that the numbers join
To seal the victim's fate.
of the RNID!

To promote the welfare
Of deaf people everywhere
The Board's duties as guardians
To stand for the principles
The Constitution shows.
Does no one question this?
Or feel some discomfort?
Remember the purpose

Where are your principles
Fine Trustees on the Board?
You who appointed him
Where now is your support?
Support for your Deaf Chief
And restraint of your Chair
Answer to the people
'Cos we're all aware
And we'll always be there.

Resign

Resign and bow your heads in shame
Ye Trustees of the Board.
Can you not see our grief and pain?
Ye have betrayed us yet again
Resign, I say, resign!

Finally, the following Negro spiritual is particularly relevant to Deaf people:

When Israel was in Egypt land,
Let my people go,
Oppressed so hard they could not stand,
Let my people go.
Go down, Moses,
Way-down in Egypt land,
Tell old Pharaoh
To let my people go.